Jesus in the Trinity

Jesus in the Trinity

*A Beginner's Guide to the
Theology of Robert Jenson*

Lincoln Harvey

scm press

© Lincoln Harvey 2020

Published in 2020 by SCM Press
Editorial office
3rd Floor, Invicta House,
108–114 Golden Lane,
London EC1Y 0TG, UK

www.scmpress.co.uk

SCM Press is an imprint of Hymns Ancient & Modern Ltd
(a registered charity)

Hymns Ancient & Modern® is a registered trademark of
Hymns Ancient & Modern Ltd
13A Hellesdon Park Road, Norwich,
Norfolk NR6 5DR, UK

All rights reserved. No part of this publication may be reproduced,
stored in a retrieval system, or transmitted,
in any form or by any means, electronic, mechanical,
photocopying or otherwise, without the prior permission of
the publisher, SCM Press.

The Author has asserted his right under the Copyright,
Designs and Patents Act 1988
to be identified as the Authors of this Work

978-0-334-05881-6

British Library Cataloguing in Publication data

A catalogue record for this book is available
from the British Library

Typeset by Manila Typesetting Company

For Tereza, Anna, Georgia, Rose and Rachel

Contents

Acknowledgements	xi
1 A Not-So-Gentle Introduction to Jenson's Theology	1

Part One | A Cluster of Jensonian Concepts — 21

2 The Strange God of the Gospel	23
3 Time, Eternities and the Story of God	37

Part Two | Jenson and the Tradition — 61

4 In the Name of the Father, Son and Holy Spirit	63
5 We Believe in One Lord, Jesus Christ	88

Part Three | Jenson's Doctrine of God — 107

6 Adopting and Adapting Barth's Doctrine of Election	109
7 One Dramatic Act, Two Terms	130
8 Easter First, Creation After	153

Part Four | And So — 181

9 What on Earth Do We Do?	183
10 Concluding Postscript	210

Bibliography	215
Selected Works by Robert W. Jenson	215
Selected Secondary Literature	219
Index of Names and Subjects	224

How could I have agreed to work with them?
Who could possibly have thought that a majority
would ever lead me to a course of action, in
preference to following the divine Word?
Gregory Nazianzus

Acknowledgements

Like all the good things in my life, the opportunity to write this book has depended on the generosity of others. I am therefore grateful to the Board of Trustees at St Mellitus College for granting me a period of study leave over the summer term of 2018, and to my colleagues who cheerfully surrounded me with prayers despite picking up extra work in my absence; theology is certainly a collegial business. The old adage that teaching is the best way to learn also rings true, and I am especially indebted to all the postgraduate students who have enrolled on the Jenson module over the last four years, not least for their patience as I slowly worked out what I think about Jenson. I am also deeply grateful to Vastiana Belfon, Sam Durley, Chris E. W. Green, Douglas H. Knight, Donna Lazenby and Stephen J. Wright for reading drafts of the various chapters and for their constructive feedback on the project as a whole. They have helped me to revise both the form and content of the final manuscript, and I think it is a much better book due to their charitable labours. Of course, any deficiencies remain entirely my fault. David Shervington at SCM Press has been a great help in ensuring the project came to print, not least in accepting that this book isn't the one he initially expected. However, I am most grateful to my beloved Tereza, not only for her encouragement during the process of writing, but for her extra patience during the frustratingly longer process of *not*-writing – that limbo state that plagues so many academics in this bureaucratic day and age. Admittedly, our wonderful children didn't provide me with quite as much space as I originally envisaged, but I don't think I could have written this book without their noisy innocence alerting me to the intrinsic goodness of family life. Finally, I must say this book has been an absolute joy to write. My hope is that the reader will delight in it also, and that it will help them bear witness to the resurrection of Jesus of Nazareth, who – as I have learned from Robert W. Jenson – is one of the Trinity, without qualification.

I

A Not-So-Gentle Introduction to Jenson's Theology

1.1 The remarkable nature of Jenson's work

Robert W. Jenson thinks God is 'one big excitement'.[1] And not just any old excitement. God is the ecstasy of his own choice to be a particular God. That is to say, God 'behappens himself' in such a spectacular way that 'doer and act' are precisely the same.[2] What is more, the personal act of God's sheer decision centres on the resurrection of Jesus of Nazareth, a decisive event that is at one and the same time an eternal 'implosion of freedom' and a timely 'explosion of love'.[3] In other words, what happens over that first Easter weekend is the event by which God renders himself always and forever God-with-us, and with God constituted by the eternal act of the Crucified bursting from the grave, everything that exists 'spirals around' the resurrected Jesus 'like a helix', with the entire creation springing into life as God envelops us from every conceivable direction to draw us into the endless harmony of his own infinite life.[4] In short, the living God 'is a great fugue',[5] and 'the end is music'.[6] That is God's glory, and we too should be excited. Or so says Robert W. Jenson.[7]

Admittedly, I have launched us in at the deep end here, with the opening paragraph likely to have left the reader somewhat bewildered. In many respects, that is how we should feel when we read any theology book. Theology is a lot like baptism, in that the last thing you want to do is keep your head above water. We are attempting to speak about God, and so we will necessarily be out of our depth. Of course, secondary literature is often designed to keep the reader on dry land for as long as possible, in effect providing the gentlest of gradients into the depths of any theologian's work.[8] But this book will be somewhat different. Though it will mimic standard approaches in many respects, I will not abstract every building block from Jenson's constructive proposal, thereby breaking down the whole into more manageable parts before laying them out in isolated form in the hope that the bite-sized chunks enable the reader to digest Jenson's proposal more readily. Instead, the book is designed to convey the startling nature of Jenson's theology by keeping the prose flowing so that the barrage of ideas conveys the exciting liveliness of his systematic proposal, thereby stretching the reader right from the start as we trace the gospel-shaped reasoning that informs Jenson's astonishing account of what makes God the God that he is. This approach means we will often race ahead into deep waters, before slowing down and returning to simpler matters, thus introducing themes ahead of time before circling back to earlier ideas with the expectation that the accumulation of repeating insights will work one upon the other in mutual development. My hope is that the paragraph with which we began will make sense by the end of the book. I think the tactic works, though appreciate that the reader will be best placed to judge if it has.

The adopted method means – as Jenson recognized when he engaged with the work of other theologians – that it is not always clear where my interpretation ventures beyond the substance of Jenson's proposal.[9] This is especially true when I attempt to show how classical concepts like *aseity* – that is, God's unique act of self-causing – can be reimagined in the context of Jenson's account of Easter. My attempt to draw these technical ideas into positive conversation with Jenson's theology inevitably places great strain on both his work and the classical concepts, and one to which Jenson never subjected them to the best of my knowledge.[10] Nonetheless, I hope to have remained faithful to Jenson's register throughout, trusting that my unusual handling of his proposal evidences the way his theology is best worked with, rather than upon.

In fact, Jenson's theology is little short of an extended invitation for others to join him in the theological task he undertakes, which he fears has been too often neglected.[11] As a result, there is more than enough room for the creativity of others alongside him, because Jenson was only ever offering an 'experimental' approach to the theological task.[12] Jenson therefore encourages his readers to replicate the risks he takes, and so that is what I will on occasion do. I want to see what we can learn from Jenson's theology, and where we can push his proposal even further than he might have liked, thereby pursuing lines of thought that his own work only gestures towards. Of course, this approach is something of a gamble. Plenty of details will be overlooked and many stones left unturned as I focus on key areas, but I think I have still managed to capture Jenson's signature moves in what follows, thereby demonstrating the way his understanding of the gospel enabled him to redefine the trinitarian concepts of person and nature in such a startling way that both God and creation – as distinct communal realities – can be set in mutual harmony within the pure contingency of the dynamic event in which the once dead Jesus is raised into the futurity that is God's own unending life. In other words, this book is something of a Jensonian introduction to Jenson.

As this brief summary indicates, we will be venturing into the epicentre of Jenson's proposal, with the hope that this guidebook thereby assists the reader in grappling with Jenson's own written work, where he can be found wrestling with the idea that Jesus of Nazareth is one of the Trinity 'without qualification or evasion'.[13] Overall, I want to encourage readers to study Jenson for themselves, because there can be no substitute for the primary texts.[14] And Jenson certainly wrote. He authored over a dozen monographs, co-authored many more – including one with his then eight-year-old granddaughter, Solveig[15] – penned countless essays and peer-reviewed articles, edited and introduced numerous collections, published two biblical commentaries, wrote unnumbered editorials, hammered out book reviews, crafted authorized liturgies, helped determine ecumenical statements and even published a short poem on the Epiphany.[16] The number of publications is nothing short of remarkable, as the select bibliography at the end of this guide makes clear.[17] The range of subjects is likewise astonishing, with Jenson covering pretty much everything under the sun, branching out from – but never beyond – his doctrinal roots to tackle all sorts of cultural and political conundrums. You can read Jenson's thoughts on civil rights, abortion, war, political upheavals, euthanasia, marriage, contemporary art, modern science, prisons, theatre, financial markets and even 'plots not to kidnap Kissinger', as well as his views on just about every doctrinal debate you might care to mention.[18] Jenson's scattered writings thereby provide his readers with an almost encyclopaedic analysis as to what it means to be human in a world created by the triune God, allowing us to work out what needs to be said on any given subject by paying close attention to the Christian gospel. In short, Jenson wrote a great deal about a great deal.

Karl Barth once joked that the inkbottle was to his family what the wine bottle was to others, implying that he liked a drop or two.[19] Barth famously wrote at length, piling up the rhetoric as he approached every imaginable point from every conceivable angle, which is one of the reasons Barth's *Dogmatics* stands at over six million words and even then remains an unfinished work. Jenson like Barth is never at a loss for words, having something to say on just about every topic, although brevity is the name of Jenson's game.[20] His prose is incredibly tight, and so you will regularly find him condensing a century or so of complex thought into just a couple of compact sentences that somehow rehearse the tradition while reconfiguring it in drastic fashion.[21] As David Bentley Hart once said, it can take Jenson only a few carefully crafted words to detonate our usual way of seeing things, thereby opening up new perspectives onto the subject in question by locating its answer in a startling conception of the dynamic nature of God's eternal decision to be a particular God, a God who in the turn of a phrase can look at once recognizable yet in a strangely original way.[22] By the time Jenson's compact prose runs over the course of his two-volume *Systematic Theology* – albeit at only 600 or so pages – you realize that he has summarized and reconfigured almost the entire doctrinal tradition. In short, Jenson packs a surprising lot into a surprising little.[23]

As these comments imply, Jenson is no easy read.[24] For a start, he is not interested in operating in textbook mode, treading idle water for the sake of patient pedagogy – which is where a guidebook like this may come into use.[25] Jenson is driven by his own revisionary agenda, and is therefore focused on changing the way we think about what we assume we already know, thus correcting what he considers to be a number of conceptual missteps and setting our thoughts on a surprising new track. He therefore writes with the urgency of a polemicist, racing from subpoint to subpoint to reach his astonishing conclusions.[26] As a result, important points can be glossed and significant details squeezed out as he hurtles along towards his next explosive point. That is why, for example, he can state – almost apologetically:

> To do it completely [i.e. unpack the point as 'promised'], I would have to discuss something I have elided, the 'third identity' of the Trinity, the Scripture's pervasively present 'Spirit of/from the Lord.' I will not now make up that deficiency, only ask readers to remember the general biblical role of the Spirit, who enlivens Israel in its darkest moments and, as the creed of Nicea-Constantinople has it – 'spoke by the prophets.' That noted, we are in a position to proceed.[27]

And proceed he will, invariably at pace.

Jenson's readers can also be sure he will throw them a curveball at some stage in an argument, constructing a line of thought by which he intends to reconfigure our understanding of the subject in question by giving it a gospel-shaped twist, and often in the space of just a sentence or two. With his revisionary agenda fuelling his super-tight prose, Jenson's writing rewards close reading. Blink, and you can miss the subtle reasoning that motivates his unusual conclusions. Blink, and you can miss the constructive point the preceding paragraphs were set to serve. But read closely and Jenson can blow your mind. He will introduce you to a God who is much stranger than the one you previously imagined, not least by being a great deal more down to earth.

As Christoph Schwöbel once commented, 'the originality of [Jenson's] thought is always astounding',[28] although Schwöbel knows this can be taken the wrong way. Jenson is no fan of novelty for the sake of novelty and was never an advocate for falling into step with the intellectual fashions of contemporary culture. As Jenson sees it, in theology, 'diversity is often a good thing, but entrepreneurship is not'.[29] This means his theology is hard to place, with his thinking resisting the standard categories with which we pigeonhole. On one occasion he will strike us as progressive, on another as reactionary, and on most issues both at once. This is perhaps inevitable given Jenson wants to be more traditional than most theologians have been, thereby demonstrating that the original message of Jesus' resurrection is a lot more liberating than anything a progressive or reactionary mind could conjure up. The underlying question for Jenson is whether we have really managed to keep pace with the apostles' original proclamation, which he thinks offers a trajectory in thought that opens out into a vision of our future within the life of a God who is nothing other than the crucified and risen Jesus with his Father in their Spirit. Jenson therefore wants to find new ways to say what has always been said, thus enabling our startled minds to be drawn afresh towards our promised future by first returning to what the church has always discovered itself to have proclaimed about Jesus in the past. In effect, he wants to move us ahead by getting us to focus on where it all started, with any steps forward requiring us to ponder afresh what exactly happened in that darkened tomb over the first Easter weekend. As he sees it, the eternal gospel should therefore 'never [be] told the same way twice',[30] and, to that extent, Jenson is a revolutionary thinker.[31]

1.2 The evangelization of metaphysics

Stanley Hauerwas once argued that a lifetime of theological education is required to write – not read! – a single Jensonian sentence, and Jenson certainly devoted his life to the theological task.[32] On entering Luther College in Decorah, Iowa, as an undergraduate in 1947, Jenson studied classics and philosophy before training for ordination at Luther Seminary in St Paul Minnesota. Jenson went on to pursue further studies at Heidelberg and Basel, learning and teaching along the way, and taking up teaching posts at Luther College Decorah, Mansfield College Oxford, Gettysburg Seminary and St Olaf's Minnesota, right through until he accepted a research post at Princeton's Center of Theological Inquiry in 1998.[33] As these appointments suggest, Jenson enjoyed the privileges of the academic life, benefitting from ample time to read widely and think deeply, but never in the sense of ivory-clad isolation. The bulk of his career was dedicated to teaching candidates for the priesthood, lecturing and tutoring in the seminary context and thereby seeking an immediate impact on the church's ongoing life of worship and mission. Simply put, this revolutionary wore his clerical collar.[34]

Jenson always understood himself to be a servant of the church, although it was an institution that frustrated him because of its ongoing failure to grasp what the good news of the resurrection really means.[35] Jenson's work should be understood as a labour both *within* and *towards* the church that he loved, because his writing is intended to reinvigorate the community's thinking by making his contemporaries grasp the radical implications of what the baptized have always been called upon – but keep on forgetting – to confess. As Jenson sees it, the church has somehow 'lost her exegetical nerve', and so he never intends to venture far from his Bible as he diligently excavates past teaching in an attempt to show that the gospel promises a much better future than the one we usually imagine.[36] He will always listen closely to what has been said by others as he attempts to work out 'what to say to be saying the gospel' today, measuring patristic, medieval, modern and contemporary theology against his own understanding of the canon and creeds.[37] As a result, Jenson describes his own 'investigation' as 'a blend of exegesis and conceptual analysis', which combine to summon the church to proclaim the gospel more faithfully in this day and age.[38]

Right up until his death in 2017, Jenson's adult life was devoted to finding appropriate ways to speak the Word that God *is*, wrestling with both the form and content of the church's message. Despite aiming to be orthodox, Jenson would invariably come up with a unique way of seeing things, even though he was keen to trace a continuous thread of doctrinal support for what he says. Jenson would often find himself in the tiniest of minorities and occasionally discover that he was the only person to have said what he thinks needed to be said.[39] He can occasionally admit he must 'develop an alternative, also suggested – though perhaps *only* suggested – in the tradition',[40] or instead back up his original proposals with throwaway comments, such as the possibility of 'recruit[ing] some prestigious if sporadic support from theological history'.[41] Of course, this puts Jenson in something of a precarious position, finding himself at the extreme margins of Christian theology while claiming to have a better insight into what it means to stand at its centre. He therefore describes the theological task as 'an irremediably hubristic enterprise',[42] in that it demands we run the risk of saying what we believe to be true even if the rest of the world is firmly set against us – a possibility that never stopped Jenson, even when it became an actuality. What results is a strange-looking orthodoxy. Jenson's work is pretty much unique.[43]

The peculiar nature of Jenson's theology is one reason why his work is worth studying. His audacious attempt to use the church's authoritative teaching to reconfigure what the church has in practice not been teaching unearths buried assumptions about what must be true of God. Reading him therefore benefits those who reject his proposals just as much as those who accept them, in that he forces us to justify what we had previously presumed to have gone without saying.[44] As a result, Jenson is never short of plaudits even among his critics, being widely recognized as an incredibly gifted theologian, with Josh Gaghan, for example, comparing him to Aquinas as he places 'these two giants alongside one another . . . to sharpen one another'.[45] Jenson is not out of place in such company, which is why his work has been described as 'the most ambitious and unflagging attempt any American theologian has yet made fully to grasp the uniqueness of Christ',[46] with Jenson thereby saluted as 'the most sophisticated and original of contemporary Lutheran theologians in the English-speaking world'.[47] Even his most vehement opponents will always extol his virtues, celebrating the force of his intellect, his scholarly acumen – except for his contested reading of Augustine and the Fathers[48] – and the literary gifts with which he was blessed. In short, his colleagues think he is brilliant, but brilliantly wrong. Or, as Stephen R. Holmes once put it, Jenson is wrong 'for all the right reasons'.[49]

But it is those 'right reasons' that make Jenson worth studying. Here is a theologian who takes Jesus seriously. Of course, I'm not suggesting that he is alone in this respect, because every theologian knows how important Jesus is for an adequate account of who God is and what he is up to. But Jenson's undivided attention to the reality of Jesus sets him apart from the crowd, enabling him to offer his reader a gospel-shaped vision of an oddly gospel-shaped God who thereby shatters our assumptions about what a 'putative god'[50] should be like – and mainly because Jenson thinks 'Mary's child and Pilate's victim' is one of the Trinity, without qualification.[51] In short, there has never been an unfleshed Word.

Of course, it is strange to argue that the *enfleshed* Jesus is eternally one of the Trinity, but Jenson is quick to point out that it appears strange because our theology is wrongly configured. Our metaphysics cannot handle the gospel's chief protagonist, which is why – since as early as 1969 – he would describe his task as the *evangelization of metaphysics*.[52] Roughly speaking, metaphysics is the investigation of first principles, those primary building blocks of thought that constitute the scaffolding which supports our construction of reality, those subterranean beliefs about time, space, causation, existence and the like which enable us to make our claims about the fundamental nature of our life together. Evangelism is of course the task of conversion, the calling into eternal life of that which is dead through the proclamation of the resurrection of the crucified Jesus. As such, Jenson thinks his work – as the 'evangelization of metaphysics' – allows the good news of Jesus' victory over death to redefine our most basic conception of the most fundamental nature of reality. Working on the assumption that the embodied person of Christ is 'the founding metaphysical fact', he proceeds to bend everything – including the nature of God! – around the events of Good Friday and Easter Sunday.[53] Over the course of his career, he therefore reimagines the structure of time, space, causation and the like, as well as the infinite nature of the triune eternity of God, refusing to define any concept by any other means than a sustained analysis of the peculiar news that this one Israelite has been raised from the dead.[54] And the results are startling. Jenson thinks the living God 'really has a mother who does not need to be a goddess to achieve this',[55] because the one this creature births is one of the Trinity, around whom time spirals 'like a helix'[56] as the creature is drawn into the endless musicality of the God who always and forever identifies himself with 'the hanged man of Golgotha'.[57]

As the previous paragraph suggests, there is a startling originality to Jenson's thought, although its novelty should be not be overstated. His work can be situated within a great company of theologians, piggybacking as he does on the Cappadocians, Cyril, Maximus, Aquinas, Luther, Edwards and countless others besides. However, his work is most profitably located alongside that of Karl Barth, because in many respects Jenson is the theologian Barth would have been if the older Barth had taught the young Barth.[58] Of course, the old Barth didn't teach the young Barth. The intellectual leaders of the modern liberal establishment taught the young Safenwil pastor, and so Barth had to spend many years unlearning the things he had been schooled to think. It was only over the course of the 50-odd years between *Der Römerbrief* and the final pages of his unfinished *Dogmatics* that Barth managed to extricate himself from his original teachers in order to construct the remarkable Christology that we find in the fourth volume of his major work. Jenson, however, can begin where Barth left off. He can launch with the idea that the man Jesus of Nazareth is God's decision to be eternally with us, thereby making Jesus eternally decisive to the life of the Trinity, and not in the everyday sense of that claim – namely that Jesus is somehow related to an eternal Trinity that was happily perichoresing around in splendid isolation long before Jesus came to save us – but in the sense of a genuinely strict identity: one of Three, who together make God what it is to be God, is 'Mary's child and Pilate's victim',[59] with as much weight as possible being placed on that 'is', which Jenson states loudly and 'without qualification'.

Of course, we will need to do a lot more work before we can make sense of the claim that 'The second person of God is a male Jew of the first century'.[60] But before we do, it is worth noting that Jenson assumes his readers will instinctively disagree with his proposal. We know God doesn't *really* have a mother. We know God doesn't *really* die. And even if we sometimes talk as if God is born of a woman and dies at the hands of men, we are certain – if we stop to think – that these kinds of statements amount to little more than a play on words, with the boundary markers of our creaturely mortality being in no way essential to God being the God he forever *is*. God is without origination and end, don't forget, and so a womb and a tomb can have no place in his eternal life. As a result, Jesus of Nazareth cannot have been one of the Trinity eternally. We know something more sophisticated needs to be said.

To put the point otherwise, Jenson has the bulk of the tradition against him, although he is prepared to proceed with his revisionary project nonetheless.[61] He thinks the rest of us have got it wrong, and mainly because we have been unwilling to allow the gospel message of one man's resurrection to shape our understanding of the epicentre of God's godliness. In fact, Jenson suspects most of his readers would prefer to lean on the teaching of the ancient philosophers, thereby positing a faraway eternity in which God can forever be the God we assume he must always be, without mother, without killer and essentially having little to do with the gospel event.[62] Of course, Jenson accepts the best theologians have ensured their vision of God is linked closely to the story of Jesus, but he thinks they have only drawn the gospel events as near as possible into the orbit of our philosophically determined God, thereby ensuring that there remains some kind of 'gap' between God eternally in himself and the historical events of his move towards us. As a result, Christian theologians – whose metaphysics Jenson is trying to evangelize – spend all their time papering over the chasm they themselves have created, devoting their energies – according to Jenson, not me! – to an attempt to join up a series of dots across a metaphysical gap, thereby positing mysterious 'extensions' and 'expressions' that get them from the eternal God to the gospel narrative.[63] Jenson thinks these bridging concepts function as a mysterious ellipsis – a dot, dot, dot – across the yawning divide between God and Jesus, thereby amounting to little more than an attempt to hide the fact that we know very little about God in himself. God thereby gets reduced to little more than an apophatic blank, onto which we can project our preferential imaginings, or before which we can collapse in exhausted silence, essentially cut adrift on the far end of an analogical interval, conjoined at best, but no more than that.[64] The problem is this unknown God can never be trusted fully. However, Jenson thinks the God of the gospel can. And that is because there is not so much as a hairsbreadth between God and Jesus of Nazareth, not now, not ever. 'Mary's child and Pilate's victim' is precisely one of the Trinity.

Of course, I've raced ahead again here, and we will need to retrace these steps at a much slower pace if we are to draw out the logic of Jenson's critique and counterproposal. However, it is helpful to have dragged the strangeness of Jenson's theology out into plain view, because it will at times be easy to lose sight of the wood for the trees. The force of Jenson's rhetoric is often compelling, and so it will be important to keep the oddity of his proposal at the forefront of our minds, not least when we begin to see that our desire to protect God from the wombs of women and the tombs men dig has created a conceptual fiction; the *Logos asarkos*, the unfleshed Word. Somewhat oddly, Jenson will ask us to ditch this treasured concept.

1.3 Always forever *enfleshed*

The *Logos asarkos* plays a pivotal role in pretty much every technical description of God. The unfleshed Word is usually one of the Trinity in 'eternity past', so to speak, who then – during 'times past' – became incarnate for our salvation.[65] But Jenson rejects this claim. Time and again, he will argue that the *Logos asarkos* is no more than a manmade construct, amounting to little more than an unfortunate consequence of the conceptual dead-end we have travelled along. And that is a strange claim.[66]

To justify his conclusion, Jenson will remind his reader that the doctrine of the Trinity is first and foremost about 'Jesus the Israelite and the Transcendence he addressed as Father, and their Spirit as the enlivener of the believing community'.[67] He thinks metaphysical prejudice alone could create the need to insert an unfleshed Word into the drama of these Three. Jenson thereby challenges us to remain where the church's reflections began, and he is confident – if we do! – that we can discover new ways of understanding how the 'aggressively incarnate' Jesus is himself one of the Trinity.[68]

As this introduction is making clear, Jenson is highly peculiar in thinking that the *Logos asarkos* has no positive role to play in our theology. However, he thinks that this drastic conclusion is demanded by the church's dogmatic decisions.[69] He will argue that the concept of an unfleshed Word only became useful because we ignored official teaching, thereby remaining functionally Nestorian by refusing to allow the concept of the hypostatic union to shape our conception of God. Nestorius, to recall, argued that there must be two most basic realities in Jesus, with one being eternally divine and the other temporally human, thereby leaving enough of a gap between these 'conjoined' entities to protect God from the things common sense said the gods mustn't do.[70] Of course, theology students soon learn that Cyril emerged victorious from the resulting argument, thereby helping establish the Chalcedonian teaching that there is only one most basic reality in Jesus, a single *hypostasis*. But Jenson thinks we tend to ignore this fact, thereby failing to devote our time to working out what the dogma implies for our conception of God. He suspects most theologians duck the difficult thinking required and instead use Leo's appended *Tome* – the details of which we will explore in a later chapter[71] – to legitimize their under-the-counter smuggling of a Nestorian duality back into our understanding of God. They thereby continue to posit two most basic realities in their account of Jesus' life, with the *Logos asarkos* being employed as a protective barrier between God and the bloody and dusty reality of the gospel event. But Jenson thinks God needs no such protection. 'Jesus, the human protagonist of the Gospels, is the second identity of the Trinity', and so 'proper Christology would be clarification of this form of the gospel claim'.[72]

Jenson's conclusion will rightly strike the reader as odd.[73] Most of us will be confident that this is not how things stand with God, not least because we have been taught how the story of creation and redemption goes. We will be quick to point out that there *was* a time in our time when Jesus did not exist – the temporal span from our Adamic origins through to Mary's pregnancy – and so conclude that the Word *became* flesh, with that highlighted concept clearly positing some prior state of *be*-ing from which the unfleshed Son *came*. But Jenson asks us to hold our nerve. Instead of allowing a previously determined conception of God to prise open an ontological space within the concept of 'becoming', he wants us to do the difficult work of constructing an alternative metaphysics in which it makes sense to say that 'Mary's child, the hanged man of Golgotha'[74] is one of the Three who always and forever together make God what it is to be God. In other words, Jenson will radically redefine what it means to say that 'the Word became flesh', seeking to take seriously the church's belief that Jesus is the Son he claimed to be and then bending our conception of the most basic features of God's reality around what the gospel says about him. In effect, he thinks we must all try to make sense of the strange claim that 'a strolling carpenter's apprentice' – in G. K. Chesterton's words – 'said calmly and almost carelessly, like one looking over his shoulder: "Before Abraham was, I am"'.[75]

Jenson's work is therefore a sustained meditation on the startling nature of the innocuous-looking verb in the predicate 'became flesh', with Jenson wanting to situate the concept of 'becoming' in a revisionary account of the two-way trajectory of the Son's single *hypostasis* – i.e. his personhood – effectively drawing the mystery of 'becoming' into the depths of God's unique way of eternal being, so that the verb captures the epicentre of a simultaneously imploding and exploding personal act of God's decision to be a particular God. Clearly, we will need to do more work before grasping what this means, but we should already be spotting that Jenson is ploughing a lonely furrow here. You can count on one hand – probably only one and a half fingers! – the number of theologians who deny the existence of a *Logos asarkos*.[76] This therefore means a great cloud of witnesses can be lined up against Jenson, with his opponents being able to draw from the most influential theologians to show how he is out of step with long established norms. He can therefore be made to face a long list of charges, with all manner of heretical errors being levelled against him.[77] As Stephen Wright helpfully summarizes, Jenson's account of an always enfleshed God is accused of collapsing the distinction between the being of God and the works of God, thereby implying that creation is somehow necessary for God to be God.[78] That is to say, Jenson's God only becomes the God that he is over the course of our temporal history, with the vital difference between God and the world dissolved in their perfect identity, with our world being rendered essential to making God the God that he in fact *is*. In short, God is no longer Almighty, but depends on us just as much as we depend on him.

Jenson knows his proposal can be read in this way, although he is quick to point out that critics haven't grasped what he saying.[79] This is one of the reasons he describes his project as an experiment, thereby reminding his colleagues that he is not claiming to be speaking the final word on the subject but instead wants to show what might be possible if we stop equating Greek philosophy with the teaching of the apostles, and instead work solely with the raw materials of the gospel message.[80] As a result, Jenson accepts, 'some readers may well think my proposal is too daring', and is open to constructive criticism throughout, but he insists that any negotiation must be undertaken on the condition that we are speaking about the man Jesus.[81] In short, there must be no bypassing the embodied God. We must wrestle with 'the Jesus who appears in the Gospels, as he is in fact the Son of God he was accused of claiming to be'.[82]

Jenson's own analysis of the experimental nature of his work clearly raises a tantalizing question, allowing us to speculate about how things would be different if other theologians had tried to do the work Jenson thinks he is doing. But of course, they didn't, which is why Jenson is so heavily outnumbered. Reading critiques of his work can sometimes feel – to borrow Feyerabend's phrase – like 'arranging a fight between an infant and a grown man, and announcing triumphantly, what is obvious anyway, that the man is going to win'.[83] *Of course*, the greatest theologians have said something different. *Of course*, that makes it look like Jenson gets it completely wrong. But that is partly Jenson's point. He thinks orthodoxy has never been decided by the rule of a timid majority but is instead 'opposed to a culture's common sense' – sometimes even that of the most faithful of Christians. As a result, the oddity of Jenson's proposal isn't enough to reject it. We need to find better reasons than that.

Jenson's frustration with the way his proposal is handled does spill out on occasion, notably in a series of exasperated responses to critics such as Hunsinger and Molnar.[84] Jenson thinks these theologians beg the principle, in that they have taken a stand in a different metaphysics to the one he is developing and from that remote position proceed to judge his conclusions as inadequate on the grounds of the very metaphysics Jenson wants to evangelize.[85] I think this can often be the case, although it is important to note that incommensurability – the lack of a common measure – can't provide any theologian with a get-out-of-jail-free card, with none of us able to claim that we are instigating a paradigm shift and thereby conclude that any criticism is mere evidence of the previous paradigm's dominance. Orthodoxy doesn't quite work like that, even if we agree with Feyerabend that scientific revolutions do. Instead, a theologian needs to convince their sisters and brothers about the strengths of their proposal, thereby showing their workings and displaying the biblical logic that determines their novel judgement, which is precisely what Jenson tries to do. He argues his case theologically.

1.4 The route ahead

Jenson's rejoinder to his critics alerts us to the need to read Jenson carefully, both in the sense that his proposals might be dangerously wrong – as Hunsinger, Molnar and others have claimed – but also in the sense of testing out whether Jenson's proposal springs logically from a shared premise, that Israel's God raised the human Jesus from the dead. Bearing this in mind, I will endeavour to guide the reader into the heart of Jenson's proposal, drawing out the way in which what he says about the resurrected Jesus informs what he says about the nature of divine and human reality. My intention is to give Jenson a fair hearing, thereby holding back on the criticism and instead slowly unpacking the points he will often make at pace.

This approach also means I will often use simple examples to illustrate complex points, drawing from outside Jenson's work to open up some of the areas where his ideas get congested. By translating his complex proposals into layman's terms, I hope to demonstrate why he believes what he believes and thereby show how solid his grounds are. Of course, the risk is that I will alienate experienced theologians by this pedagogical process, as they will, for example, have no need to get to grips with the ABCs of Greek metaphysics or be introduced to the technical meaning of terms such as *hypostasis*. Such readers might therefore tire of my attempts to translate Jenson's ideas into simpler terms, but that is a risk I am willing to take if it means this guidebook can enable newcomers to understand what Jenson is up to, and thereby help them get to grips with the primary texts.

To get our investigation started, I will use the next two chapters to introduce a series of points which I think are central to Jenson's proposal.

We will first explore how he handles the scandalous particularity of the gospel message, never shying away from its historical claims, but instead weaving contingency, time and stories into his doctrine of God. This step-by-step approach will mean that some of the initial ideas will remain underdeveloped in the first two chapters, only receiving fuller treatment later in the book, with this tactic creating an inevitable degree of overlap between different sections and chapters, and an element of repetition proving unavoidable in places. However, I think the accumulative development of the ideas is the best way to create the necessary space for our own thoughts to move beyond where we begin and get to where Jenson wants us to go, in effect allowing the process of evangelization to happen in our heads over the course of the book.

Having flagged up a cluster of concepts in Part One, we will then turn our attention to the way Jenson believes a series of trinitarian and christological concepts developed within the early life of the church. This apparent detour – where we will engage with trinitarian discourse in the broader sense – will show why Jenson seeks to redeploy the tools he receives from the tradition, thereby overcoming the established metaphysics, which the missionary church encounters, and thus create a relational ontology by which the most basic identity of Jesus can be understood to participate at one and the same time in the two communal realities of divinity and humanity. This analysis of Jenson's reading of the dogmatic tradition will set us up nicely for Part Three of the book, where we will attend to his revisionary doctrine of God directly, with three substantive chapters being devoted to showing how Jesus of Nazareth is one of the Trinity, with the eternal life of the Three centring on what happens over the first Easter weekend. These three chapters – including one on Jenson's development of Barth's doctrine of election – include my attempt to align his proposal to some of the classical concepts in theology, seeking to articulate the way in which the doctrine of divine *aseity* and the doctrine of creation need to be reconfigured in light of his understanding of the resurrection of Jesus. These sections are where I press Jenson the most, thereby running the risk that I will step beyond the bounds of his own thinking at certain points. If that happens, I hope to remain on the same trajectory as Jenson and thereby speak in tune with his proposal.

Once the complex matter of God's eternal self-determination in Jesus has been examined, we will turn our attention to what the reader can take from Jenson's account of the gospel message. Part Four of the book will therefore be devoted to deciphering the way in which his proposal informs our religious practice, not least in the way it locates our encounter with God and our neighbour in the here and now of the concrete rituals that define our local churches. The closing chapters will thereby show how the strangest thing about Jenson's work is the way it keeps our feet planted firmly on the ground, albeit with the ground being strangely situated within the eternal life of a God who is forever incarnate. However, to see how Jenson gets us to that point, we must first examine his understanding of the explosive consequences of our everyday Christian speech. And to that opening task we finally turn.

Notes

1 Robert W. Jenson and Solveig Lucia Gold, *Conversations with Poppi about God* (Grand Rapids: Brazos Press, 2006), 15.

2 Robert W. Jenson, 'Karl Barth on the Being of God', in *Thomas Aquinas and Karl Barth: An Unofficial Catholic-Protestant Dialogue*, ed. Bruce L. McCormack and Thomas Joseph White (Grand Rapids: Eerdmans, 2013), 47.

3 Jenson, 'Karl Barth', 51. Emphasis removed.

4 Robert W. Jenson, 'Scripture's Authority in the Church', in *The Art of Reading Scripture*, ed. Ellen F. Davis and Richard B. Hays (Grand Rapids: Eerdmans, 2003), 35.

5 Robert W. Jenson, *Systematic Theology, Vol. 1, The Triune God* (New York: OUP, 1997), 236.

6 Robert W. Jenson, *Systematic Theology, Vol. 2, The Works of God* (New York: OUP, 1999), 369.

7 I could have inserted something like, 'the American Lutheran theologian' at this point. However, such adjectives could mislead. Even though Jenson was on the 'clergy list' of the Lutheran Church throughout his career, he thought 'a theologian who described her or his own work as "Lutheran" or "Reformed" or whatever such, and meant by that label to identify the church the work was to serve, would either deny the name of church to all but his or her own allegiance or desecrate the theological enterprise.' Instead, Jenson wrote for 'the unique and unitary church of the creeds', though offered a 'statement of confessional limitations' where his own 'particular location in the landscape created by the divisions' is set out. See Jenson, *Systematic Theology*, Vol. 1, vii–viii. Jenson elsewhere offers an account of why he remained officially in the Evangelical Lutheran Church of America despite worshipping in an Episcopal church. See Robert W. Jenson, 'Reversals: How My Mind Has Changed', *The Christian Century* (20 April 2010), 33.

8 Extensive secondary literature on Jenson's theology is detailed in the bibliography. For a fine concise introduction to the way Jenson thinks, see Chris E. W. Green, *The End Is Music: A Companion to Robert W. Jenson's Theology* (Eugene, OR: Cascade, 2018).

9 For example, see Jenson's description of his engagement with Gregory of Nyssa, in Robert W. Jenson, *The Triune Identity: God According to the Gospel* (Philadelphia: Fortress, 1982; reprint, Eugene, OR: Wipf and Stock, 2002), 162.

10 For example, Steve Wright argues that Jenson tends to avoid the term *aseity*, although he employs the concept, notably by engaging with Aquinas's argument about existence and essence. See Stephen John Wright, *Dogmatic Aesthetics: A Theology of Beauty in Dialogue with Robert W. Jenson* (Minneapolis: Fortress, 2014), 54–63.

11 One quote nicely captures the spirit of Jenson's invitation to other theologians: 'Readers will undoubtedly sometimes decide that the commentary's proposal of a theological story is unconvincing. Given the character of our text, they can without sarcasm be invited to do better. It may be that the chief purpose of a commentary on this text is not to provide interpretation but to provoke it.' Robert W. Jenson, *Song of Songs: A Biblical Commentary for Teaching and Preaching* (Louisville: John Knox Press, 2005), 12.

12 Robert W. Jenson, 'A Reply', *Scottish Journal of Theology* 52.1 (1999), 132.

13 Jenson, *Systematic Theology*, Vol. 1, 144.

14 Chris Green alerts us to the importance of reading beyond Jenson's *Systematic Theology* to grasp his entire project. Green makes the case that there is consistency *and* development through Jenson's written work. See Green, *End Is Music*, 2–5, 10–12.

15 Jenson and Gold, *Conversations*.

16 It is worth noting Jenson believed a lot of his books were co-authored with his wife, Blanche. As he puts it, 'In my judgment, both our names should appear as co-authors on most of these books. She, however, does not agree. The best I can do, therefore, is state the reasons for my view. Through the course of my theological work, I have had few thoughts or insights that she has not suggested or occasioned.' Robert W. Jenson, *Unbaptized God: The Basic Flaw in Ecumenical Theology* (Minneapolis: Fortress, 1992), v. Jenson's love for Blanche regularly shines through his work, culminating in an aside offered shortly before his death: 'I do not seem to want a heaven that does not include that head now on the next pillow.' Robert W. Jenson, 'Dante's Vision', *Studies in Christian Ethics* 30.2 (2017), 168. For Blanche's own account of his academic career, see Blanche Jenson, 'You shall love the Lord with all your mind', *Pro Ecclesia* 27.3 (2018), 248–54.

17 Even though this book's bibliography is extensive, it is not exhaustive. Adam Eitel also offers an *almost* comprehensive list of Jenson's works. See Robert W. Jenson, *A Theology in Outline: Can These Bones Live?* transcribed, ed. and introduced by Adam Eitel (Oxford: OUP, 2016), 117–34. It is therefore uncertain whether anyone knows exactly how much Jenson published, and – in personal correspondence – Chris Green informs me that Jenson himself didn't possess a list of everything he had written.

18 See details in Eitel's bibliography, e.g. Robert W. Jenson, 'The Plot Not to Kidnap Kissinger', in *Dialog* 11.2 (1972), 88–9.

19 Eberhard Busch, *Karl Barth: His Life from Letters and Autobiographical Texts*, translated by John Bowden (Grand Rapids: Eerdmans, 1994), 26.

20 In correspondence, Chris Green and Steve Wright suggested 'precision' is a better term to use. However, I don't want to thereby suggest Barth is not precise.

21 Jenson once described Ezekiel as, 'the most intellectual of the prophets, and a prose artist adept at manipulating established oral and literary genres to novel effect.' I'm tempted to say that it takes one to know one. Robert W. Jenson, *Ezekiel* (London: SCM Press, 2009), 17.

22 David Bentley Hart, 'The Lively God of Robert Jenson', *First Things*, October 2005.

23 In a preface, Jenson says he understands why the likes of Aquinas and Barth went to the lengths they went, because there is *always* more to say about the gospel. Nevertheless, it remained his 'doubtless superficial determination to be brief'. Jenson, *Systematic Theology* Vol. 2, v–vi.

24 Jenson aimed 'to make the trinitarian tradition lucid – which does not mean easy'. Jenson, *Triune Identity*, xii. He recognizes – in another book – that 'readers

may complain that this account of our knowledge of God is too simple, perhaps even simply too brief. But brevity and naiveté belong to the account given. This may of course be a sign of its incorrectness. But greater prolixity or argumentative complexity would not improve it' (Jenson, *Systematic Theology*, Vol. 2, 303).

25 For Jenson in teaching mode, see the transcribed lectures in Jenson, *Theology in Outline*.

26 As Jenson confesses, 'my report of the tradition, while as accurate as I could make it, is not systematically neutral. It is not offered as a replacement for the standard historical summaries – though naturally I hope it improves on them.' Jenson, *Triune Identity*, xii.

27 Robert W. Jenson, 'What Kind of God Can Make a Covenant?' in *Covenant and Hope: Christian and Jewish Reflections*, ed. Robert W. Jenson and Eugene B. Korn (Grand Rapids: Eerdmans, 2012), 15. Or, another example: 'I should not throw such heavy dogmatic propositions at you without exposition or argument. But if I were to supply these, I would get nothing else down. So I have to hope that the dogmatic propositions are at least to some extent evocative in themselves, and that the following applications will be themselves some argument and exposition.' Robert W. Jenson, 'Liturgy of the Spirit', *The Lutheran Quarterly* 26 (1974), 190.

28 Stated in personal correspondence.

29 'An Interview with Robert W. Jenson', *The Christian Century* (May 2006). www.religion-online.org/article/an-interview-with-robert-w-jenson.

30 Robert W. Jenson, *Story and Promise: A Brief Theology of the Gospel About Jesus* (Philadelphia: Fortress Press, 1973; reprint, Eugene, OR: Wipf & Stock 2014), 11.

31 Jenson knows the desire to offer something new is dangerous, because, 'Making such a judgement may locate me in a fictitious godlike position above the parties.' Robert W. Jenson, 'Lutheranism and the *Filioque*', in *Ecumenical Perspectives on the Filioque for the 21st Century*, ed. Myk Habets (London: T&T Clark, 2014), 162.

32 Stanley Hauerwas, 'How to Write a Theological Sentence', *ABC Religion and Ethics*, 26 September 2013.

33 For details, see Robert W. Jenson, 'A Theological Autobiography, to Date', *Dialog* 46 (2007), 46–54. See also, Blanche Jenson, 'You shall love the Lord', 248–54.

34 Obituaries evidence Jenson's impact on the clergy. See, for example, Gregory Fryer, 'A Parish Pastor Speaks of Robert W. Jenson', *Newsletter of the Center for Catholic and Evangelical Theology* (2017), 2–4, and Alvin F. Kimel, 'Robert W. Jenson: Reminiscences and Memories', *Eclectic Orthodoxy*, 7 September 2017. However, as Steve Wright points out, Jenson's work is shaped by the liberal arts teaching he undertook. As Wright argues, Jenson thought that 'precisely because they will be serving in the church, seminarians need exposure to difficult poetry and edgy plays'. It would therefore be wrong to 'diminish the importance of college teaching for Jenson'. Wright, in personal correspondence.

35 Jenson did plenty of ecumenical work, although it eventually frustrated him, leading to the conclusion, 'An act of God is needed' to 'reestablish communion once broken', adding hopefully that 'God may act tomorrow'. Jenson, *Systematic Theology*, Vol. 1, viii.

36 Jenson, 'What Kind of God', 16.

37 Jenson, *Systematic Theology*, Vol. 1, 32.

38 Jenson, 'What Kind of God', 6.

39 For example, when dealing with the 'patrological problem', Jenson knows the 'title of this chapter is something of a neologism'. Jenson, *Systematic Theology*, Vol. 1, 115.

40 Robert W. Jenson, 'On the Ascension', in *Loving God With Our Minds: The Pastor as Theologian*, ed. Michael Welker and Cynthia A. Jarvis (Grand Rapids: Eerdmans, 2004), 334.

41 Jenson, 'What Kind of God', 10. In short, Jenson thinks his work is 'fair to the tradition, but is not itself traditional'. Jenson, *Triune Identity*, xiii.

42 Jenson, *Systematic Theology*, Vol. 1, vii.

43 For example, Jenson states: 'But so far as I know, previous theology has not explicitly said that "Father, Son, and Holy Spirit" is a proper name.' Jenson, *Triune Identity*, xiii.

44 David Bentley Hart makes this point. Hart, 'The Lively God.'

45 Josh Gaghan, 'Reason, Metaphysics, and their Relationship in the Theologies of Jenson and Aquinas', *New Blackfriars* 99.1082 (2018), 540.

46 Hart, 'The Lively God.'

47 Rowan Williams, *Christ The Heart of Creation* (London: Bloomsbury Continuum, 2018), 158.

48 For one summary of Jenson's critique of Augustine, see Jenson, *Systematic Theology*, Vol. 1, 110–19. For an examination of his use/misuse of patristic sources, see Morwenna Ludlow, *Gregory of Nyssa, Ancient and (Post)modern* (Oxford: OUP, 2007), 8–10. For Jenson's rejoinder to the charge of misreading patristic sources, see Robert W. Jenson, 'A Decision Tree of Colin Gunton's Thinking', in *The Theology of Colin Gunton*, ed. Lincoln Harvey (New York: T&T Clark, 2010), 10–12. As Jenson later stated, 'I will take this occasion to remark that several defenders of Augustine have expressed their outrage at this book [*The Triune Identity* and its critique of Augustine], but none has engaged my actual argument to show that anything is the matter with it.' Jenson, 'Lutheranism and the *Filioque*', 161, n4.

49 Stephen R. Holmes, in conversation and used with permission. The most (in)famous critique of Jenson remains George Hunsinger, 'Robert Jenson's Systematic Theology: A Review Essay', *Scottish Journal of Theology* 55 (2002), 161–200. For Jenson's rebuttal, see Robert W. Jenson, 'Response to Watson and Hunsinger', *Scottish Journal of Theology* 55.2 (2002), 225–32. The work of Paul Molnar is also of note, see Paul Molnar, *Faith, Freedom and the Spirit: The Economic Trinity in Barth, Torrance and Contemporary Theology* (Downers Grove: InterVarsity Press, 2015), 232–42, and Paul Molnar, 'The Perils of Embracing a "Historicized Christology"', *Modern Theology* 30.4 (2014), 454–80. For Jenson's succinct reply to Molnar, see Jenson, 'A Reply', 132. For a sharp critical analysis of Jenson's proposals, see Oliver Crisp, *Word Enfleshed: Exploring the Person and Work of Christ* (Grand Rapids: Baker Academic, 2016), 19–31.

50 This is the first use of the word 'putative' which Jenson regularly uses to indicate any/all alternative gods that are thought to exist. See, for example, Robert W. Jenson, 'How the World Lost Its Story', *First Things*, 1993. Citations will not be offered on every use going forward.

51 This is also the first use of this phrase, variants of which Jenson will often use. For one instance, see Robert W. Jenson, 'What if It Were True?', *Neue Zeitschrift für Systematische Theologie und Religionsphilosophie* 43.1 (2001), 11. I will shift the language from 'child' to 'boy' to press the specific particularity. Jenson does use 'boy', but drops Pilate in one instance, see Robert W. Jenson, 'Jesus in the Trinity',

Pro Ecclesia 8 (1999), 309. With the first reference to this essay, the origin for the title of this book is revealed.

52 An early description of theology as 'revisionary metaphysics' can be found in Robert W. Jenson, 'The Futurist Option of Speaking of God', *The Lutheran Quarterly* 21.1 (1969), 22.

53 Jenson, 'Interview in Christian Century', 35. For an account of what 'revisionary metaphysics' means in practice, see Robert W. Jenson, 'Watson and Hunsinger', 225–32.

54 Hence, Jenson concludes, 'Rationality is epistemic openness to God's future: it is obedience to the command, "Be prepared to change your mind. Test your opinions by whatever are in any circumstances the appropriate warrants"'. Jenson, *Systematic Theology*, Vol. 2, 146–7.

55 Robert W. Jenson, 'For Us . . . He Was Made Man', in *Nicene Christianity: The Future for a New Ecumenism*, ed. Christopher Seitz (Grand Rapids: Brazos Press, 2001), 83.

56 Jenson, 'Scripture's Authority', 35.

57 Jenson, *Systematic Theology*, Vol. 1, 145.

58 As we will see, Jenson engages with Barth because Barth's *Dogmatics* 'is an enormous attempt to interpret all reality by the fact of Christ'. Jenson, *Systematic Theology*, Vol. 1, 21. However, Barth's influence is complemented by the works of other theologians, with Jenson – as Steve Wright helpfully shows – never becoming a mere 'acolyte' of Barth. Wright argues: 'Readers of Jenson who wish to claim him too quickly for Barthianism overlook the complexities of Jenson's formation' (156), although recognizes Jenson's early engagement with Barth 'shaped all of his subsequent theology' (159). Wright's article helpfully sets out the various influences in a chronological account of Jenson's development, and should be read to mitigate the broad claims made in this introduction. Stephen John Wright, 'Sounding Out the Gospel: Robert Jenson's Theological Project', *Pro Ecclesia* 28.2 (2019), 149–66.

59 Jenson, 'What if', 10.

60 Robert W. Jenson, *A Large Catechism* (Delhi, NY: American Lutheran Publicity Bureau, 1991), 28.

61 For example, Jenson can state that 'we follow a minority tradition of dogmatics; the minority, we claim, is right'. Robert W. Jenson, 'The Triune God', *Christian Dogmatics*, ed. Carl E. Braaten and Robert W. Jenson (Philadelphia: Fortress, 1984), 84.

62 See, for example, the way Jenson thinks the church must overcome 'pagan antiquity's revulsion at the obtrusively temporal facts of gestation and childbirth'. Nonetheless, he does accept that engagement with 'Plato or Aristotle' is part of the church's mission, but insists it is a mistake to think their teaching is 'more "natural" or "rational" than truth taught by Isaiah or Paul.' Jenson, *Systematic Theology*, Vol. 1, 49.

63 Jenson's diagnosis of the inherent futility of trying to figure out how a *timeless* God can act *in time* is set out succinctly in Jenson, 'What Kind of God', 7.

64 Jenson makes this point, for example, in Jenson, *Systematic Theology*, Vol. 1, 59–60.

65 I'm indebted to Chris Green for the phrasing here.

66 As Steve Wright points out, Jenson's early work on Barth criticized Barth's handling of the *logos asarkos*, with Jenson thinking that the concept was in some sense indispensable. However, Jenson soon moved beyond his initial hesitance and rejected the concept. See Wright, *Dogmatic Aesthetics*, 20–7.

67 Robert W. Jenson, 'Jesus, Father, Spirit: The Logic of the Doctrine of the Trinity', *Dialog* 26.4 (1987), 249.

68 Jenson, *Systematic Theology*, Vol. 1, 139. With this phrase, Jenson indicates God's unstoppable desire to be in this particular way, i.e. embodied.

69 This is a regular line of attack in Jenson's arguments. For example, see Jenson, 'Jesus in the Trinity', 308–18.

70 For details of the debate, see Jenson, *Systematic Theology*, Vol. 1, 127–33.

71 For Jenson's view, see Jenson, *Systematic Theology*, Vol. 1, 130–3.

72 Robert W. Jenson, 'How Does Jesus Make a Difference?' in *Essentials of Christian Theology*, ed. William C. Placher (Louisville: WJK Press, 2003), 201.

73 As Jenson exclaimed when spotting that Barth posits the eternal pre-existence of Jesus, 'But surely Barth is going wild . . .! Is not Barth branching off into gnostic mythology?' Robert W. Jenson, *Alpha and Omega: A Study in the Theology of Karl Barth* (New York: Thomas Nelson & Sons, 1963; reprint, Eugene, OR: Wipf and Stock, 2002), 71–2.

74 Jenson, *Systematic Theology*, Vol. 1, 145.

75 The phrase is Chesterton's but captures Jenson's point nicely. G. K. Chesterton, *The Everlasting Man* (Mineola, NY: Dover, 2007), 192. For Jenson's argument on the pre-existence of Jesus, see, for example, Jenson, *Systematic Theology*, Vol. 1, 138–44.

76 On my reading, Bruce McCormack does, and – if he is right! – half of Barth as well. (Whether that is the more Barthian half is not the question here.)

77 Again, the go-to critique, detailing multiple charges, remains Hunsinger, 'Jenson's Systematic Theology'. Of course, the combination of opposite heresies could suggest something is not quite right about Hunsinger's charges. Steve Wright has shown, for example, that the charge of 'Hegelian' is fair neither to Jenson nor to Hegel. Stephen John Wright, 'Restlessly Thinking Relation', in *Essays on the Trinity*, ed. Lincoln Harvey (Eugene, OR: Cascade, 2018), 140–60.

78 Wright, 'Restlessly Thinking', 146.

79 See, for instance, his response to Hunsinger, in Jenson, 'Response to Watson and Hunsinger', 225–32.

80 Jenson describes his project as 'revisionary metaphysics', which he defines as seeking to change the 'conceptual ways commonly followed by all disciplines within an historical culture'. He claims Christian theology should dislocate culture's 'common sense', but some are unable 'to entertain the proposals made, *even as experiment*'. Jenson, 'Reply', 132, emphasis added. Hunsinger also highlights the experimental nature of Jenson's project, while hoping his critique brings the experiment to an end. Hunsinger, 'Jenson's Systematic Theology', 200.

81 For example: 'If readers prefer another mapping, they have this author's blessing to develop it, so long as they do not under the hand construe a disembodied risen Jesus'. Jenson, 'On the Ascension', 339.

82 Jenson, *Systematic Theology*, Vol. 1, 134.

83 The phrase is Feyerabend's, and not about Jenson directly. Paul Feyerabend, *Against Method*, 3rd edn (London: Verso, 1988), 108.

84 See Jenson, 'Reply', 132, and Jenson, 'Response to Watson and Hunsinger', 225–32.

85 While shifting the point away from specific theologians, Jenson argues, 'irrationality is indeed a crime. When I maintain my opinions merely because I already hold them, I shut myself against the future and so against new possibilities others represent to me. And so I violate community.' Jenson, *Systematic Theology*, Vol. 2, 147.

PART ONE

A Cluster of Jensonian Concepts

2

The Strange God of the Gospel

2.1 The scandalous ABCs of Christian speech

Throughout his work, Jenson's intention is clear. He wants to identify the true God from all other claimants to that title. Jenson thinks the gospel is essential to that task, because 'the blessing of the gospel is that it unexpectedly and wonderfully identifies who the true God is, and . . . newly and amazingly permits us to worship him and even explain how that is possible.'[1] As a result, Jenson's entire project is an exercise in pinpointing God so that Christians may praise and petition him in appropriate ways.

With this aim in sight, Jenson invites his readers to return to the most basic things Christians believe, although he thinks we are in for something of a shock when we do. That is because the 'most Sundayschool-platitudinous of Christian claims . . . contain cognitive explosives we fear will indeed blow our minds', mainly because they commit us to the project of 'revisionary metaphysics . . . on a massive scale'.[2] In other words, he suspects most of his readers will have lost sight of the 'mind-boggling'[3] nature of the Christian gospel, with its earth-shattering truth being obscured by the '*conceptual dissonance*'[4] our ingrained patterns of thought inevitably trigger. With that emphasized phrase, Jenson highlights the way our habitual thinking will be deeply disturbed by the gospel's alignment of one single man with universal truth. Ever alert to the discord this coupling creates, he plans to drag the plain sense of our speech out into the open so we can see how the eradication of this 'conceptual dissonance' demands nothing short of the evangelization of our metaphysics.[5]

As a result, Jenson encourages his readers to undertake a patient re-examination of the ABCs of Christian speech, and – once done – invites us to join him in facing up to the unexpected consequences. To put that another way, he intends 'to assert faith's simplicities: to say them, hear them . . . [and] hammer them against the metaphysical structure of traditional theology until they make more systematic difference than heretofore'.[6]

To understand how this project plays out in practice, we can start with a simple enough example, which Jenson uses to launch one essay: what do Christians mean when we confess that 'Jesus is Lord'?[7] Jenson thinks there 'could hardly be a more direct and basic confession of faith' than the lordship of Christ, and so at first glance it is hard to see what the catch might be.[8] However, he is keen to show his readers that there is more to the statement than first meets the eye.

Jenson notes that the declaration begins with a person's name, and – as we will see – personal names play a vital role in Jenson's argument.[9] It is therefore important to understand how names function in everyday speech if we are to decipher their use in his theology. Before we do that, however, we should first note something in passing. Jenson refuses to draw out the second-order implications of the gospel too hurriedly, resisting the temptation to cash the message out into the promotion of an abstract ideal or general property, such as love or forgiveness.[10] These ideals may well be a logical outworking of the claim that 'Jesus is Lord', but he is suspicious of hasty abstractions, preferring instead to posit the concrete actuality of what happens historically and only then work things out from there. The reason for his suspicion is simple: 'abstractions don't need a mother', which is what God in fact has.[11]

As this preamble suggests, Jenson wants us to think carefully about what it means to name a particular man as Lord. In everyday speech, a personal name is the primary means by which we pick one individual out from another.[12] For example, I can ask Jane and not Mary to pass the ketchup, or Bill and not George to answer the phone, and, in both cases, the name *identifies* the person in question. As the use of italics indicates, 'identity' is another concept that will play a prominent role in Jenson's project, denoting as it does the brute fact of being who or what anything is in distinction from who or what other things are. He will argue that the concept of 'identity' encapsulates the concrete *this-ness* of the unavoidably particular within the class in which it stands, and will thereby claim that our personal names function as a shorthand indicator for the cluster of personal characteristics by which we are individuated one from another, thus being the proper noun that picks out our specific *who-ness* amid the nexus of attributes that we share in common.

Jenson will look to knock the concept of identity into the specific shape he needs through the course of his labours, especially when he explores how the concept of 'identity' is better suited to denote what we usually mean by 'person' in trinitarian theology, thereby concluding that God is 'three identities of one action', which is captured by the proper name Father, Son and Holy Spirit, which functions as a condensed summary of the dramatic work that these three pick-out-ables do as the living God establishes – through Christ's death and resurrection – the type of God he is.[13] However, we will return to this matter later. The thing to grasp here is how Jenson wants his readers to recognize that a name picks out a particular person. As a result, he will want us to remember that 'The Son has a human proper name: *Jesus*.'[14]

In making this point, Jenson also wants his reader to notice how a single name may not be enough to identify the person in question.[15] That is partly because we all hold our names in common, in the sense that none of us enjoy exclusive rights to their use. The declaration 'Jesus is Lord', for example, refers to someone named 'Jesus', and, although we already know which Jesus we are referring to, Jenson wants us to slow down for a second and imagine instead that we don't. To demonstrate his point, we might call to mind how 'Jesus' is a popular name in some parts of the world today, and so, in certain circumstances, it might be necessary to clarify which Jesus we mean. If that were the case, we could indicate we are talking about Jesus of Nazareth, rather than Jesus of Mexico City or Jesus of Puebla, with the named subject being located – plotted, as it were – by the addition of the geographical descriptor.

At risk of labouring the point, someone – if only for the sake of being awkward – could of course remind us that a number of people called 'Jesus' have hailed from Nazareth, and if we were pressed in this way, we would need to clarify exactly which Nazarene we mean. Jenson thinks we would do this by explaining that Jesus lived around 2,000 years ago, journeyed from village to village to teach people about the kingdom of God, before landing himself in all sorts of trouble with the ruling authorities, who eventually put him to death by public execution outside Jerusalem's gates around the year AD 33.[16] Jenson's point is therefore simple enough: if we did this sort of thing for long enough, the identifying process could come to an end at some stage, with the singular subject being pinpointed by 'name and narrative description'.[17] 'Ah, *that* Jesus of Nazareth. Mary's boy and Pilate's victim.'

Having highlighted how we are talking about a single pick-out-able man, Jenson turns our attention to the next word; that is, '*is*'. The meaning of this word will occupy our thoughts in the next part of the book, where we will examine Jenson's understanding of its place within a classical analysis of *Being*. He will argue that Christian theologians constructed a trinitarian ontology in conversation with the existing Greek metaphysics, by which God's godliness came to be defined as the communal substance of three persons in subsisting relation, thereby transforming our understanding of '*is*-ness'. But at this stage of the argument, we need only register how the word 'is' functions as the verb in the declaration, thereby linking the subject to the predicate, and that it does so tightly. We are not saying that Jesus of Nazareth 'seems to be' Lord, or that Jesus of Nazareth is 'sort of' Lord, or that Jesus of Nazareth is 'related' to the Lord. In fact, no conditions or qualifications are attached.[18] Instead, we are making the strong claim that Jesus of Nazareth is what we are about to say about him. In short, we are dealing with the identified one's identity.

And 'so far so good', as Jenson will often say, though that piece of rhetoric is usually a precursor to him doubling down on the difficulty stakes.[19] And that is certainly the case here. This is where Jenson thinks things start to get interesting, mainly because the final word in the sentence is 'Lord'. Of course, in everyday speech 'Lord' can be used simply to predicate power and authority to the subject in question, and in many contexts that predication might not be a big deal. We might be stating a political fact, for instance, in the way that 'Caesar is Lord' once did. But Jenson thinks that is not the way the word is being used here. The Old Testament unlocks the intended meaning, and Israel's Scriptures know of only one Lord; that is, God. As a result, 'God' is what this Jesus of Nazareth is being declared to be.[20]

Now, another quick aside before we come to the central issue which the expanded declaration has brought into focus. The move Jenson makes pivots on his reading of the Old Testament, and in many respects this illustrates how his entire project is little more than a sustained work of theological exegesis of Israel's life.[21] He wants to draw out the logic of the Scriptures at each point in his argument, seeking to trace his doctrinal proposals back to the overarching narrative by which the Old and New Testaments hang together in their mutual but distinct witness to the God of Israel.[22] As Jenson sees it, 'the church – that is, the community of interpretation that for its specific purpose put the Bible together in the first place – intends this book, for all the diversity of documents collected in it, as one continuous story of Israel's God with his people and his creation',[23] and so he will look to read Israel's Scriptures very closely as he makes his case, seeking always to make sense of the God to whom the entirety of texts bears witness. Jenson's work is therefore undergirded with biblical references throughout and is often shaped by the exegetical work he undertakes in conversation with leading biblical scholars, with Jenson resolutely determined only to 'ride the waves' of the single plot that he thinks runs through both Testaments.[24] But, for now, we need only notice how his reading of Scripture leads him to the conclusion that the commonplace declaration 'Jesus is Lord' is a declaration that 'Jesus of Nazareth is God'.

With the declaration expanded in this way, Jenson is confident that his readers will be feeling a little less comfortable than we were at the outset. He suspects the copula '*is*' will be feeling the pressure, and we ourselves may immediately want to add a qualification or two, maybe clarifying that only a part of the Nazarene is divine or that God only seemed to hail from Nazareth. Whatever qualification we want to affix, Jenson thinks we will attach it because of a gut feeling that something more nuanced needs to be said. In short, we feel uncomfortable with the strong sense of that '*is*'. Nonetheless, Jenson is adamant. '"Jesus is the eternal Logos" is an identity statement.'[25]

Jenson believes the reason for our discomfort is easy to discover. The expanded declaration is pushing together two things – one of which is not a thing! – which we have been taught to separate: the infinite God and a finite creature. This is why he thinks a degree of 'conceptual dissonance' will be kicking in, making it almost impossible for us to see how the plain sense of the words could be true.[26] He is therefore confident any reader could assign a long list of attributes to both sides of the pairing, thereby demonstrating how incompatible the two realities are.[27] A finite man is born and then he dies, for instance, whereas the infinite God has neither beginning nor end; and the list could go on. As a result, it is hard to see how a finite man could be identified with the infinite God, without, that is, causing substantial damage to one or the other.[28]

With this in mind, Jenson assumes his readers will be wary of making a category error, and so he thinks we will be tempted to shroud the on-the-face-of-it oxymoron in mystery, thus mitigating the 'dissonance' that the expanded declaration generates by celebrating the paradox of the gospel message.[29] However, Jenson thinks this would be a mistake.[30] The gospel compels us to make sense of this very strange claim, and so he thinks it is wrong to shrug our shoulders in pious resignation in an attempt to dodge it. We must instead get to grips conceptually with the fact that 'The first-century male Galilean Jew, Jesus of Nazareth, prophet and rabbi and healer, is one of the three whose life together *is* God'.[31]

As this opening section indicates, Jenson wants to work with the expanded version of the declaration and fathom out what sort of metaphysical structure could handle such a claim. He will therefore be found emphasizing on regular occasions that Jesus of Nazareth is God, 'without qualification or evasion',[32] and with no conditions attached. His work is therefore devoted to showing what sort of metaphysics could stop us retreating into 'mystery' and 'paradox' at this point, seeing – as Tee Gatewood has argued – that the 'essential Christological task is to begin with this person and bend the use of "nature" to the logic of our confession'.[33]

In pursuit of a suitable metaphysical framework to make sense of the gospel, Jenson sets about interrogating the assumptions his readers hold dear, thereby seeking to overturn the established conceptual order that created the 'dissonance' and provide an alternative structure within which it can make sense. However, he is under no illusion. He accepts that his project will cause something of a scandal, although that is precisely what the gospel should provoke. A theological statement about Jesus is only 'adequate precisely insofar as it comprehensively and ingeniously *offends* what "everybody" at a time and place "of course" knows to be true of God'.[34] As a result, Jenson is utterly fixed on one idea: 'a temporal figure, Jesus of Nazareth, is one identity of the eternal God'.[35] To see what he makes of it, we need to pick up the earlier point about names and narrative and run with it a bit further.

2.2 Name and narrative identify

We should first recognize that the declaration we have been working with – namely, the lordship of Jesus Christ – is in fact an outworking of the gospel message, rather than its most basic form. Jenson intends to strip things back even further, seeking to identify the fundamental premise from which all second-order statements arise. He concludes that the gospel is most basically an item of news and the 'message with which the Apostles raced through the world is, in starkest simplicity, "Jesus is risen"'.[36]

Jenson's entire project is an attempt to work out the consequences of this primordial form of the gospel message, in that he will argue that the resurrection of Jesus pinpoints the event by which we identify who we mean when we use the concept 'God'. What is most remarkable, however, is that Jenson thinks the validity of this logic pivots entirely on the fact that God defines who he eternally is by the exact same event, so that the resurrection is also at the heart of what God is forever. To see how Jenson reaches this conclusion, we should first trace the way he thinks the announcement of a resurrection is a specific type of news, i.e. good.

Jenson will regularly point out that resurrection in itself may not be good news. The vague declaration that 'resurrection happens', for example, doesn't convey enough information to bring comfort to its hearers, and even if the declaration was made more specific we might not conclude it is good.[37] Jenson will regularly remind his readers that 'The message, "Attila is risen", would be no gospel', and he knows we wouldn't be celebrating if people were racing around proclaiming Hitler had been raised.[38] However, the news is about Jesus of Nazareth, the one who brought good news to the poor and recovery of sight to the blind and proclaimed liberation to the captives and healing for the lepers and the forgiveness of sins, and so on, and it is only because *that* Jesus 'now lives with death behind him' that we can describe the news as good.[39] In other words, we know the identity of the Last Judge and he is no tyrant.

Jenson's point is well made, and not just in positing those horrendous alternatives. It is hard to imagine how the identity of the resurrected one doesn't inform the message we proclaim about him.[40] But Jenson wants his readers to notice what was involved in reaching that conclusion. The personal name must be tagged to a particular life. Jesus, who preached good news to the poor, and proclaimed liberty to the captives, and so on, has been raised and *that's* why the news is good.

Of course, this move is no big deal in some respects. We regularly link personal names to the lives people live.[41] If I ask my dad, 'Have you heard what happened to Edward?' my dad might say, 'Edward at the golf club?' and I would reply, 'No, Edward who's married to Brenda and works at the store.'[42] In other words, we habitually identify people by situating them within the nexus of the relations they inhabit, a method that allows the person's identity to be established by picking them out through a process of narrating how they did this, that or the other. As Chris Green puts it, 'Names, in other words, work to identify only as and through *story*. Or, more precisely, they depend upon the kind of coherence that only dramatics makes possible.'[43]

As Green suggests, Jenson thinks that names and narratives identify within the dramatic act of the life we live together, although Jenson accepts that people don't usually take this approach with God. God isn't thought to possess the necessary attributes to be narratable in this straightforward sense, because God is held to have nothing to do with the 'befores' and 'afters' and the 'thens' and 'theres' that are essential to the telling of stories. Jenson, however, takes the opposite view. He thinks the process of narrative identification is central to the gospel and so it must be central to the task of identifying God, but that can only really work if God himself is somehow narratable, with 'befores' and 'afters' to be found in him.[44] Or to put that a different way, Jenson will argue that the gospel's God cannot be timeless, because the punctiliar – that is, the absolute compression of a single point – cannot be told, whereas the gospel most definitely can.

Again I am wary of racing too far ahead here, and so I only want to flag up the kinds of issues we will be tackling later, not least when we explore the way Jenson's understanding of personhood is irrepressibly relational, being best understood not as a static property but as a vector within a nexus of mutual activity that amounts to God's self-determining act of enveloping us within the story he tells himself about himself from God's unprecedented First through to his unsurpassable Last via the twists and turns of the timely life, death and resurrection of Jesus, the Nazarene. But that can wait for now. Here we need only see how Jenson thinks the gospel can be classified as good news because we can specify the character of the one who has been raised by situating him in the contingent relations of the finite life he lived unto death. As a result, Jenson concludes, 'the coherence of Christian theology depend[s] on a proper identification of Jesus Christ'.[45]

With this being so, Jenson knows we must hear stories about the way Jesus lived if we are to identify the risen One. He thinks this is why 'the subject-term of the gospel message . . . once grew into whole writings of a new sort, the Gospels', which function as extended narratives that allow us to identify what sort of life Jesus lived.[46] 'Ah, Jesus, the one who said such and such to Zacchaeus . . . and who sat with Mary, as Martha worked . . . who spoke to the widow at Nain . . .' has been raised from the dead and so our future is good.[47] But what is most remarkable about Jenson's handling of the narrative identification of Jesus is the way he thinks the identity of Jesus can only be accurately narrated because his life came to an end. Or to put that another way, termination is central to Jenson's project of identification.

To see why this is so, we must venture another step into Jenson's proposal, one which will allow us to catch first sight of the way he thinks the crucifixion determines what sort of God the living God is. He will argue that the public execution of Jesus amounts to a specific question being posed within the life of God, the answering of which determines that God is the sort of God he has always chosen himself to be, namely, the merciful God who eternally lives for his creatures unconditionally.

2.3 Termination and determination

Jenson argues that incompletion and incomprehension are closely related, and his point is easy to grasp if we consider the structure of a sentence. In many ways, the meaning of a sentence depends on it coming to an end; it must have a full stop. For example, if the speaker at a conference announced to the assembled delegates that 'Jenson is . . . uhm', or 'Jenson said . . . uhm', we wouldn't know what they mean, even if we had a good idea who it is they were talking about. In other words, the petering out of a dwindling sentence renders its meaning underdetermined, and Jenson thinks our identity works in much the same way, as, for that matter, does God's.

To show how this works itself out, we should note an important definition that will drive Jenson's entire proposal. He thinks that the 'difference between a live person and a dead person [is that] a live person or a community has a future; a dead person or a community does not.'[48] As Jenson sees it, having a future is vital, in that this alone means we are not trapped in a flat polarity between a fixed beginning and the present moment, locked in as it were within a closed binary that amounts to little more than a static singularity in which everything is essentially frozen. It is therefore only because time lies ahead of us that the encroaching future can pose an open question to the already-determined nature of the present, thereby opening it up and enabling us to continue to act, negotiate and manoeuvre, one to another, for better or worse. In short, to live.

With this definition in mind, Jenson concludes that our identity cannot yet be established, because the future gives us the potential to surprise one another. His point makes sense to me, though it is not without controversy. For example, I can think of people who claim to know me very well, and some of those people have good cause. We have spent a lot of time together, and so they have seen how I operate in close proximity, becoming familiar with my idiosyncrasies as they witness my character develop as I navigate my passage through the contingencies of time. But because I have a future – at least at the time of writing! – Jenson thinks these people don't really know me just yet. When we next meet, for example, I could do something so impressive that the ones who don't rate me would have to reconsider; 'Ah, we were wrong about Lincoln. He's pretty amazing.' Or I could do something so atrocious that the people who think highly of me would need to change their minds. In other words, my *Lincoln-ness* – that is, the *who*-ness of my concrete individuation situated and set apart within the various episodes of my temporal relations – is a question that is still being posed. As a result, 'who or what I am is not determined until "the moving finger" has written the last line of my story'.[49]

As this suggests, Jenson is arguing that the 'death of any person defines the person: it is both the concluding event of a life and the seal that no further turns must be expected'.[50] He therefore concludes:

> When I try to understand and evaluate myself, the 'self' I have to work on is my past history. I trace out the dramatic coherence of a sequence in time of events, which I identify as together the happenings of my life precisely by this dramatic coherence. I am a plot. We experience ourselves as stories. But we also experience ourselves as unfinished stories. It is the last act, the catastrophe and denouement, of a drama which makes sense of the whole series of enacted occurrences, which makes of them a coherent whole so as to be a plot, a story, at all. Only, therefore, from its end can I grasp my life as my true self, as a meaningful whole. Thus not until I die can I know what my life is about, what its plot is, what or who I am. But then it is too late. This is the agony of mortality: I cannot achieve myself, I cannot live to any purpose, I cannot justify my actions, except by dying.[51]

Now, it is important to realize that Jenson will run with this point, arguing that God's identity works in much the same way, albeit somewhat differently. God remains faithful to who he will always forever be in the pure act of his self-determination towards the particular temporal end he already is as the self-possession of his unsurpassable Spirit by which he is always his own Future, and by which he enlivens himself. Of course, that string of ideas will need a lot of unpacking, but even at this early stage we can understand how Jenson will weave the insight into his doctrine of God if we look at how it relates to the gospel message. This can be done if we imagine Jesus was still alive today, in the everyday sense of having not yet died.

If Jesus had just celebrated his 2019th birthday, for instance, and was rattling around an old people's home in a suburb of Nazareth, we couldn't be sure whether he would head down the corridor for breakfast and suddenly reveal a previously hidden side to his character – a mean and spiteful Jesus, for example, or a bullying and deceitful one. But Jenson thinks the good news of the gospel pivots on the fact that the one who is risen did die. 'It is finished,' Jesus cried, and 'just so' – another of Jenson's favourite phrases[52] – the news of his resurrection is good, because the one 'whose death is behind him'[53] is identifiable by the end that he met.

In other words, Jenson thinks 'the point of Jesus' death is that his identity is now settled and knowable',[54] and that means we can trust that our future is good because we know Jesus is unshakeably the friend of tax collectors and sinners because the final truth about him is that he lived so fully for others that he offered himself unto death.[55] This is why Jenson thinks it is so important that Jesus resisted the last temptation, thereby refusing to put himself first by coming down from the cross, with his refusal to succumb to that final temptation showing that he lived fully for others come what may.[56] That is to say, what transpired – suffering execution at the hands of men – means the identity of Jesus is fixed as unconditionally selfless, because his death was utterly free, and that means, in turn, that we can celebrate that it is the 'Man for Others' who has been raised, and therein be assured that the one who awaits us is wholly good. In other words, his identity is sealed for our salvation.

This logic drives Jenson's conclusion that the gospel is *'unconditional promise* . . . made by the narrative of Jesus' death and resurrection',[57] in that we are freed from whatever imprisons us in the past or present because the identity of the Last Judge has been determined by his termination for us. The gospel thereby proclaims that 'because Jesus, who has bound himself to you unto death, lives with death behind him, you will surely be fulfilled'.[58] Clearly this is yet another important point, and so it must be added to the growing list of things that require further development through the course of the book. We will later see how it is linked to Jenson's handling of the theological concept of person, and how he defines 'person' as '"a subsisting relation" . . . that is its own term', which is to say that the relation is not between polar entities, so to speak, 'things' that relate one to another, but that the relation is its own end/terminus and therefore utterly constitutive of what it is.[59] Jenson will thus argue that a person is 'a relation that can be and *do* things',[60] which is how he then situates the unconditional nature of Jesus' death on the cross within the eternal life of God so that the death of Jesus is the act by which God chooses only to be God if the rest of us are thrown in, that is, his identify is so fixed relationally for others that God *does* the binding of himself to others in the event of raising this Nazarene.[61] For now, however, we need only register the link Jenson is making between identity and termination and press on to explore his understanding of what makes a good story, because we are already seeing how the narrative structure of the gospel message drives the extraordinary character of his conclusion. In fact, his entire proposal will pivot on the claim that the gospel is the story that God tells himself about himself within our presence, and so we need to spend time examining the way Jenson systematically links narrative and reality, a task that will involve us exploring the novel way in which he imagines the relation between eternity and time. Thus, we come to the subject of the next chapter.

Notes

1 Robert W. Jenson, 'The God of the Gospel', *Baltimore Paper*, 2.

2 Robert W. Jenson, 'What if It Were True?' *Neue Zeitschrift für Systematische Theologie und Religionsphilosophie* 43.1 (2001), 4.

3 Robert W. Jenson, *Systematic Theology, Vol. 2, The Works of God* (New York: OUP, 1999), v.

4 Robert W. Jenson, *Systematic Theology, Vol. 1, The Triune God* (New York: OUP, 1997), 125, emphasis added.

5 Watson therefore praises Jenson for showing 'the sheer oddity' of the Christian faith. Francis Watson, '"America's Theologian": an appreciation of Robert Jenson's *Systematic Theology*, with some remarks about the bible', *Scottish Journal of Theology* 55.2 (2002), 215.

6 Robert W. Jenson, 'About Dialog, and the Church, and some Bits of the Theological Biography of Robert W. Jenson', *Dialog* 11.1 (1969), 39–40.

7 Robert W. Jenson, 'Jesus in the Trinity', *Pro Ecclesia* 8 (1999), 308.

8 Jenson, 'Jesus in the Trinity', 308.

9 See, for example, Robert W. Jenson, *The Triune Identity: God According to the Gospel* (Philadelphia: Fortress, 1982; reprint Eugene, OR: Wipf and Stock, 2002), 7–10.

10 See, for example, Jenson, *Systematic Theology*, Vol. 1, 50.

11 The phrase is Pope Benedict's but captures Jenson's thinking nicely. See Aaron Riches, *Ecce Homo: On the Divine Unity of Christ* (Grand Rapids: Eerdmans, 2016), 225.

12 Jenson, *Triune Identity*, 3.

13 This point is covered in the first volume of his systematics. For example, Jenson, *Systematic Theology*, Vol. 1, 106. See also Robert W. Jenson, 'Three Identities of One Action', *Scottish Journal of Theology* 28 (1975), 1–15.

14 Robert W. Jenson, *A Large Catechism* (Delhi, NY: American Lutheran Publicity Bureau, 1991), 26, emphasis added.

15 Jenson, *Systematic Theology*, Vol. 1, 31.

16 For the identifying narrative in 'maximum compression', see Jenson, *Systematic Theology*, Vol. 1, 176–8.

17 Jenson, *Systematic Theology*, Vol. 1, 44.

18 The title of one essay states it boldly: '*With No Qualifications*'. See Robert W. Jenson, 'With No Qualifications: the Christological Maximalism of the Christian East', in *Ancient and Postmodern Christianity: Paleo-Orthodoxy in the 21st Century*, ed. Kenneth Tanner and Christopher A. Hall (Downers Grove: Intervarsity Press, 2002), 13–22.

19 For an example of use: Robert W. Jenson, *Canon and Creed* (Louisville: Westminster John Knox Press, 2010), 28.

20 Jenson, *Systematic Theology*, Vol. 1, 92, and Jenson, 'Jesus in the Trinity', 308.

21 Jenson's understanding of Scripture is set out in several places: Jenson, *Canon and Creed* and Robert W. Jenson, *On the Inspiration of Scripture* (Delhi, NY: ALPB, 2012). It is also worked out in commentaries, see Robert W. Jenson, *Ezekiel* (London: SCM Press, 2009) and Robert W. Jenson, *Song of Songs: A Biblical Commentary for Teaching and Preaching* (Louisville: John Knox Press, 2005). Peter Leithart makes the same point in 'Jenson as Theological Interpreter', in *The Promise of Robert W. Jenson's Theology: Constructive Engagements*, ed. Stephen John Wright and Chris E. W. Green (Minneapolis: Fortress, 2017), 45–58. Thanks to Chris Green for the reference.

22 Jenson, *Systematic Theology*, Vol. 1, 58.

23 Robert W. Jenson, 'How Does Jesus Make a Difference?' in *Essentials of Christian Theology*, ed. William C. Placher (Louisville: WJK Press, 2003), 195.

24 Robert W. Jenson, 'What Kind of God Can Make a Covenant?' in *Covenant and Hope: Christian and Jewish Reflections*, ed. Robert W. Jenson and Eugene B. Korn (Grand Rapids: Eerdmans, 2012), 12. I will use variations of this phrase going forward. This citation signals the debt.

25 Colin Gunton and Robert W. Jenson, 'The *Logos Ensarkos* and Reason', in *Reason and the Reasons of Faith*, ed. Paul J. Griffiths and Reinhard Hütter (London: T&T Clark, 2005), 75.

26 The phrase 'conceptual dissonance' indicates the clash between metaphysical assumptions about God's impassibility and telling a story about suffering and death. Jenson, *Systematic Theology*, Vol. 1, 125.

27 See comments on there being no need to unpack what is assumed because the pairings are so 'commonsensical', in Robert W. Jenson, 'Creator and Creature', *International Journal of Systematic Theology* 4 (2002), 216.

28 In short, it is difficult to understand how 'a particularly embodied human is Lord of all things'. Robert W. Jenson, 'On the Ascension', in *Loving God With Our Minds: The Pastor as Theologian*, ed. Michael Welker and Cynthia A. Jarvis (Grand Rapids: Eerdmans, 2004), 340.

29 Jenson thinks, 'Much of church history can be interpreted as the continuing disaster of this attempt'. Jenson, *Systematic Theology*, Vol. 1, 224–5.

30 For example, see Jenson's analysis of the difficulty of imagining a changeless God creating without the act of creating constituting a change. Jenson, *Triune Identity*, 124.

31 Jenson, 'How Does Jesus', 201.

32 Jenson, *Systematic Theology*, Vol. 1, 144.

33 Tee Gatewood, 'A Nicene Christology? Robert Jenson and the Two Natures of Jesus Christ', *Pro Ecclesia* 18 (2009), 36.

34 Robert W. Jenson, 'Basics and Christology', in *In Search of Christian Unity: Basic Consensus/Basic Differences*, ed. Joseph A. Burgess (Minneapolis: Fortress Press, 1991), 47.

35 Robert W. Jenson, *Unbaptized God: The Basic Flaw in Ecumenical Theology* (Minneapolis: Fortress, 1992), 119.

36 Jenson, *Large Catechism*, 27. Hence, 'The short statement of the gospel is "Jesus is risen".' Jenson, *Systematic Theology*, Vol. 2, 293.

37 Hence Jenson's critique of Bultmann's project of demythologization. Jenson, *Systematic Theology*, Vol. 1, 168.

38 Robert W. Jenson, 'Story and Promise in Pastoral Care', *Pastoral Psychology* 26.2 (1977), 114. Jenson will regularly change villains when making the point; consider, for example, '"Stalin is risen" would be no gospel'. Jenson, *Large Catechism*, 27.

39 For the origin of the phrase 'lives with death behind him', see Jenson, *Large Catechism*, 30.

40 Again, this is why Jenson opposes Bultmann's desire to strip the life of Jesus from the reality of eternity. Jenson wants to do the opposite: strip eternity of any feature that cannot accommodate this specific life. Jenson, *Systematic Theology*, Vol. 1, 165–71.

41 Jenson, *Triune Identity*, 3.

42 For Jenson's own way of making the point, see Robert W. Jenson, 'The Triune God', in *Christian Dogmatics*, ed. Carl E. Braaten and Robert W. Jenson (Philadelphia: Fortress, 1984), 88.

43 Chris E. W. Green, *The End Is Music: A Companion to Robert W. Jenson's Theology* (Eugene, OR: Cascade, 2018), 15.

44 As Jenson puts it, 'In the Bible the name of God and the narration of his works thus belong together.' Jenson, *Triune Identity*, 7.

45 Gatewood, 'Nicene Christology', 28.

46 Jenson, *Large Catechism*, 27. See discussion in Jenson, *Systematic Theology*, Vol. 1, 31–2.

47 Jenson, *Systematic Theology*, Vol. 1, 58.

48 Robert W. Jenson, *A Theology in Outline: Can These Bones Live?* transcribed, ed. and introduced by Adam Eitel (Oxford: OUP, 2016), 30.

49 Jenson, *Song of Songs*, 94. Hence we cannot conceive of our death, because that would be to grasp ourselves as a whole – but who but God could do such grasping? See Jenson, *Systematic Theology*, Vol. 2, 327–8, and Robert W. Jenson, *On Thinking the Human: Resolutions of Difficult Notions* (Grand Rapids, Eerdmans, 2003).

50 Jenson, *Large Catechism*, 29.

51 Robert W. Jenson, *A Religion Against Itself* (John Knox Press, 1967; reprint, Eugene, OR: Wipf and Stock), 16–17.

52 See his repeated use of this phrase in a single paragraph, in Robert W. Jenson, 'Evil as Person', in *Theology as Revisionary Metaphysics: Essays on God and Creation*, ed. Stephen John Wright (Eugene, OR: Cascade, 2014), 141.

53 Jenson, *Systematic Theology*, Vol. 2, 332.

54 Jenson, *Systematic Theology*, Vol. 1, 198.

55 In short, it shows, 'The death was for our good'. Jenson, *Large Catechism*, 29.

56 Jenson, *Systematic Theology*, Vol. 1, 181.

57 Eric W. Gritsch and Robert W. Jenson, *Lutheranism: The Theological Movement and Its Confessional Writings* (Philadelphia: Fortress, 1976), 42. As Jenson adds, 'The gospel, rightly spoken, involves no ifs, ands, buts, or maybes of any sort . . . The gospel says, "Because the Crucified lives as Lord, your destiny is good."'

58 Jenson, *Triune Identity*, 26. As Jenson puts it elsewhere, '"Gospel!" is the news of God's completely remarkable affirmation of just this rebel [i.e. sinful man], the Last Judgment let out ahead of time and revealed as, of all things, acquittal.' Robert W. Jenson, 'A Dead Issue Revisited', *Lutheran Quarterly* (1962), 55.

59 The classical definition comes from Thomas Aquinas: 'The divine persons are the subsisting relations themselves' (*Summa Theologiae* I, 40, 2).

60 Jenson, *Triune Identity*, 123.

61 Robert W. Jenson, 'Once More the Logos Asarkos', *International Journal of Systematic Theology* 13 (2011), 133.

3

Time, Eternities and the Story of God

3.1 Stories and contingencies

Jenson believes the gospel tells us what happened to Jesus: *the God of Israel raised him from the dead*. However, he thinks we can only know this is good news because we can identify Jesus by narrative. That is to say, we hear stories about the life he lived, thereby seeing how he related to others through the episodic twists and turns of his own existence right up until the series of events reached their definitive conclusion in his crucifixion, whereby his identity as the 'Man for Others' is finally sealed. As a result, stories are central to establishing the character of the gospel message we receive, and so stories need to play a determinative role in Jenson's revisionary metaphysics.

Jenson's preoccupation with the nature of stories is partly driven by his understanding of Scripture. He thinks the Bible is one loosely structured metanarrative.[1] Its various books, with their multiple authors and many genres, together make up a single plot in their mutual but distinct witness to the Christ of Israel. As Jenson sees it, this leaves each of us with a decision to make, as to whether to give ontological weight to the narrative they tell or instead make Scripture's story somehow abstract, in the sense that it speaks of a reality that is ultimately *non*-narratable in essence.[2] As expected, Jenson thinks the second option – a non-narratable reality – could only be embraced if our ingrained prejudices decide the matter, with the relegation of narrative being decided on premises that are themselves established outside the scriptural story. As a result, he encourages his readers to give ontological weight to the narrative. And that is certainly what Jenson does.[3]

To that end Jenson makes use of Aristotle's theory of narrative.[4] Aristotle thought stories are simple enough in their structure, in that 'the plot must be a self-contained narrative with a clearly marked beginning, middle, and end'.[5] But Aristotle spotted how a story can begin in any way, in that the tale isn't necessary in itself but instead begins with a *given*; 'Once upon a time', as it were.[6] A series of episodic events then flow from this sheerly contingent beginning, with the plotted sequence made up of one thing leading to another, with each step shaped by what preceded it as the narrative twists and turns until the episodic events finally come together in their dramatic fulfilment. As Aristotle understands it, a story is therefore the coherence of the serially contingent as a singular whole, so that to *storify* – to use an odd verb – is to draw together the episodes to create a single completed order.

Now, this is all pretty straightforward, although it does suggest the outcome determines the plotted sequence of prior contingencies, with the sequence predictable only in hindsight. That is to say, the ending can only ever be guessed at as we journey towards it, because the episodic events are free to surprise us as they happen, with one contingency relating to other contingencies and thus lacking predictability, even if each step appears the right step within the logic of the final plot. As Jenson puts it, there is a freedom with narrative, in that 'Within the sequence of events a specific opening future liberates each successive specious present from mere predictability, from being only the result of what has gone before, and just so opens each such present to its own content, given precisely as what it does not yet encompass.'[7] As a result, it is only a completed story that shows – not tells! – how the outcome had to happen, which is to say narrative is a free logic that relates an initial 'happenstance' to a final 'it-has-to-be-stance' through the mediating middle of its contingent episodes.

To put the point otherwise, Aristotle thinks the unavoidable outcome of a good story creeps up on us, as it were, but is thereafter utterly definitive of the tale that is told. In effect, the end fixes meaning, and thereby identifies the story for what it is. Jenson thinks Aristotle is right in this respect, though with an important qualification. He agrees that a story involves retroactive determination, by which the ending makes sense of the episodes that preceded it, rather than being an already-determined unfolding of an initial necessity (like the solution of a primordial equation or some such equivalent).[8] That is to say, only at the end of a story can the reader see the couple just had to get together or that it was always going to end in tragedy, but at each step of the story it always appears like *it could be otherwise*. This caveat is important to Jenson, because he wants to embrace the evident contingencies of the gospel, which he thinks 'is the one example of a story that satisfies Aristotle's criterion without fudging: the resurrection of Jesus could not be believed in advance but afterward is plainly the only thing that could have happened.'[9]

Of course, in some respects, it is obvious that narrative contingency is central to the gospel. The series of events happened at a particular time and particular place, and it is difficult to see why Jesus had to be crucified under Pontius Pilate outside Jerusalem, rather than Queen Elizabeth II, for example, in the suburbs of London. This means the contingency of the event can either be seen as a problem or – as Jenson judges – an 'ontological perfection', in that it is definitive of the nature of the reality we inhabit with God.[10] And that is precisely why he must part company with Aristotle. As Jenson puts it, 'Aristotle got the logic of true narrative exactly right . . . [But] he did not believe it applied to anything but fiction, since his cosmos had no narrative'.[11]

As we will see in the next part of the book, Aristotle – like other Greek philosophers – thought that contingency was finally a problem, and necessity was the solution. Jenson therefore knows this means the Greek philosophers are not offering us a gospel-shaped account of the reality we inhabit, and so Jenson needs to find a more positive place for contingency within the structure of reality if the gospel is to be the final word about it. But this leads him towards some drastic conclusions, and to see what these are we should first clarify what Jenson means by contingency.

In some respects, contingency is best understood negatively, in that the concept denotes the opposite of necessity. It thereby indicates a specific form of freedom, in that it contrasts with things having to be as they are (the latter being a rough definition of necessity). However, this definition could mislead. Jenson doesn't think contingency is somehow chaotic, capricious or mere happenstance, in that things happen to be how they are by chance. Instead, the concept conveys a sense of ordered freedom in that it indicates 'the way in which any historical event or institution could have been otherwise', but without undermining the authority of what is.[12] An example will help clarify the point.

Consider the sacraments.[13] Jenson thinks Christians gather to tell the story of God with 'visible words',[14] which are 'bodily concentrations'[15] of the gospel message, a series of tangible acts by which God is signified *and* does what is signified by the event; in other words, a sacrament is a sign and instrument of God doing God in our midst. Jenson thinks these acts are contingent in their form, in that it didn't have to be bread and wine, for example, that God uses in our encounter with him. If Jesus had been born in northern Europe, for example, Jenson believes it could have been 'beer and bread' that we use, and, similarly it wouldn't have been a watery initiation that marks our entry into church if Jesus had been born in the frozen Arctic. Nonetheless, *that* the meal or the bath could have been otherwise – with Jesus instead doing a circle dance rather than a meal with friends[16] – doesn't undermine the authority of what is. It simply implies there is nothing intrinsic to bread and wine – or water, for that matter[17] – which makes them irresistible to God. Or, to put the point negatively, Jenson argues that 'We are not able to create a different ceremony of initiation – say, the giving of a particular lifelong haircut – and declare that this will now mean what baptism has meant. The reason is that we possess no semantic rules to control the translation.'[18]

With this noted, Jenson thinks we must accept 'sacramental specificity' as an authoritative given.[19] The acts are free unto God, rather than being necessary in any way. Hence, they are utterly contingent. As this suggests, Jenson wants to show how the sacramental ordering of the church's life is only what it is because it has been freely willed by God as the form of the life he lives with us. In effect, God alone decides bread and wine – as opposed to 'a daisy-chain'[20] – is to be the mode of his presence, and that decision is what authorizes their use. This illustrates the way Jenson never ducks the determined nature of our situation – inventing updated symbols, more fitting for our context – but at the same time refuses to cash this 'is' into 'should'. What is most remarkable, however, is the way Jenson thinks we can only do this if we draw contingency into the nature of God.[21] He therefore argues that God chooses how God will be, thereby being the very act of his own decision, which is the freely willed act of triumphing over the death to which he was put by the ungodly. In other words, God is the act of this decision, without being so necessarily other than in the pure act itself. God is therefore identified as 'the one absolute contingency', who wills to be the specific God that he is with us, although – as the one pure contingency – God amounts to the one necessity, because he alone is absolutely free in his self-ordering.[22] As a result, 'This God *is* what he might not have been',[23] and that is to say, 'there is no penetrating behind contingency' with the God of the gospel.[24]

As this is beginning to reveal, even with God, Jenson refuses to cash 'is' into 'should'. This is the only way Jenson can ensure that God is completely at home in the contingent particularities of his history with us. In other words, God's contingency ultimately underwrites the sheer contingency of Abraham's summons, of Israel's entire history and that of the church, thereby enabling Jenson to embrace the scandalous particularity of God's elective act without looking for any further justification than God's freedom to do what happened to whomever, wherever. In short, contingency is not a problem to be solved, because it is at the heart of the gospel, and that can only mean the God of the gospel is irreducibly free in the contingency of his own life. And that is something Aristotle would find ridiculous.[25]

A lot of Jenson's argument is circular here, although he is keen to point out that not all circles are vicious.[26] His basic move is therefore straightforward enough, in that he is reading from the historical events of the gospel up into God, but in so doing refuses to fillet the historical out of that history in order for the history to serve our theological statements. And that is why Jenson needs to underwrite his metaphysics with an account of the ontological quality of narrative. Because the narratable gospel is God's first and last word – a word that identifies him – reality must also be a lot like a good story, and to make that move, Jenson requires a storied God to justify the claim, so that history is what it is because it is created by a God who is God from the beginning to the end of his own narratable eternity.[27] The only other option would be to conclude that the gospel is at odds with the reality to which it gestures, but that is something Jenson refuses to countenance. The gospel is God's first and last word about us, and about himself.

With this point noted, we can see how Jenson allows stories to drive his metaphysical proposal, thereby seeking to counter the standard assumption that what really '*is*' is finally non-narratable.[28] The gospel shows how 'creation's temporality is not awkwardly related to God's eternity, and its sequentiality imposes no strain on its participation in being',[29] but this means Jenson must argue – somewhat strangely – that God himself must be *storied in nature*. In effect, God must be ordered by his own End, which makes sense of the pure contingency of the brute Beginning, from which the twists and turns of a plot that 'could have been otherwise' springs as God's first and last word about the peculiar identity he chooses himself to be.[30] And – what's more! – in God's story of God, there must be a genuine movement from one to the other, with pivotal twists and turns within its contingent ordering as the storied God tells himself the story that is the event of Jesus dying for the ungodly and being raised into the life of the Spirit. In short, Jenson can only conclude that the crucifixion is the determinative ending, and the resurrection the plot twist that constitutes the Beginning of an Infinity that is God's endlessly opening up of his thereby determined life to everything that exists in the dramatic coherence of his Spirit. If this wasn't the case, 'The very story of Jesus . . . [would] be frozen into an icon of timeless eternity'.[31] And, of course, Jenson wants to avoid such an outcome.[32]

No doubt, a storified God is difficult to think. How can God be the story he tells himself?[33] We usually imagine there first must be a *someone* to tell the story, but things here are different. Jenson is arguing that 'doer' and 'act' are one in God, in that God 'behappens himself', being the event of his own personal decision, while giving this insight a narrative twist, in that God can be the story he tells in its telling, thereby constituting himself as the specific converse that we see taking place in the life, death and resurrection of Jesus the Nazarene in relation to his Father.[34] And that is why Jenson concludes, 'the triune God is in himself a great Conversation'.[35] However, Jenson's conclusion therein positively relates God to time, if only because a story can never be punctiliar. Stories need space to unfold. Therefore, Jenson's decision to prioritize the narratable character of the gospel means he must also make the highly unusual claim that God has a temporal structure within himself as the story he tells himself, and to see how that works itself out, we must first investigate Jenson's understanding of time in relation to eternity.[36] What we will see is that eternity is best conceived as the transcendence of time, the means by which the fleeting moments cohere as a meaningful whole. And that is to say: eternity is the temporal presence of whatever we mean by 'God'.[37]

3.2 There can be no escaping the passage of time

Jenson thinks we can identify God by telling the story of Jesus' life. But because telling this story takes time – requiring space for the narrative to unfold – he concludes that 'time is *narrative* in its own reality'.[38] This is an inescapable conclusion as Jenson sees it, and so he sets out on the assumption that the 'one ineluctable metaphysical experience is the passage of time'.[39] As a result, any misunderstanding of the nature of time will render our construal of reality inadequate.

Before we get into Jenson's account of temporality, it is worth noting that space has a positive role to play in his account.[40] He knows each human is situated on a populated plane, and within this territorial field we relate to a host of identifiable particulars: mountains, trees, oceans, dogs, cats, sun and stars, as well as recognizably other persons. Each identifiable particular – of whatever taxonomy or provenance – has a spatial beginning and a spatial end, being pick-out-able from all the others within the physical realm. Just so, Jenson will certainly address the question of 'space' within his proposal,[41] although it is fair to say he focuses on time's priority, with space best conceived as 'the horizon of the present tense', in that it is the act of God 'making room for us' within his life.[42]

To put the point another way, Jenson thinks it is only because there is a temporal flux that the spatial nexus of relations between bounded particulars can be open to the possibility of new manoeuvres and renegotiation of their shared space; in other words, nothing is static, but only because there is time for things to change. Time is therefore best conceived as God's way of stopping everything happening at once, so that space can be the place where everything doesn't happen to me, because, without time's movement, everything would collapse into a singularity, and without each other it might as well do so.[43] That is because – as Jenson puts it – 'It is as you, a person who differs from me, confront me, that I face the possibility of being other than I am, that is, that an actual future comes on for me. It is you and I together who experience time.'[44] In other words, he thinks time and space are functions of communal relation, in that they enable otherness-in-difference so that we can live one to another. This is a point to which we will return.

With his handling of space flagged up, our focus re-centres on time. Jenson thinks time is what makes our relationships genuinely alive, and it is the future that gives time its lively character. That is to say, if there were no time ahead of us, things would be fixed as a claustrophobic *Thing*. The directionality of time into the opening expanse of a future will therefore prove pivotal in Jenson's theology, and so it will preoccupy us at a later stage of this book, where we will see how Jenson rejects the notion of a timeless God and instead reimagines God's eternity as a temporal infinity in which God is his own Unprecedented Beginning and Unsurpassable End, within which our time spirals like a helix around the eternal Presence of the resurrected Christ in whom God makes time for us within the story he tells himself to make himself what he is within the opening expanse of eternity to eternity.[45] Here, however, we need only note that Jenson thinks we are all – as time-bound creatures – trying to catch up with a somewhat threatening series of episodes. And he argues the only way to catch up with this movement is to posit some form of *eternity*.[46]

Now, the nature of time is notoriously hard to understand, and it is therefore difficult to see how the concept of eternity will make it any easier to grasp. Augustine, for example, has long since identified the slippery quality of time, and the way in which past and future appear to have no reality other than in the irresistibly transient present.[47] With even the greatest of minds struggling to make sense of time, it should come as no surprise that the rest of us are somewhat bewildered.[48] We find ourselves situated within a dynamic structure of relations, being set one to another, participating as both a contributing agent and suffering subject as we navigate and negotiate life's irresistible flow, and – as we do – we become increasingly aware that we are hurtling towards a muddy grave or dusty urn. That is to say, we fear this threatening movement towards our mortal end, with the seamless passing of one moment into another overshadowed by the termination we know to lie ahead, with our present moment thereby forming an ungraspable reality within a limited span.[49] As a result, the question we face is whether this threatening movement has any point. Or to put that otherwise, we need to find something that 'bridges over the nothingness that threatens as the future becomes past'.[50]

Jenson thinks this is the key issue we face, because if the complex sequence we inhabit doesn't hang together then the nihilists are right; nothing ultimately matters, because we are at sea in a meaningless flux in which we can only Canute-like impose a self-curated order on the chaos, like a collective or individual Übermensch participating in some group therapy in which we collude in the charade that things have genuine meaning. Or, as Jenson puts it, if 'every moment of our lives seems to go immediately from the future into the past, from what we are not yet into what we no longer are, [and] if this seeming is veridical [i.e. only a "seeming"], temporal creatures are finally nothing, and creation fails'.⁵¹ However, contra the nihilistic vision of disintegrating futility, Jenson knows we can instead assume that the dynamic movement is ultimately ordered, cohering as a genuine unity within which life's episodes are meaningful in the end.⁵²

As Jenson sees it, if we think time is ultimately meaningful then we can define temporality as a genuine *history*.⁵³ It will come as no surprise that he thinks time is historical, in the sense it is meaningful in the way it hangs together as a coherent whole in the end – even if that doesn't immediately answer the question as to what its meaning is. But rest assured, Jenson will get to that, arguing that the resurrection of Jesus is the in-breaking of that End into the middle, thereby opening up a future beyond our temporal end, which is to share in the eternal life of the God who is defined by the life of the Spirit of the crucified and risen Nazarene.⁵⁴ But before we get to that, we should first explore – with his distinction between time and history in mind – what Jenson means by 'eternity'.

As Jenson sees it, for time to cohere as a meaningful history, we must posit something transcending time, so to speak, something situated in positive relation to time to determine the series as a coherent whole. He argues that whatever we think guarantees time to make it a history is what we mean by *eternity*.⁵⁵ Or to put the point otherwise, eternity is time's transcendence, constituting its Beginning and End by which the flowing present makes sense.

Jenson claims every culture will posit some kind of eternity and structure their understanding of life in relation to it, although not always in the positive way that Jenson uses the concept. The norm in the West, as he reads it, has been to posit an unmoved Mover or Absolute One at time's immobile beginning or centre, from/around which we are either falling away into non-being or to which we are in some state of migrational return. The details don't matter just yet, although we will look closely at them in the second part of the book when we analyse Jenson's reading of ancient philosophy and the substance metaphysics that informed that discourse. For now, we need only see how he thinks every culture will pose at least one form of eternity – either negative or positive – to legislate the coherence of time and thereby turn time into a genuine *history*.⁵⁶ In other words, he thinks 'humans are religious beings, that is, hung up on the infinite'.⁵⁷

As this is beginning to suggest, Jenson thinks we cannot live in non-historical time, because that would render life meaningless.⁵⁸ 'Only if the moment between future and past is not in fact a merely "passing" moment, only if it dwells in some reality that transcends the abrupt difference between the future as it comes on and the past as it departs, can we live stories that are coherent through time, that is, can we *live* at all.'⁵⁹ In other words, every culture has to make sense of life somehow, and in making that point Jenson draws out an important distinction between two conceptions of eternity.

Jenson argues that, if you can talk to the bracketing eternity that we posit – if you address it in some way as a personal eternity, somehow active and related in a positive sense to present time – then you have 'a God or a Pantheon', in that a 'god or pantheon is then the embodiment of some eternity'.[60] As a result, Jenson thinks the word 'God' posits a talkative eternity who defines our time as a meaningful history by underwriting its coherence by actively transcending it.[61] That is to say, 'the only way to speak of an *absolute* beginning and *absolute* end is to speak of God as Beginning and End, as the one who . . . "embraces" time and is not himself embraced'.[62]

Put otherwise, 'God' is the temporal presence of the personal eternity that makes time historical, in that 'a particular community will use the word "god" or some equivalent to invoke whatever it is that this community relies on to survive moving from its past to its future – or perhaps we should say, from its future to its past'.[63] We will return to the complexities associated with Jenson's way of seeing things – especially the priority of the future – shortly, but it is worth noting that he sees such God-talk as the unavoidable vocation for the specifically human creature. He will argue that we are 'praying animals', in that we are creatures situated in relation to the One who made us by summoning us into existence and inviting us to respond to his ongoing address.[64] In short, a talkative eternity wants to be listened to and talked to within time – and, as we will see, we can only talk about God because God talks about us *and* to us in forever discussing himself.[65]

As this is beginning to suggest, Jenson thinks we can't help but be religious, caught up as we are in some call and response to the eternity we think addresses us, petitioning 'God' in praise and intercession as we navigate the brute experience of time's passing in the belief that our temporal existence hangs together in the end. However, he knows that humans can posit all sorts of eternities – i.e. all manner of 'putative gods' – or can instead fall silent in philosophical speculation of a mute infinity, which has no interest in us at all.[66] Either way, it raises an obvious question. We must ask *which* talkative eternity we are talking to when we make sense of time? And that brings us back to the primary task of identification: which 'God/eternity' is the true meaning of life?[67]

3.3 Identifying the talkative eternity

Jenson has spotted how a question arises from his analysis of time and eternity. With all manner of 'putative gods' available, we must enquire as to which one we are referring to when we use the word 'God'.[68] Jenson's question is simple enough, and he is right in saying the word 'God' doesn't signify much on its own. Many of us will have chatted with self-confessed atheists and noticed how the God they don't believe in is an entity we don't believe in either. What is of interest, however, is that Jenson thinks big ticket words like 'create' or 'redeem' cannot define the concept of 'God', signifying next to nothing in themselves unless the identity of the God to which they are tagged is known in advance. In other words, to say 'God saves' tells us very little about either God or salvation unless we know *which* God we are talking about.[69] As Jenson puts it, 'X redeems' means nothing other than 'X restores whatever state X defines as good'.[70] As a result, only when we have clarified who is specified by the concept 'God' can the meaning of the verb be understood and life thereby make sense. Jenson's example is that 'God creates' *can* mean Marduk 'slays the great Slime and divides her body into plowland', and thereby ensures another harvest to save the Mesopotamian world.[71] But 'creates' will mean something else when predicated of a different God.

Of course, Jenson thinks the gospel identifies what Christians mean by 'God', and therein determines what it means to say we have been created and redeemed by him. However, this is where the earlier point about narrative kicks in. Because the gospel is a narratable event, Jenson thinks we can proceed with our identification of God in the same way as we identify other temporal entities. Just as I can say to my wife, 'You know Yvonne', and she can reply 'Which Yvonne?' and I explain that I am referring to the one who is married to Albert and works at the petrol station, we can adopt the same method when we identify God, that is, name him by situating him in the narrative of his temporal relations with us. But how does that work?

'To see how it *should* work', Jenson draws our attention to the form of corporate prayers in church.[72] As he writes:

> Typically, the address to God is first a name or title, followed by a narrative identification of this God, e.g., 'Almighty God, who through thine only begotten Son hast overcome death . . .' The item of biblical, and usually directly Christological, narrative used is chosen to open a gate for the petition that follows, as the identification just quoted opens to the petition for life in the living Christ.[73]

The truth of Jenson's argument will be obvious to many. For example, I went to church this morning and prayed the Collect for the 'Visit of the Blessed Virgin Mary to Elizabeth', with that part of the liturgy identifying God by naming him and narrating an episode in the story of his act with us. The name and narrative – in my case, about Elizabeth and Mary – picked out which God among the 'putative gods' we were addressing as we proceeded to petition this specific God to 'please do this that or the other for us'.[74] In short, we addressed God by specifying historical people who are caught up in his work with us, and then sought to navigate the contingencies of our lives in relation to that specified God.

Of course, Jenson knows Christians are not the first to identify God in this way, and so he will make much of the fact that we are only doing what Israel has always done. Israel, as Jenson understands her, defines herself as a particular people distinct from all other nations in that God chose Abraham, created a people and proceeded to get them out of Egypt, and so on. Thus, 'To the question "Whom do you mean, 'God'?" Israel answered, "Whoever got us out of Egypt."'[75] However, Jenson appreciates Israel's approach is somewhat odd. In Western history, for example, God is usually uncoupled from historical events, with our religious speaking signifying something lurking the far side of a metaphysical chasm, being situated in a timeless realm; in other words, our words gesture towards a God who is not 'with' the identifying activity, even if accurately indicated 'by' it. However, Jenson thinks the narrative of Scripture precludes such a move. The Shekinah presence in the Temple, the bread and wine on the altar, the gospel rightly preached, and of course Jesus Christ are all events *with* which God is identified, not only *by* them.[76] In other words, Jenson thinks God does God-with-us, and that is why he can be identified.

As Jenson makes clear, his entire project pivots on making this move.[77] He will not settle for identifying God by specific events alone, but only *with* those very same events.[78] But that brings us back to an earlier question. Can the infinite God be identified in this way?

It will come as no surprise that Jenson thinks he can, and that is because the gospel specifies a talkative eternity who is identified with the life of one particular person. What Jenson means is that the gospel specifies 'the temporal infinity' of Jesus of Nazareth as the talkative eternity that gives meaning to our lives.[79] And that is why Jenson thinks the gospel is unavoidably scandalous. It specifies a God who is identified *by* and *with* the infinity of one historical man.

To understand why this is so, we must remember that the gospel message is about what happened to a nameable someone who lived with us, Jesus of Nazareth. Because Jesus ate and drank with us, healing the leper, giving sight to the blind and saying 'Father forgive them' as he drew his last breath, this Jesus can be identified by a narrative that is complete; i.e. he died.[80] However, though this makes the gospel intrinsically tellable – because it is the identifying narrative of a completed life – the gospel is nonetheless *surprising*. It is the announcement that this nameable man has been raised from the dead and now lives with 'death behind him', and, because he lives with 'death behind him', this identifiable someone is in some sense *in*finite, because he lives in a state that is no longer bounded by the full stop that is the threatening termination of everything finite as it hurtles through time.[81] As a result, Jenson thinks the gospel event is speak-about-able in the same way as other historical events, but it is odd because it concludes with a blurting-out exclamation: '*Life* beyond death!' '*Infinity* opens within time!'[82] In other words, the resurrection triggers the blurting exclamation: '*God!*'[83]

As Jenson sees it, we say 'God' because the experience the apostles had 'of the risen Jesus did not conform to the supposition that he had merely come *back* from the dead [i.e. being resuscitated]; rather, if their meetings with him rightly displayed the risen Jesus' location in reality, death had been *undone* with him, so that it was left *behind* him.'[84] And just so, 'This puts him alongside Israel's God in his infinity, somehow identified so that God "just *is*" the one who raised him – i.e. the event of this particular resurrection.'[85] And with that being so, Jenson's argument is in fact simple: the gospel is an item of religious news – in that is specifies a particular eternity – but it does so in a way that makes us identify this eternity as the infinity of a particular someone, whose End interrupts the rest of us ahead of time. In short, 'The envelopment of our time by God is itself accomplished in the course of our time',[86] and that is the scandal. It is to make the claim that the bracketing meaning of history somehow breaks out in the middle of that history, with the transcendent end of time somehow made present within time, with the eschatological interruption of the resurrection being nothing less than the being of God who is nothing other than this event of transcending time, so that our specific history is his history through which he gives meaning to himself.

Now, we will need to do a lot more work to make sense of this. But we can already see that Jenson – as a result of this logic – thinks there is a straightforward answer to the question, 'What do you mean by God?' Jenson will simply reply, 'Whoever raised Jesus from the dead.'[87] Jenson thinks this answer is accurate because, 'a God is always some sort of eternity, some sort of embrace around time, within which time's sequences can be coherent, and if Jesus is risen he is to be both remembered and awaited.'[88] As a result, Jenson's understanding of time, eternity and history leads to a simple conclusion: 'The content of the gospel is that God can now be known as "whoever raised Jesus from the dead".'[89] As a result, when 'Humankind cries out: *Where* may we turn? To *whom* may we pray? *What* power may we invoke? By *what name*? Christianity answers: We may pray to Jesus's "Father," whom in his Spirit we too may address as Father.'[90]

3.4 Speaking to and about the God who speaks to and about us

We can hopefully see the way Jenson's work disorientates his readers, not least because he is doing something very different from the norm.

Jenson is refusing to evacuate our time in order to speak about eternity, and instead proceeds as if the stories we tell about the historical Jesus are in fact stories about who God eternally *is*. Of course, in many respects, this is simply the occupational hazard of any theologian. We are all compelled to link the eternal to time somehow, getting on with our task in the belief that God is in some sense a pick-out-able subject, albeit identified with neither everything in general nor nothing in particular. Theologians therefore spend their days learning how best to specify what makes God to be God, both in distinction from and in relation to everything else that exists, with certain characteristics being attributed to him and thereby identifying him as totally *other* to everything else. That is to say, we agree that God is in some sense identifiable as the *Something* – even if not a thing! – who is like this, that or the other.

With that being said, our usual approach is to highlight the inherent contradiction between finite words and the infinite Subject we are describing, noting, for example, how this determines the type of language we use, thereby emphasizing how the non-circumscribable God is like-but-not-like the finite concepts we deploy. Analogical speech is therefore the preferred idiom, if only because it offers us sufficient wriggle room for our words to identify by *non*-identity, thus allowing the infinite God to be genuinely *other* to the finite concepts with which we pick him out.[91] But we can now see that Jenson is doing something different.[92] In fact, he thinks the standard approach is little more than, 'pious mystery-mongering of the vacuity', and that is simply because Jenson's God has *narratable content*.[93]

Jenson argues that Christian speech about God – our metaphors, concepts, parables and dogmatic statements – are not inadequate gestures across a metaphysical chasm. That is because we are speaking about someone who is 'aggressively incarnate',[94] and therein graspable – and not only in the sense of being able to nail him down on a cross. Because Jesus of Nazareth defines the infinity of God, this God can be unequivocally signified if we tell stories about the life Jesus lived.[95] Sentences like 'God is born', 'God eats', 'God tires' and even 'God dies' are therefore not linguistic tricks, but instead state a matter of historical fact which are simultaneously eternally true because they are about Jesus who is genuinely infinite. Thus, for Jenson, no analogical interval is needed, because there is no metaphysical gap for our words to bridge. Jesus of Nazareth is still one of us in his infinity.[96]

To put the point a different way, Jenson is arguing that the 'challenge is not posed by any of the predicates [i.e. born, dies, infinite, etc.], odd as some of them are in themselves, but by the unity of the subject'.[97] We must simply proceed as if God really is all about Jesus, with that assumption meaning we must say it is 'one and the same . . . who is crucified and who orders the galaxies . . . lies muling and puking in his mother's arms and the while restrains Satan'.[98] The words are true in their plain sense, with there being no need for us to imagine a way of getting beyond these signifiers, leveraging a space between the narrative and the God there identified. Instead, our words pick Jesus out, because he is truly one of us, and therein identify God because Jesus is infinite.

Jenson's understanding of the capability of our finite words trades on his theology of prayer. Chris Green has made this point, highlighting the way Jenson's account of our speech about God depends entirely on who God is, with the efficacy of our words ultimately depending on the fact that we are situated in direct relation to a God *who speaks* – which is to say theologians adopt the posture of prayer.[99] Of course, Jenson is hardly the first to offer this insight. He understands how prayer and theology have always been connected, in that the old adage of *lex orandi lex credendi* – the law of prayer is the law of belief – captures the way 'the school of [Christian] logic was the church's liturgy'.[100] The creeds we recite, for example, draw from existing rites of initiation by which a worshipping community identified the God to whom they prayed as they petitioned him and one another to become a faithful church. For Jenson, this implies we can talk accurately about God to each other, because this is a God who can first be talked to, conversed with, argued with, lamented with and even advised as we praise him for his mighty acts.[101] In short, 'The life of humanity before God is an antiphony of God's word to us and our word to God', and that is what underwrites our speech to each other.[102]

As always, Jenson is prepared to draw out a startling conclusion from this insight. He argues that prayer works, because God is himself an eternal conversation. As expected, the story of Jesus drives Jenson to this conclusion,[103] arguing for example that 'Jesus' prayer in the seventeenth chapter of John can only be understood as inner discourse of the Trinity exposed to our overhearing'.[104] As Jenson reads this passage, he concludes that conversation is God's life, in that it is the way in which he is resolutely personal, but only to the degree that the conversation he speaks between Father and Son establishes the way of his being in the Spirit. Thus Jenson can argue that 'When the Gospels quote Jesus' report of his sending by the Father and Jesus' prayers to the Father, they cite exchanges in a conversation by and in which God is God',[105] with the life of Jesus thereby showing that the Father speaks this Word, whose response is liberated by the Spirit, who thereby opens up the constitutive address between this Father and Son into the endless futurity that is God's own infinite life. And, what is more, we are able to listen in on their conversation.

Now, this is obviously a complex issue to raise so early in our task, and so we need to return to it better equipped later on. Here, however, the point has to do with the way our language can identify the way God *is*, because Jesus is one of us and one in the Conversation God is. As Jenson sees it, the issue is simple enough: the Wordiness of God's life underwrites the wordiness of narrative identification. Because God bespeaks himself as the story he tells himself about Jesus – a pure dramatic act, as it were – 'unabashed petitionary prayer is the one decisively appropriate creaturely act over and against the true God'.[106] And that must be true because, 'We know God in that the Word of God that is God, that is *homoousios* [i.e. of one being] with the Father, is actual only as conversation with us.'[107] In other words, Jenson thinks Jesus shows how our creaturely being depends entirely on God's speech about himself, in which we are mentioned along with Jesus.[108] We are thereby invited to participate in their conversation, which is already about us, as well as about them. And that is our being.[109]

To put this otherwise, Jenson thinks we exist in the eternal conversation, which is the act of God's self-transcendence to include us with him through the Word who is his Son. Or, as Chris Green puts it, 'In the creative, creating utterance of God, the Father says "Let there *be*" and the Spirit says "*Let* there be". And just because God is the beginning and end of this utterance, Jesus is *there* for us, always already present to us here and now for our good.'[110] As a result, 'in prayer, we tell God what we think, and God, who first graciously invited us to speak, listens, and responds'.[111] In effect, this God, who is the dynamic conversation of his own self-address, should be talked to by those he creates, meaning that our 'prayer to him is, unmitigatedly, talk to a person',[112] and therein Jenson thinks, 'The sort of mysticism that advises us "pray not with your mouth" has no place in the Church'.[113]

In other words, because God is his own speech of speaking to us, we are invited into the ultimate conversation, and that alone is the ground of any confidence we might have in the capability of our speech about God.[114] Therefore, if we can converse with this God who speaks us into being within the conversation that he is, why would we want to undermine the way our words work by introducing the loosening concept of analogy when we speak to each other about him? Jenson thinks that approach could only be indicative of a false humility or – even worse! – constitute evidence that our knowledge is of a different God.

Of course, Jenson knows, 'our knowledge of God is now "through a glass darkly"', but that is 'because it is knowledge across the eschatological boundary, across the discontinuity of our own death and resurrection'.[115] The good news, however, is that Jesus is alive and the Spirit of his life with his Father transcends that final boundary, coming to us as God's Future as a down payment of what he will be for us, as he is for the man Jesus. As a result, we can already enter into the call and response of our life with God because God is the overcoming of any 'gap' through the resurrection of Jesus of Nazareth. Thus, our words can identify God as they pick out this pick-out-able man. Jenson therefore dares to say that 'being' is a univocal concept in respect to God and us, but with the stress being placed on the *vocal*: the act God does for himself and the act of creation is but a singular speech-act, with the enfleshed Word being at the heart of both. And just therein lies the difference between us and God. '[W]hen we say, "Creatures are", we give thanks, but when God says, "Creatures are", he creates.'[116] The point, however: both of us speak as one conversation.

3.5 Gathering thoughts and moving forward

At this stage of the book, Jenson's overall intention has become clear. Like other theologians, he wants to identify God. That much is obvious, and hardly contentious. However, we can begin to see how the situation gets a bit more complicated, because he doesn't think the word 'God' is self-evident in meaning, as if it is clear what a God must be like. Jenson readily accepts that there is 'a different divine offering on every street corner', and he knows these alternative gods can help people make sense of their lives.[117] As a result, we must labour to pick out the true God from all the other claimants to that title, and Jenson thinks the success of that work depends on whether we attend to the message of the gospel.[118]

Proceeding with confidence, Jenson believes we can identify the God of the gospel, because God is genuinely present in the event of his self-introduction. In many respects, this remains standard procedure. Any Christian theologian proceeds in the belief God acts, and that his act is true to who he is, in the sense that God is not playing tricks with us by pretending to be a different God in relation to us. That is to say, theologians believe God does himself with us, and so his being is in his act. As a result, Jenson's work is in keeping with the vast majority of Christian theologians. However, we have also seen that he is somewhat peculiar because he doesn't think any 'gap' exists between God's act towards us and God's being in himself, believing instead that only ingrained prejudices would make us want to leverage open a space between God's being and act. Resisting that temptation, Jenson decides to press ahead on the assumption that God's being is in his act, and that his being is therefore 'active', and that – somewhat strangely – the activity God *is* is precisely what he does in our midst. Were that not the case, Jenson thinks God and the gospel would finally go their separate ways, effectively meaning that we were back to square one.[119] God must therefore be identified *by* and *with* this event.

What is even more unusual, however, is that Jenson believes the gospel demands that we conceive of God's presence as somewhat episodic in form, in that God acts in very particular ways and at very particular times, allowing us to point – along with Israel – to specific events and exclaim '*There!*' '*That's God!*' Otherwise put, Jenson thinks God's presence is in some sense 'roomy', because it is utterly specific, rather than being the featureless reality of a blanket universal.[120] This means he is prepared to say that God was here and not there, doing this and not that, which in turn means he thinks that these specific God-happenings can be strung together to make a series, and thus – in their sequence – together make a plot. As Jenson sees it, it is only because God is plottable in this way that we are able to tell the story of God, which we know can only be a true story about him if it is his own story about what makes him to be the God that he is. In other words, he has spotted that God must finally be identified *through* these specific events, if he is really known *by* them and *with* them. If not, we can again only gesture with greater or lesser accuracy across a metaphysical divide towards a God who is essentially uncoupled from the gospel narrative.

However, this summary is far too abstract. Jenson thinks God's narratable work of self-identification centres on a single Israelite whose life is at one and the same time historically with us and infinitely with God. However, the identity of this singular Nazarene must never be construed in static terms, but instead allowed to exhibit its dynamic character over the span of the life he lives. That is because a punctiliar point could have no identifiable character but must somehow be extended if it is to be known, thereby making a narratable span through the plot of its timely episodes, which – we have seen – must terminate if they are to make a coherent unity. As a result, Jenson argues the span of this singular Israelite does make a narrative plot, but only because – just like a meaningful sentence or story – the series of dynamic episodes cohere in the end. In short, the death of Jesus underwrites our confidence that he is who he truly was in the run up to it.[121]

With this move being made, Jenson argues that the death of Jesus means his character can be properly identified, but the resurrection means he must simultaneously be identified as the infinite one. In effect, this specifiable man lives with death behind him, and so is both accommodated to the contingencies of our time, while also transcending its boundaries.[122] With these moves made, Jenson can therefore conclude that the only way we can identify this God is by undertaking 'the *interpretation of God* by what happened and will happen with Jesus Christ',[123] because what did happen with Jesus is the Father willed the Spirit to raise the one who lived fully for others from the dead, thereby enabling him to interrupt our lives by opening up the future of God-with-us, which is the meaning of time. In other words, Jenson thinks God is this specific conversation, in that he is the speaking of an eternal Word that is not empty, but instead amounts to the fulfilled invitation and response we see in Jesus, which is begun eternally in the Father and ends eternally in the Spirit, with the one born of Mary and crucified by Pilate somehow being the way God knows himself because it is who he decides to be with us in his infinity.[124]

With all this in mind, Jenson's project has its focus. Because 'the Man for Others died rather than seek his own kingdom', Jenson thinks it 'settles that he is the Man for Others and so determines the salvific import of the message that he lives as Lord'.[125] That is to say, what we mean by 'God' is captured by the story we tell of Jesus and the Transcendence he called Father and the life of the Spirit they share, with these Three together making the basic plot line of the narrated conversation that is 'God'.[126] But the twist in the drama is that God wills our presence through Christ's terminated life unconditionally for others. In other words, Jenson is claiming that this specific span – which is a narratable series – is constitutive of what makes God to be God, because the resurrection renders the one who is infinite one of our brothers, and the only way for Jenson to do this is to lay out the historical plot the Son in fact lives upon the eternal begetting of the exact same Son from the Father, so that eternity and time are strictly identified in him. As a result, Jenson thinks Mary is the Mother of God, 'without being a goddess to achieve this', because the span from conception through to death coincides with the substance of the Father's eternal begetting, which comes before anything else exists so that it may share in the life of the Spirit.[127] In effect, both God and ourselves turn towards the crucified Jesus to know God and creature in an act of identification. In short, the gospel picks out a God who is nothing other than he is for us.

With this being so, Jenson has picked out a 'talkative eternity', but only by claiming that God in himself – as 'the talkative eternity' – is in some sense 'storied', so that he can be identified with the story of this particular temporal life. Thus, Jenson concludes God possesses the character of a story, being best imagined as his own Beginning, Middle and End through which God determines who he will always forever be, and – even more astonishingly – this story must finally be no different to what happens to Jesus over that first Easter weekend in which he dies and lives for the ungodly. Of course, these final comments have taken us way beyond a rehearsal of what has been covered so far, and we have thereby opened up the expanse into which we must venture as we press on with our investigation. Our next task is to see if any of this relates to the church's official teaching, and to do that we will explore Jenson's reading of the doctrinal tradition. As this will demonstrate, Jenson thinks he can find all the resources he needs to align his proposal to dogmatic teaching, but in so doing he spots that the history of the church evidences a colossal failure in nerve. All too often, we have denied that Jesus is the Son he claimed to be, and thereby lose sight of the gospel the church is called to proclaim by leveraging open a space between God and the story of this Israelite. Simply put, our metaphysics are unevangelized.

Notes

1 Robert W. Jenson, *Systematic Theology, Volume 1, The Triune God* (New York: OUP, 1997), 57.
2 Robert W. Jenson, 'Choose Ye This Day Whom Ye Will Serve . . .' in *Essays on the Trinity*, ed. Lincoln Harvey (Eugene, OR: Cascade, 2018), 14–19.
3 Jenson, 'Choose Ye This Day', 14–19.
4 See, for example, Jenson, *Systematic Theology*, Vol. 1, 64.
5 Anthony Kenny, 'Introduction', in Aristotle, *Poetics*, translated by Anthony Kenny (Oxford: OUP, 2013), xx–xxi.
6 Thanks to Donna Lazenby for this phrasing.
7 Jenson, *Systematic Theology*, Vol. 1, 66.
8 Jenson, *Systematic Theology*, Vol. 1, 159.
9 Robert W. Jenson, *Unbaptized God: The Basic Flaw in Ecumenical Theology* (Minneapolis: Fortress, 1992), 141.
10 Jenson, *Systematic Theology*, Vol. 1, 64.
11 Robert W. Jenson, 'What Kind of God Can Make a Covenant?' in *Covenant and Hope: Christian and Jewish Reflections*, ed. Robert W. Jenson and Eugene B. Korn (Grand Rapids: Eerdmans, 2012), 17–18.
12 Robert W. Jenson, *A Large Catechism* (Delhi, NY: American Lutheran Publicity Bureau, 1991), 47. This phrase will be used regularly in what follows, but the origin will not always be cited.
13 On this, see Robert W. Jenson, *Visible Words: The Interpretation and Practice of Christian Sacraments* (Minneapolis: Fortress, 2010).
14 Cf. title of Jenson, *Visible Words*.
15 Jenson, *Large Catechism*, 46.
16 Robert W. Jenson, 'Story and Promise in Pastoral Care', *Pastoral Psychology* 26.2 (1977), 118.
17 Robert W. Jenson, *Systematic Theology, Volume 2, The Works of God* (New York: OUP, 1999), 259.
18 Robert W. Jenson, 'The Father, He . . .' in *Speaking the Christian God: The Holy Trinity and the Challenge of Feminism*, ed. Alvin F. Kimel, Jr (Grand Rapids: Eerdmans, 1992), 107.
19 Jenson, 'Story and Promise in Pastoral Care', where one section is entitled, 'sacramental specificity'.
20 Jenson, *Large Catechism*, 48.
21 Jenson makes this point regularly, setting out the logic in various ways. See, for example, Jenson, *Systematic Theology*, Vol. 1, 47–8.
22 Robert W. Jenson, 'For us . . . He Was Made Man', in *Nicene Christianity: The Future for a New Ecumenism*, ed. Christopher R. Seitz (Grand Rapids: Brazos, 2001), 77.

23 Jenson, *Large Catechism*, 48.

24 Robert W. Jenson, 'Anima Ecclesiastica', in *God and Human Dignity*, ed. R. Kendall Soulen and Linda Woodhead (Grand Rapids: Eerdmans, 2006), 69.

25 For a discussion of the way God's life establishes contingent history, rather than the other way around, see Stephen John Wright, *Dogmatic Aesthetics: A Theology of Beauty in Dialogue with Robert W. Jenson* (Minneapolis: Fortress, 2014), 129–40.

26 Jenson can argue, for example, that 'The circle just traced is benign.' Jenson, *Systematic Theology*, Vol. 1, 58.

27 Francesca Aran Murphy attacks Jenson on this point in *God is Not a Story: Realism Revisited* (Oxford: OUP, 2007). Thanks to Chris Green for this reference.

28 As Jenson sees it, '*At this precise point*, the Western tradition must simply be corrected.' Jenson, *Systematic Theology*, Vol. 1, 113.

29 Jenson, *Systematic Theology*, Vol. 2, 35.

30 As Jenson puts it, 'we cannot rightly talk of this God in any way which would make the temporal sequences, the stuff of narration, unessential to his being'. Robert W. Jenson, *The Triune Identity: God According to the Gospel* (Philadelphia: Fortress, 1982; reprint, Eugene, OR: Wipf and Stock, 2002), 22.

31 Jenson, *Unbaptized God*, 143.

32 The danger is the church would thereby 'saw off the limb of the narrative identification on which all its talk of God sits'. Jenson, *Triune Identity*, 25.

33 Jenson, *Systematic Theology*, Vol. 1, 222–3.

34 Or, to put the point otherwise, 'the being of God is primally hypostatic: to be God the Father, or God the Son or God the Spirit, does not require that there antecedently be something one could call God.' Jenson, *Systematic Theology*, Vol. 1, 215.

35 Jenson, *Large Catechism*, 22.

36 Jenson, *Systematic Theology*, Vol. 1, 217–18.

37 Jenson, *Systematic Theology*, Vol. 1, 222.

38 Jenson, *Unbaptized God*, 145.

39 Jenson, 'What Kind of God', 3.

40 For instance, see 'Time, Created Being, and Space', in Jenson, *Systematic Theology*, Vol. 2, 29–49.

41 Partly to appease his friend Colin E. Gunton. See Jenson, *Systematic Theology*, Vol. 2, 46 n75.

42 Jenson, *Systematic Theology*, Vol. 2, 46–7.

43 Chris Green has drawn my attention to Susan Sontag's coinage of this idea, but to put it in Jenson's technical terms: 'Space . . . is the a priori of otherness.' Jenson, *Systematic Theology*, Vol. 2, 46.

44 Jenson, 'What Kind of God', 4.

45 Robert W. Jenson, 'Scripture's Authority in the Church', in *The Art of Reading Scripture*, ed. Ellen F. Davis and Richard B. Hays (Grand Rapids: Eerdmans, 2003), 35.

46 See, for example, Jenson, *Triune Identity*, 1.

47 See Jenson, *Systematic Theology*, Vol. 2, 29–35.

48 Jenson, 'What Kind of God', 3–4.

49 As Jenson states, 'It is above all birth and death that establish temporality, both as to fact and as to our knowledge of the fact.' Jenson, *Systematic Theology*, Vol. 1, 49.

50 Jenson, 'What Kind of God', 4.

PART ONE | A CLUSTER OF JENSONIAN CONCEPTS

51 Jenson, 'What Kind of God', 3.

52 Jenson thinks the threat of nihilism already has a place in the church's witness. Hence, 'With one footnote to Ecclesiastes, Nietzsche could have spared us a great deal of his rhetoric.' Jenson, *Systematic Theology*, Vol. 2, 56 n21.

53 For Jenson's theological analysis of time as history, see Jenson, *Systematic Theology*, Vol. 2, 29–35.

54 As he puts it, 'Against the threat of anthropological nihilism, the disillusioned heirs of Athens could find new hope in Jerusalem.' Jenson, *Systematic Theology*, Vol. 2, 58.

55 See discussion in Jenson, *Systematic Theology*, Vol. 1, 54–7.

56 Jenson uses the concept of eternity *positively*, i.e. to render time meaningful, but it can be used negatively in stark contrast to time and thereby undermine time. I'm grateful to Steve Wright for helping to clarify this point.

57 Robert W. Jenson, 'Election and Culture: From Babylon to Jerusalem', in *Public Theology in Cultural Engagement*, ed. Stephen R. Holmes (Milton Keynes: Paternoster, 2008), 49.

58 See Jenson's critique of idolatry, which pivots on the idea that it is impossible to live without worshipping *something* (even nothingness), and thereby posit an 'eternity/god' in some form. Jenson, *Systematic Theology*, Vol. 2, 134–8.

59 Jenson, 'What Kind of God', 3–4.

60 Jenson, 'What Kind of God', 4. By 'pantheon', Jenson simply means a plurality of gods.

61 Jenson, *Triune Identity*, 2. See also, Jenson, *Systematic Theology*, Vol. 1, 55.

62 Robert W. Jenson, 'Creation as a Triune Act', *Word and World* 2.1 (1982), 39.

63 Jenson, 'What Kind of God', 3.

64 Robert W. Jenson, 'The Praying Animal', *Zygon* 18.3 (1983), 311–26. See also, Jenson, *Systematic Theology*, Vol. 2, 58–9.

65 Robert W. Jenson, 'What if It Were True?' *Neue Zeitschrift für Systematische Theologie und Religionsphilosophie* 43.1 (2001), 13.

66 As Jenson summarizes, 'what we usually call "philosophy" is theology suffering under the handicap of getting along without Scripture'. Robert W. Jenson, 'Response: The Philosophy that Attends to Scripture', in the Symposium on Kenneth Oakes, *Karl Barth on Theology and Philosophy*.

67 Jenson, *Systematic Theology*, Vol. 1, 55.

68 Jenson, *Systematic Theology*, Vol. 1, 56–7.

69 Jenson, *Triune Identity*, xi. Or, as he states elsewhere, 'the proposition "All gods save" is indeed indisputable but only because it is wholly empty.' Jenson, *Systematic Theology*, Vol. 1, 56.

70 Jenson, *Triune Identity*, xi.

71 Jenson, *Systematic Theology*, Vol. 1, 48.

72 Robert W. Jenson, 'Joining the Eternal Conversation: John's Prologue and the Language of Worship', *Touchstone* 14 (2001), 34. See also, Robert W. Jenson, 'The Triune God', in *Christian Dogmatics*, ed. Carl E. Braaten and Robert W. Jenson (Philadelphia: Fortress, 1984), 89.

73 Jenson, 'Joining the Eternal', 34.

74 See comments about the function of Collects in Jenson, *Triune Identity*, 3.

75 Jenson, *Triune Identity*, 7. See also, Jenson, *Systematic Theology*, Vol. 1, 44.

76 Or, as Jenson puts it, 'Invested in palace and temple at Jerusalem, God's will was invested in the reality of this world.' Jenson, *Systematic Theology*, Vol. 1, 69.

77 Jenson, *Systematic Theology*, Vol. 1, 59.
78 Jenson, *Systematic Theology*, Vol. 1, 60.
79 In short, 'The story told in the Gospels states the meaning of creation.' Jenson, *Systematic Theology*, Vol. 2, 27.
80 Jenson, *Systematic Theology*, Vol. 1, 198.
81 Jenson, *Triune Identity*, 23. See also, Jenson, *Systematic Theology*, Vol. 1, 143.
82 See discussion in Jenson, *Systematic Theology*, Vol. 1, 142-3.
83 For Jenson's outworking of this point, see Jenson, *Systematic Theology*, Vol. 1, 198-201.
84 Robert W. Jenson, 'How Does Jesus Make a Difference?' in *Essentials of Christian Theology*, ed. William C. Placher (Louisville: WJK Press, 2003), 191.
85 Jenson, 'How Does Jesus', 191.
86 Jenson, *Systematic Theology*, Vol. 2, 27.
87 Jenson uses this term so often that examples abound, in this instance see variation in Jenson, *Systematic Theology*, Vol. 1, 42.
88 Jenson, *Triune Identity*, 23.
89 Jenson, *Triune Identity*, 8.
90 Jenson, *Triune Identity*, xii.
91 See discussion of Aquinas' development of analogy to solve the puzzle, in Jenson, *Systematic Theology*, Vol. 2, 36-7.
92 Though Jenson agrees with the mainstream consensus that God's *being* is finally unspeakable, he puts a twist on why that might be: God is *too* close for comfort, as we will see.
93 Jenson, *Triune Identity*, 126.
94 Jenson, *Systematic Theology*, Vol. 1, 139.
95 Hence, his opposition to standard approaches to mystery. See Jenson, *Systematic Theology*, Vol. 1, 233.
96 See Jenson, *Systematic Theology*, Vol. 2, 302-3.
97 Robert W. Jenson, 'Christ in the Trinity: Communicatio Idiomatum', in *The Person of Christ*, ed. Murray Rae and Stephen R. Holmes (London: Continuum, 2005), 62.
98 Jenson, 'What if', 9.
99 For an analysis of Jenson's theology of prayer, see Chris E. W. Green, 'Participation in Providence: Robert W. Jenson's Theology of Prayer', *Pro Ecclesia* 28.2 (2019), 167-77. I am grateful to Chris for advice on much of what follows in this section.
100 Jenson, *Systematic Theology*, Vol. 1, 92.
101 Jenson, 'The Triune God', 92.
102 Jenson, *Systematic Theology*, Vol. 2, 59.
103 Jenson, *Systematic Theology*, Vol. 2, 61.
104 Jenson, *Systematic Theology*, Vol. 1, 93.
105 Jenson, *Systematic Theology*, Vol. 2, 270. Thanks to Chris Green for this reference.
106 Jenson, *Systematic Theology*, Vol. 1, 222.
107 Jenson, *Systematic Theology*, Vol. 1, 228.
108 Jenson, *Systematic Theology*, Vol. 2, 26, 35. As a result, 'The creatures . . . have their being not as *phenomena*, things appearing, but as *legomena*, things told of.' (Vol. 2, 160).
109 Jenson, *Systematic Theology*, Vol. 1, 228.

110 Green, 'Participation', 169, citing Jenson, *Systematic Theology*, Vol. 2, 26.

111 Green, 'Participation', 168. Of course, in doing so, we 'piggyback' on the Son's address to his Father. Jenson, *Systematic Theology*, Vol. 2, 184.

112 Robert W. Jenson, 'Some Platitudes about Prayer', *Dialog* 9 (Winter 1970), 64. Thanks to Chris Green for this reference.

113 Jenson, *Systematic Theology*, Vol. 1, 223. See also, Jenson, 'What if', 13.

114 Hence Jenson makes clear: 'to be is to be *heard of*'. Jenson, *Systematic Theology*, Vol. 2, 36.

115 Jenson, *Systematic Theology*, Vol. 1, 230.

116 Jenson, *Systematic Theology*, Vol. 2, 38.

117 Jenson, *Triune Identity*, ix.

118 As Jenson puts it, specific identification is everything, because 'A theology of no-god-in-particular, or of all-gods-at-once, would be, if not quite vacuous, wholly unhelpful'. Jenson, 'The Triune God', 84.

119 Jenson, *Systematic Theology*, Vol. 1, 59.

120 As we will see, Jenson's understanding of the 'roominess' of God is central to his account of our place in his life with us. See, for example, Robert W. Jenson, 'Aspects of a Doctrine of Creation', in *The Doctrine of Creation: Essays in Dogmatics, History and Philosophy*, ed. Colin E. Gunton (London: T&T Clark, 2004), 24–5.

121 Jenson, *Systematic Theology*, Vol. 1, 198.

122 Or, as Jenson puts it, 'The one Lord Jesus Christ is at once one of the Trinity, in God the Father's identification with him, and one of the human community, in his identification with us. In that he is one of the Trinity, he can have death *behind* him; were he not one of us, he would not have *death* behind him.' Jenson, 'How Does Jesus', 193.

123 Robert W. Jenson, 'Basics and Christology', in *In Search of Christian Unity: Basic Consensus/Basic Differences*, ed. Joseph A. Burgess, (Minneapolis: Fortress Press, 1991), 46.

124 Jenson, *Systematic Theology*, Vol. 1, 222.

125 Jenson, *Systematic Theology*, Vol. 1, 181.

126 Jenson uses variations on this wording at regular intervals. For example, Jenson, *Triune Identity*, 12, and Jenson, *Systematic Theology*, Vol. 1, 108.

127 Jenson, 'For us . . .', 83–4.

PART TWO

Jenson and the Tradition

4

In the Name of the Father, Son and Holy Spirit

4.1 General guidance on Jenson's approach

One point will have come across loud and clear so far: Jenson's proposal is somewhat odd. At the same time, we should also have seen the way his proposal is strangely familiar, in that his attention to the gospel narrative means he is drawing on a story that is extremely commonplace, even if the use to which he puts it subverts normal practice. As a result, his attempt to work out a revisionary metaphysics by way of a gospel-shaped logic means his proposal should be closely scrutinized, rather than being dismissed on the grounds of its oddity alone. To press on with that task, we will now explore the way in which Jenson situates his constructive proposal within the established discourse of trinitarian theology.

Jenson thinks the doctrine of the Trinity is 'the Christian faith's repertoire of ways of *identifying* its God, to say *which* of the many candidates for godhead we mean when we say, for example, "God is loving" or "Dear God, please . . .".[1] On this basis, a series of technical concepts – such as *person* and *nature* – are employed to track the gospel narrative, rather than being set to decipher a reality somehow abstracted from the story of Jesus.[2] As Jenson reads it, the church's early theologians refused to ponder a 'religiously vacuous and intellectually uninteresting' generalized concept of God, but instead stuck closely to the historical events around Jerusalem.[3] As a result, the doctrine of the Trinity is a compression of the gospel story, by which we pick out the God of Israel defined by the life, death and resurrection of Jesus.[4]

We should already see that Jenson's approach is somewhat contentious, but it is the only way to align his odd proposal about narrative, identification, time and eternity to the original teaching of the church.[5] He accepts that his approach is idiosyncratic, but that is because most of us have forgotten how trinitarian theology is meant to be about the 'aggressively incarnate'[6] Jesus, and 'the Transcendence he calls Father', and the life of the Spirit they share.[7] In short, we have allowed our minds to wander away from the story we tell about the first Easter weekend.

His proposal is therefore a corrective to this perceived pathology, with his reading of the development of trinitarian doctrine underwriting the positive and negative aspects of his revisionary account. To understand what he is up to, we would therefore be wise to excavate his historical groundwork before getting into the substance of his proposal. To calibrate our sights, we should note a series of subsidiary points in passing.

First, as is already evident, Jenson will read the history of doctrine in two ways, at once both positive and negative. He thereby 'alternates between lamentation and admiration'.[8] Negatively, he will often accuse the vast majority of theologians of sawing off the branch they were meant to be sitting on.[9] They wrongly think the historical contingencies of the gospel narrative are an intellectual embarrassment, mainly – as Jenson reads it – because 'we have let the great pagan Greek theologians tells us too much about what deity must be like'.[10] Rather than focus on the witness of the apostles – and then undertaking the hard labour of constructing a gospel-shaped metaphysics in line with their teaching – theologians have swallowed the philosophers' teaching, and thereby understand their task as working out how a philosophically defined God can be protected from the 'contamination' of 'wombs and the tombs women tended'.[11] Jenson thinks the outcome is disastrous, because – with the story of Jesus stripped of its ultimate value – the reality of time is undervalued as we pursue some timeless 'Being' situated on the far side of a metaphysical chasm. God the Son is thereby reduced to 'a demigod or symbol, rather than a human person, that is one truly born, with a specific mother, and truly dead, with a specific grave',[12] which is another way of saying that most of us are working with 'a doctrine of God only partly bent to the gospel'.[13]

The details of Jenson's critique can be put on hold for now, because we need to note that he also has many positive things to say about the development of doctrine. He thinks the early church encountered deeply engrained patterns of thought, but rather than capitulate to the dominant metaphysics, the early theologians managed to evangelize the way people think. Existing philosophical concepts were thereby taken and reworked into a specifically Christian shape, which allowed the refashioned concepts to be deployed in the construction of an alternative metaphysics within which the most basic building blocks of reality were reconfigured in light of the fact that Jesus has been raised from the dead.[14] As a result, Christian theologians discovered a way to describe God that was very different to anything an ancient philosopher could have imagined, even if the same philosophers would have immediately recognized the concepts the church had recruited into its analysis.[15] Or, to put that differently, the emergence of the doctrine of the Trinity marked a revolution in thought, because its account of 'Being' centred on what happened to Mary's boy and Pilate's victim over the first Easter weekend.

Again, the details can wait. The point to grasp is that both the negative and positive readings need to be kept in mind when grappling with Jenson's constructive proposal, because it is the combination of the two that enables him to develop his revisionary account of the Trinity in line with what he considers to be the church's best insights. In short, his twofold reading of dogmatic history underwrites his claim to be speaking orthodoxy better than the majority of theologians have managed.

And that brings us nicely to the next point. Despite criticizing the majority of theologians, Jenson accepts there is a plank in everyone's eyes, *including his own*. Not once will he suggest that any of us are immune to the conceptual struggle he will recount, but instead he expects the 'double history' to be happening in everyone's mind.[16] That is to say, he never imagines some hermetically sealed capsule of orthodoxy, which is somehow shrink-wrapped and protected from contamination from the philosophical world, in which 'real' Christians – like him! – can resist the alternative metaphysics by simply telling the gospel story.[17] Instead, the 'double history' – at once both positive and negative – is a personal negotiation each of us is required to make.[18] In effect, the struggle between alternative metaphysics characterizes our own ongoing conversion in the Spirit-agitated[19] work of renewing our minds in tune with the gospel-happening that *is* the life of God. We must continually struggle to be orthodox.

As these comments make evident, Jenson thinks trinitarian theology is an ongoing conversation in which what we say about God is worked out in relation to the existing way of seeing things. Of course, this is simply another way of saying all theology is contextual, although Jenson doesn't think all contexts are equally influential in the task we are undertaking.[20] The gospel is carried from its initial epicentre in time and place – a group of women run in startled shock from a garden tomb outside Jerusalem's gates – and is shared by one person to another as it makes its way towards the ends of the earth, *but the trajectory of that movement is primarily westward*.[21] The first Christians thereby encounter the dominant Greco-Roman culture of the day, which meant their message was interpreted by the norms of the already established discourse of the Greeks.

As we should expect, Jenson thinks this westward trajectory was entirely contingent, in that things 'could have been otherwise'.[22] This is one of the reasons why he is keen to point out that there isn't anything necessary about the philosophical questions the church tried to answer, although he will make this point without undermining the value of the conversation that was thereby triggered. Jenson will on occasion demonstrate what gospel-shaped reasoning might have produced under different circumstances, offering a sketch of how the trinitarian logic would have worked itself out in an Islamic context, for example, or in conversation with contemporary Jewish scholars.²³ Each time the doctrine of the Trinity comes into plain sight, but the conceptual framework with which it is constructed is different to the one we can assume to be normative. Otherwise put, God looks the same even though our conceptual apparatus is different.²⁴

With the contingency of the westward trajectory noted, Jenson recognizes we still tend to imagine the Greek philosophers were doing something unique, and perhaps in the process consider their work to be rigorously 'rational', which thereby makes it somehow universal in application.²⁵ Jenson, however, thinks this is another mistake we make, and so he will go to great lengths to show how philosophy – outside 'the pure study of logic'²⁶ – is no more than a local construal of a specific eternity, which on Jenson's account makes it a rival religion that posits its own 'putative god'. As he describes it in one place, 'what we usually call "philosophy" is theology suffering under the handicap of getting along without Scripture',²⁷ thereby amounting to little more than 'the historically particular Olympian-Parmenidean religion, later shared with the wider Mediterranean cultic world'.²⁸ As a result, Jenson thinks philosophy can claim no privilege. It is just another local discourse, with no claim to universal reason.²⁹

With that in mind, Jenson sees how the dominance of the Olympian-Parmenidean religion meant the questions asked of the early church were heavily loaded.³⁰ The first missionaries proclaimed that Jesus has been raised from the dead, and were met with the response, 'What sort of being must this one be, who has death behind him?'³¹ This innocuous-looking question springs from the local conception of the world, and is therefore derived from a number of entrenched assumptions, which are themselves rooted in a substance metaphysics, the details of which we will get to shortly. The problem, as Jenson sees it, is that this alternative metaphysics is the exact antithesis of the gospel, and so the way in which the question was posed was precisely what needed to be overcome as the church sought to bear faithful witness to the story of Jesus. As a result, Western theology was birthed at the intersection of two incommensurable construals of reality, thereby amounting to an ongoing missionary task in which the way we think is transfigured as our faith is shared. In other words, the metaphysics needs evangelizing as the faith is explained in appropriate missional terms. And that task remains ongoing.³²

Of course, Jenson knows something like this had to happen, even if it might not have taken the specific form it did. Theologians are called to think after the events of the Easter weekend, and so we cannot run to some conceptual store cupboard to find a set of pristine concepts that are begging to be used to describe an event of unprecedented resurrection.

The doctrine of God is not *glossolalia*, somehow dropping down from the heavens, but is instead worked out with whatever materials lie to hand.[33] The outworking of the doctrine is therefore almost eucharistic in form, in the sense that the technical concepts of *hypostasis*, *ousia* and *prosopon* – definitions of which I will soon offer – are, just like the loaf at the supper, taken up and drawn into the Easter narrative until they break, only then being given out in transformed state in service to the peculiar God which they now identify. In other words, Jenson doesn't think these concepts – the specific form that Western theology takes – are anything other than contingent, with the Greek lexicon being in no way necessary for the task in hand. Or to put that otherwise, the original philosophical tools are to be deployed where necessary, while remaining dispensable in essence. However, the story they summarize is not.[34]

And that brings us to the penultimate point before our analysis begins. Jenson thinks the reworked concepts are set to serve the articulation of what remains a narratable event. As Jenson will regularly remind us, the concepts are about Jesus and the Transcendence he named Father in the Spirit of the life they share, with the church thereby using the concepts to capture the story of what took place outside Jerusalem's gates.[35] What the church finds in telling this story is that it demands an interconnected series of most basic concepts to make analytic sense of the narrative plot, with a number of most basic ideas thereby allowed to overlap and intertwine as they mutually define each other in an attempt to recount what remains most basically a narratable occurrence. In other words, the series of technical concepts condense the gospel narrative into a single episodic snapshot, which thereby amounts to the personal name by which we pick out what we mean by 'God'. In short, all 'the complexities about "three persons and one substance" are simply elaborate attempts to resist the temptation to fall back from this vision . . . [in which] the trinitarian formulas say, "These three are all there is to God"'.[36]

Now, this is a simple enough claim on the face of it, although the consequences are drastic. Jenson knows the technical concepts are usually thought to denote the immanent life of God, i.e. the distinct modes of origination of the Son and Spirit from the Father as one God. But because he is arguing that they are nothing more than the compression of the historical plot, trinitarian concepts like *begetting* and *spirating* end up denoting the eventful happenings in time, which are thereby nothing other than the trinitarian Persons in the dramatic mutuality of God walking in our midst.[37] Jenson therefore refuses to reify the concepts – i.e. turn them into static states, abstracted from time – but instead allows them to remain *storified*, as it were, with the meaning of each being no more than a conceptual abstraction from the ongoing event that is the tellable life of this peculiar God with us.

Of course, this discussion has quickly encroached into complex matters, and so we should slow down to prevent us racing too far ahead. The point to take on board is that Jenson thinks the contingent concepts are recruited from philosophy – which is itself little more than a local religion – then positively worked into a specific shape, and thereby used as a conceptual snapshot of what remains most basically the trajectory of a narratable plot. The doctrine that emerges thereby works as a proper name by which we tag the identity of its subject to a specific nexus of mutual relations, which amounts to little more than a condensed summary of the story the church tells about what happens with Jesus.[38] That is to say, trinitarian doctrine is Christian shorthand, providing its users with a quick way of clarifying what we mean by 'God' by binding the concept to what happens between these Three in the narratable drama of Mary's boy and Pilate's victim, in the Spirit of the one he named Father. What is most startling, however, is how this means concepts like 'births' and 'begets' coincide, and do so precisely. Jesus of Nazareth *is* one of the Trinity, without deviation.

Jenson accepts that this will sound odd on first hearing. He knows the dominant metaphysics has encouraged theologians to seek a compromise with the Greeks, with all of us tempted to render the gospel narrative somehow secondary to the established metaphysics because of the scandalous reality of an enfleshed man being constitutive of the life of God.[39] Jenson thinks theologians will tend to venture along various dead-ends, with the desire for compromise leading to Gnostic, Docetic, Adoptionist, Modalist, Arian and Nestorian heresies, each of which should be understood as little more than a failure to identify God *by* and *with* the story we recount.[40] But to understand why Jenson reaches this conclusion, we first need to get to grips with the substance metaphysics that the doctrine of the Trinity overcomes. Though this will involve us making something of a detour, we must do the initial groundwork if we are to understand why Jenson considers his own proposal to be more faithful to what the church officially teaches from the start. I will therefore sketch the basics of the substance metaphysics and thereby show why Jenson thinks it is nothing other than a rival religion from which we need to be converted if we are to identify the God of the gospel faithfully.

4.2 The substance metaphysics

Our summary of the substance metaphysics can begin with a simple enough question: *what are these 'things' we encounter?*[41] To see how the Greeks answered this question, we will work with one of Jenson's examples. As is often the case, Jenson only mentions it in passing, intending to press on to make his constructive counterpoint. But if we labour over the illustration at length, the central issue will come into focus, thereby enabling us to see why Jenson thinks trinitarian theology took the form that it did under the interrogation it suffered.

So, to Jenson's example.[42] Imagine a provincial town at the foot of a large mountain. One day – and the temporal clause will be an important feature in Jenson's analysis – a large boulder is dislodged from the cliff face and tumbles down the side of the mountain. Then – and again note the temporal implication of that word – a local sculptor uses the boulder to carve out a statue of the governing ruler, which is afterwards displayed on a plinth in the town square. A number of years pass before the people rise up against their ruler, and through the course of the revolutionary melee – in which the ruler is overthrown – the statue is toppled and smashed into hundreds of pieces. Once the social dust has settled, the 'Revolutionary Council of the People' takes power and reshapes society to improve local life, with the debris and rubble being collected and crushed into aggregate, which is then used to construct a pathway through the centre of a new civic park. With this being so, it appears the same 'thing' has existed in six successive states: mountain, boulder, statue, debris, aggregate and finally a path.

Jenson thinks the Greek philosophers knew that this sequence of events is in some sense *accidental*; or, in Jenson's terms, things 'could have been otherwise'.[43] The sculptor might have chosen a different material, for instance, carving the statue out of wood. In short, certain things happened to something, but none of these events appear essential to it being what it had always-already been. As a result, the philosophers wanted to identify whatever it is that the accidental changes happen to, seeking to work out what unites the successive states of a 'thing' to ensure there is something continuous through the course of the changes. And the Greeks had their answer. They decided something must *stand beneath* the accidents, and therein constitute whatever the various things most basically are in whatever form they currently take.

Given this conclusion, the philosophers invented the concept of *substance* to underwrite continuity through change, speculating that the *substance* 'stands under' the accidents, as the twofold stem of the English word suggests.[44] To return to Jenson's example: the philosophers thought 'rockiness', so to speak, must 'stand under' the accidental series running from mountain through to pathway, with 'rockiness' therein posited as the most basic reality at each episodic point, thereby amounting to the unformed nature of each form of the thing.

In other words, *substance*, as Jenson puts it, 'simply meant "what holds something up"',[45] although we may have noticed the word 'substance' is derived from the Latin *substantia*, rather than being rooted in the Greek language the philosophers were working with. Jenson spots how the relation between these two languages will become important once the church begins to respond to questions about the substance of God, with the resulting debate being marked by the conflicting use of linguistic synonyms and the common use of on-the-face-of-it differing terms.[46] For now, however, the twofold stem of *sub-stance* demonstrates Jenson's point nicely: whatever 'stands beneath' the appearances is the substantial nature of what accidentally is.

But Jenson knows the Greeks couldn't stop there. 'Rockiness', for example, can itself be defined, because rockiness has certain characteristics in relation to other substances, differing from 'tomato-ness', for instance, in not being edible, and from 'wood-ness' in not being burnable. As a result, Jenson thinks a process of compare and contrast could take place, which enabled the philosophers to delineate the specific nature of something like *rockiness* by relating it to other substances. In many respects this is what we still do, in that one of the ways to define anything is to locate it within a wider category and then identify its distinguishing features. For example, a chair can be defined as a piece of furniture (the wider category) that you sit on (its distinguishing feature), and the philosophers could therefore use this sort of approach to map the reality they encountered, thus creating various sets, classes and families of substances by which they could define what makes each thing to be the thing that it is. This approach therefore provided them with an interrelated topography of various substantial natures.

By the time the church was announcing that one man has been raised from the dead, the Greek philosophers had done a lot of work on their substance metaphysics, refining a cluster of concepts to make sense of the reality they inhabit. These various concepts constituted the tools of the philosophical trade, which the church's theologians were handed as they were invited to explain what sort of being the 'God' they were speaking about possesses. As a result, it is worth us dragging the technical concepts into the open, before we look at the way Jenson thinks the church refashioned them. I will take the concepts in no particular order, therein recognizing a significant degree of overlap exists as the concepts work in tandem to identify what is the most basic feature of reality. Of course, the evident overlap between the concepts can cause confusion, and it often makes it difficult to grasp the subtle distinctions between them. However, the overlapping nature of the concepts is a symptom of the problem Jenson identifies: the philosophers were papering over their fundamental belief that everything is most basically *one*. Or so Jenson will argue, as we will see.

First up, *Ousia*.[47] Jenson thinks the ancient philosophers used this term to denote what makes something whatever it really is, its 'essence, substance, being, genus, or nature',[48] and, as this suggests, various terms were in circulation at the time the church arrived on the scene.[49] For example, what makes a unicorn a 'unicorn' is that it has the characteristic of possessing a horn and four legs, and so on. But note: the *ousia* possesses these characteristics even if it does not actually exist in the world, as is the case with unicorns.[50] The concept of *ousia* – and its synonyms – is therefore more of an intellectual abstraction, existing only in the mind rather than in concrete actuality, though we should note that mental existence is not a deficiency for the Greeks, but more of a perfection. Mind over matter, and all that.

Second, the concept *Physis*. Jenson knows this concept is closely related to *ousia*, again doing the philosophical work of indicating whatever most basically makes a thing to be the thing that it is. But in using the concept of *physis* the philosophers take 'one step further' towards the concrete.[51] To continue with the example, the concept *physis* could be used to pick out what makes the particular unicorn in a fable – for example, the one the young prince owns – to be a unicorn. In this case, we are still not dealing with a concrete existent, but we are edging towards it by having a specific referent, even if the subject of the predicate remains something of an abstraction. Otherwise put, we are talking about what is most basic to a particular instance of what remains a rarefied abstraction.

Next up, *Hypostasis*. Here we cross something of a Rubicon, because the philosophers use this concept to denote 'the concrete reality of the thing'.[52] Jenson thinks the concept thereby enabled them to denote *this* actual existent of the *ousia*, rather than *that* actual existent of it; in other words, *hypostasis* picks out 'the underlying essence' of an actual thing.[53] So if we stick with our current illustration we would have to admit there is no *hypostasis* of a unicorn, because unicorns enjoy no concrete existence outside the mind.[54] However – and here is another aside – it is worth pointing out the etymology at this early stage, because *hypostasis* begins its life as a synonym for substance, i.e. it picks out what really *is* behind the appearance, with the two stems of the Greek word again directly translating as 'standing under'.[55] As we will see, Jenson thinks the meaning of this concept will change when it is drawn into the service of the gospel, because once it is evangelized the 'hypostasis' is no longer thought to stand beneath the particulars to unite them in general, but instead indicates the most basic particularity of the Three most basics that together enact the mutual communion that makes God what it is to be God. In other words, there is nothing *standing under* the Three *hypostases* that is somehow more basic than them by being held in common by them. Instead, reality bottoms out with particular persons in relation. But more on this shortly.

Finally, we come to *Prosopon*.[56] For the ancient philosophers, the *prosopon* is the observable character of a *hypostasis*, amounting to the defining properties of the existential manifestation of the substantial reality as it confronts us in the world.[57] In other words, the *prosopon* is the outward-facing phenomena of a specific *hypostasis* in relation to others in its accidental form. Again, we will soon see how Jenson thinks the concept gets a trinitarian twist, in that *prosopon* is allowed to inform the definition of *hypostasis* to give meaning to the theological concept that we now translate as 'person', thereby denoting an eccentric reality that is the outward relation between Three most basics, who are no more than the nexus of their towards-the-other relations by which the singular substance of God is constituted as Three *personae*. But again, the details of this must wait. The point here is that Jenson thinks the Greeks were using these various technical concepts to construct a sophisticated account of the most basic building blocks of our existence, thereby offering a rich conceptual account of *substance*. As a result, by wielding the concepts with skill, any philosopher could define what something like 'rockiness' and 'tomato-ness' and 'woodenness' *is* despite the accidental contingencies of their historical forms.

However, the Greeks couldn't stop there.[58] Jenson knows their search had to continue, because we are still talking about the nature of specific 'things'. As a result, the philosophers began to speculate what it is these various 'things' hold in common; which is to ask, what do rocks doing their 'rocking' and tomatoes doing their 'tomatoing' share to be doing what they do in relation to one another? Otherwise put, what is the substance of these substances?

According to Jenson, the Greek answer was straightforward. They concluded the substantial natures simply *are*.[59] That is to say, the substances 'possess *being*'.[60] However, Jenson thinks this innocuous-looking answer created a genuine problem for the church. We will see why this is so if we first recall a substance *stood under* the accidents, thereby denoting what persists through the changes to establish the unity of the thing in question. The substance of the thing could then be defined by setting it in relation to other substances, enabling its own qualities to be identified by its difference-in-relation via a method of compare and contrast. But the philosophical investigation has now dug beyond this, but with the same intent. The Greeks are trying to decipher what persists underneath the differentiated substances to make them one, and so Jenson spots how the philosophical drive is always towards the universal, meaning that the resulting concept of *Being* had to become – under this generalizing pressure – essentially generic, with *Being* thereby ending up as unspecifiable in essence. Or, as Hegel neatly put it, *Being* is the 'indeterminate immediate'.[61]

In other words, the search for generality had created a loss in content, and with disastrous results in Jenson's view.[62] For the philosophers, *Being* just had to be simple in the sense described, because if it isn't then *Being* wouldn't be *most basic* and so the philosophical search would need to continue to pursue the bottoming-out of reality – we would be looking for the substance of *Being*. As a result, *Being* must be necessarily singular, and therein amount to the precise point at which the process of identification runs its course, if only because there can be nothing alongside it with which to compare and contrast it if it is truly the universal feature of every nature in every form.[63] Jenson thereby spots that the reality of *Being* could only be considered negatively, in that the philosophers could only set it in negative relation to what – to some extent – lacks the plenitude that *Being* is thought to possess.[64] It was therefore stripped of any positive attributes and rendered in its sheer ineffability as the reality that changes not, moves not, feels not, suffers not and, as such, possesses no defining features other than its own necessity. In short, *Being* is the pure persistence of an undifferentiated One. It is simply and purely *sheer*.[65]

Jenson spots how this account of *Being* had to work itself out in practice.[66] Because *Being* is sheer simplicity, it must lack any positive specification, and that means the specifiable substances we encounter in the world – in whatever form they currently take – must somehow be deficient in *Being* precisely to the extent we are able to specify them, thereby meaning that identifiable things can only be participating in *Being* to a greater or lesser extent.[67] To put the point otherwise, Jenson sees that the specific substances must somehow be dilutions in *Being*, because they themselves possess attributes by which they can be identified in distinction from other substances.[68] What happens is that this conclusion allows the philosophers to map a hierarchy of substances, by which some things are deemed to be more real than others, but only to the extent to which they measure up to the simplicity of the indistinguishable *One*.[69]

Proceeding in this manner, the philosophers began to imagine that mental ideas, for example, are more robust than the material body, because our ideas can be shown to possess something necessary about them in their simplicity – in mathematical axioms for example – whereas our bodies cannot. What Jenson spots is that the measure by which things are evaluated is therefore the extent to which they perdure as what they necessarily are. Or to put that otherwise, the substance metaphysics cannot celebrate difference, because individual pick-out-ability is nothing less than an ontological deficit, and that has further ramifications, none of them good.

Because everything that can be specified is in some sense an unravelling of *Being*, our existence ends up amounting to little more than the fading away into *non*-being. The Greeks have effectively prioritized persistence over change, with the result – as Jenson emphasizes – that *time* is understood to be inherently problematic because the heartbeat of temporality is change.[70] That is to say, with the present falling away into the past as the future crashes in for a fleeting moment, the Greeks could only define time as the fading away of *Being*, which can of course happen at greater or lesser pace, with what is superior being prior to the current form anything takes. Otherwise put, the beginning must somehow be more real, with the end amounting to our oblivion as time sweeps us away from the perfection of simple *Being*, with history thereby becoming the story of deficiency, rather than being a positive project with its true meaning to be found as its end.[71] Put at its sharpest, 'As Greek myth dramatised it, *Chronos* eats his children'.[72]

Now these outworkings need detain us no longer, because Jenson simply wants us to see what kind of discourse this is.[73] The concept of *Being* is functioning as the 'eternity' by which the philosophers make sense of the contingencies of time. Of course, *Being* cannot strictly be described as their 'God', because this is an eternity that cannot be addressed, but Jenson sees how it defines the nature of time, albeit negatively. That is to say, because *Being* – in the substantialist account – is utterly static, it must be situated at a distance from the movement of time, making it only conceivable as the sheer point at the start of a line or the motionless centre of a turning circle.[74]

To look at the same point from a different angle, Jenson sees how the Greek account of substance is really a search for what is truly present in the fleeting moment, with the accidental form that we encounter amounting to no more than the temporal aftershadow – warped by its distance from its source – of something more substantial than the appearances that confront us as time slides away. Jenson thinks this means each of us must be somehow torn apart in the temporal slipstream of *Being*, with our spiritual nature acting like a handbrake and our accidental embodiment like an accelerator, and thereby our body being ruptured from our soul as we attempt to cling to what is really real as *presence*.[75] As a result, the contingencies of our temporal life are nothing less than our mortality, whereas our resolute grip on the timeless substance is our eternity, which is precisely why Jenson thinks the substance metaphysics becomes a religious quest to escape time. Strange religious practices duly follow.[76]

As Jenson sees it, we must keep hold of *Being*, and we will do so by curving inwards towards a residual spark – a fading memory, some dim Platonic recollection – of that undetermined necessity by which we can curve upwards, so to speak, climbing the 'great chain of being' towards something buried beneath us as the substance beyond the historical lives we live.[77] In short, we must melt into the timeless eternal, and we would be best to close our eyes as we do so, because interior contemplation is all we can do, because there is nothing out there, extrinsic to us, of any value other than fellow shadows in a cave that is essentially crumbling. In other words, *living* is a problem for the Greeks, and so its dynamics can play no part in the religious solution.[78]

Of course, Jenson's analysis of Greek philosophy is not good news. It offers us an 'eternity' that is hardly worth praising or bothering with petitionary prayer, because *Being* is not pick-out-able in itself and so 'mystery' becomes the vogue. As Jenson puts it:

> Their God is God – 'truly', 'really' God – precisely by the absence of such concern . . . It would be blasphemy to depict this deity negotiating with Abraham or dining with Israel's elders on the mountain of his self-revelation. And as for Moses seeing the God of Sinai from behind, a greater offence to the Greek dream of deity can hardly be imagined.[79]

And that is precisely the issue for Jenson. The substance metaphysics not only opposes dynamic finitude – i.e. time, space, embodied contingencies and narratable histories, and of course the coming and going from womb to a tomb – but also erases the personal character of the God we worship. Hence, the problem is crystal clear: 'the metaphysics that construes being as perdurance, and contingency as an ontological deficit, is antithetical to the gospel'.[80] Jenson therefore concludes that 'This theology is bluntly unchristian. For it dissolves the specific God of Israel, the Father of our Lord Jesus Christ, into a soup of our own miscellaneous "loves".'[81]

Which brings us back to the mission of the church. Because the substance ontology lies behind the innocuous-looking question, 'what sort of entity is Jesus',[82] Jenson sees how the church had to think carefully about its response, ensuring the metaphysical presuppositions on which the question rests are not determinative of the answer it provides.[83] The good news, however, is that the church did find an appropriate way to respond. Being handed the concepts of *ousia*, *physis*, *hypostasis* and *prosopon*, Christian theologians began to articulate what sort of 'God' our God must be if he is identified with whatever happened to Jesus. In other words, the philosophical concepts were worked into shape 'by collision with Yahweh',[84] thereby enabling us to talk about God's *Being*, not by evacuating the structure of the specific story we tell, but by 'riding its waves' and thereby celebrating the good news that the ultimate *Being* is 'roomy', 'timely' and utterly committed towards his unending movement towards us.[85] In short, the, 'direct fruit of the gospel's struggle with Hellenic worship and theology is the doctrine of the Trinity, which affirms about God nearly everything that Plato was concerned to deny of God, but does so in a language continuous with that of Hellenic reflection and at Hellenic reflection's level of sophistication.'[86] Our next task is to see how Jenson thinks this struggle played out in practice.

4.3 Evangelizing the substance metaphysics

Confronted by the Greeks, the church needed to work out, 'what is the timelessly self-identical Something that *is* all these three?'[87] Jenson thinks we couldn't duck this question, and once asked 'it has refused to go away'.[88] In effect, the church had to find a way to make credible sense of the gospel within the culture it encountered, and so began to draw on its finest minds to explain to the Greeks – in the Greeks' own terms – who God 'interpreted by what happens with Jesus' actually *is*.[89] As a result, the doctrine 'is a task: that of the church's continuing effort to recognize and adhere to the biblical God's hypostatic being'.[90]

According to Jenson, what the church arrived at is something like as follows. Broadly speaking, the 'new terminological regulation [used] two words for "what is real"'.[91] First, there is only one God to be identified, because there is one story to be told, and so the church could say this God must possess a single 'substance'.[92] However, the church quickly recognized that the nature of God is much richer than the bland singularity the Greek philosophers identified as *Being*.[93] The nature of the Christian God can never be abstracted from the reality of what happens *between* these Three identifiable agents in the drama the church recounts, meaning the conceptual metaphor of 'standing under' needed to be reimagined as more like a harmony that is lived.[94] To that end, Jenson thinks the concept of 'person' was commandeered from the existing discourse to specify the threefold distinction in the story of the one God, but it was employed in such a way that the Three specifiable identities are most basic to what God actually *is*. That is to say, the threefold identity of God cannot be surpassed in order to arrive at a substantial singularity, because the concept of *hypostasis* is now being used to distinguish the Three as what is most basic despite their evident differences.[95]

The church's theologians therefore began to use a cluster of definitions to rework the concept of *hypostasis* into the required shape, and to do this they ran two related ideas in tandem, allowing the Greek concept of *prosopon* and the Latin concept of *persona* to be determinative of the technical meaning of *hypostasis*.[96] The early theologians knew *prosopon* had originally denoted the mask that an ancient actor would wear on stage, with the word literally meaning 'a seeing through'. This dramatic definition helps indicate the way each trinitarian *hypostasis* is inherently relational, in that 'seeing through' suggests an extrinsic manifestation of the Three, one towards the others.[97] This point could be further emphasized by using the Latin concept of *persona* to inform the concept of *hypostasis*.[98] The Latin term literally meant a 'hearing through', and had been used to pick out the various roles, associations, contracts and organizational allegiances that defined each Roman citizen. By running the Latin definition alongside *prosopon*, the church found a way to say 'God' is most basically Three 'sounding forths' or 'seeing throughs', whose single identity is the ecstatic relation of the social roles they *are* in facing one another in the drama of their singular life with us.[99] Or, to put that in the simplest of terms, 'What happens between Jesus and his Father and our future *happens in God* – that is the point.'[100]

Of course, this was a very strange way of describing the singular nature of God. But Jenson doesn't want us to retreat behind the smokescreen of 'mystery' at this point, or certainly no greater mystery than applies to any person.[101] Jenson knows there is a qualitative distinction to be made between our personhood and that of God, in that, for example, our nature precedes our personhood, meaning human nature and particular personhood do not coincide. Human nature existed long before I was around, for instance, and will likely continue long after I die, and so, who I am as a hypostatic manifestation of our common nature – my *Lincoln-ness*, so to speak – is conceivable apart from the nature we share, which is why we can conceive of individuals.[102] Or to put that point a different way, my existence and my essence are finally distinct, in that you can know everything about my nature but still not know whether I actually exist.[103] But 'not so with God',[104] as Jenson sees.[105] God's existence must *be* his essence, in that if someone knows what makes God to be God they will also know *that* God exists, which – to reverse the logic – is why Jenson thinks we mustn't conceive of an individual in God because the 'one' and the 'many' coincide, with his eternal nature not preceding the eternal persons in their mutuality.[106] Or to put the point yet another way, the Three mutually constitute the nature, so that the nature doesn't make a fourth thing which can be known in abstraction from the Three. However, the point is the same whichever way we run at it: the distinctions between the Three persons are most basic to what makes God to be God through their differences.

Jenson thinks this point is of utmost importance. It shows, for example, how our modern concept of the 'self' is fundamentally misleading, because we will often posit some kind of entity in abstraction from our mutuality – one which we hold back from each other – and think this residue is somehow the real me. That is to say, I am whatever it is that is in no way public. But God has no such residue, because God is instead the pure ecstasy of an eternal moving outward – albeit inward! – of doing himself from Father, Son and Spirit. Or to put that in Jenson's own words:

The 'I' that persists behind and aloof from my acts is precisely what I hold back from my fellows... This 'I' represents what I lack of myself. God has no such lack. He is what he does for the other. God is the occurrence of relation.[107]

That is to say, to believe

> that the private layers of the human onion are somehow more 'the real person' than the public layers, or that the roles in which we face each other are somehow mere 'masks' to be stripped off, is a wholly unjustified and intrinsically implausible prejudice... It is exactly the role I play in your life, and the role you play in mine, roles made possible by inherited social structures, which are the reality of our being-for each other and so of your personal reality and of mine.[108]

In other words, just as with God, so with us: 'it's the relationship that's the metaphysically heavy fact rather than the poles of the relationship'.[109]

Now, we can already see Jenson is arguing that the term *hypostasis* is intrinsically relational. It had originally been used by the Greeks to signify the 'point of departure' in an expedition, and this original meaning indicates the way Jenson thinks the Three *hypostases* in God are defined by their dynamic relations of origin, although he will supplement this as we will discover.[110] What this definition means, however, is that the theological concepts of *begetting* and *spirating*, for example, are used to denote the dynamic origination of the Son and the Spirit from the Unoriginate Father, with their *from-ing* – so to speak! – denoting the dynamic movement that is God's liveliness.[111] The concept of *person*, therefore, as the most basic reality, should be understood as the dynamic movement that subsists as its own term in relation to the others, which is another way of saying that there is no 'pudding'[112] type blob on the end of the relations that is the 'person', but rather the person is the identifiable relation in its dynamic origination.[113] Or as Jenson puts it, 'Each person of the triune God simply *is* the third to the other two, established in its identity by its relation to them.'[114] Or, perhaps more clearly: 'a trinitarian identity is a "relation... in the mode of substance"'.[115]

As Chris Green spots, Jenson is claiming that the church had found a way to stress the freedom of God, in that 'For God, who, what, why, and how are all identical'.[116] Tee Gatewood has also captured the point nicely, arguing that the persons 'are not identically divine but each give and receive being from one another to be equally, fully, and absolutely divine', so that each 'has the divine nature in relation'.[117] Of course, Jenson knows this way of describing things is drastically countercultural, not least because the Greek philosophers had made the concept of *hypostasis* flip from the general to the particular at a certain point in their discussions. 'Humanness', for example, was thought *to distinguish* humans from whatever else we might imagine – such as rockiness or tomato-ness – and thereby unify particular instances in a single class, but then, within humanity, *hypostasis* was used to distinguish the particular *from* the class, which for the Greeks – as we have seen – makes it the point where *hypostasis* becomes an imperfection. As they understood it, what is really real is the nature by which we participate in *Being*, and so in the same way as substances are deficient in relation, the particular *hypostasis* is distinguished from the others only to the extent by which it falls short of the common ideal.[118] As a result, by using *hypostasis* for each of the Three identities of God's life, Jenson thinks the church is claiming that there is nothing more basic than personhood in communion, meaning the particular is the most basic 'standing under', which is the perfection of communion. And that is to say particularity is no deficiency but is instead the dynamic 'point of departure' within a journey that is God, and that is its perfection.[119]

This insight goes some way to explain why Jenson makes much of an image from Gregory Nazianzus.[120] Gregory had argued that the 'godhead' is an activity that these three most basic *hypostases* do in mutual relation. That is to say, the Godhead is an active 'beholding', and so we should not think of a singular 'thing' when we conceive of it, but instead imagine something more akin to three suns emitting a ray of such mutual intensity that they amount to one ray for us; 'the *beam* is God'.[121] Whatever the limits of Nazianzus' image, Jenson thinks it helps because it shifts our thinking from 'standing beneath' to something more ecstatic, a transcendent movement out from oneself, thereby allowing us to see that God is the movement of one to another, a to-ing and fro-ing that is the dynamic mutuality of these Three doing what makes God to be God. In effect, when asked what God is, Jenson thinks we can only speak of Three persons *godding*, i.e. a verb. In effect, the substance must be conceived as a predicate, because God is *done* as an act by these Three, and personhood is therefore 'not an aspect of God's being but is rather correlated to the three *who live* deity . . . it is divine personhood, not divine being, that is metaphysically primary'.[122]

Now this is highly complex stuff. But we can hopefully see what has happened here. Jenson's reading of doctrine leads him to think the missionary church created a new metaphysics in conversation with the Greek philosophers. The substance metaphysics is effectively redefined as the doctrine of God is constructed out of the reworked concepts, with the church now positing two most basics in simultaneous harmonic actuality as what is most fundamental to our existence, i.e. persons *doing* nature as the mutual coincidence that is their being. Jenson thinks this account of God's triune nature thereby allowed the church to handle the differences, so to speak, in the drama of God, without worrying about everything collapsing into one by moving beyond it. As a result, Jenson judges all of this to be a remarkable achievement, amounting to 'the Christianizing of Hellenism',[123] in that 'the doctrine affirms about God nearly everything that the Greeks denied'.[124]

With that accepted, Jenson is at pains to remind us that this is no more than a conceptual snapshot of a story. The concepts have been reconfigured in service to the gospel narrative, now offering no more than a static image of the temporal plot line that is finally only narratable because it is about a Subject who is irresistibly alive and not a stationary target.[125] In effect, these Three *hypostases* are identifying markers of the Beginning and End of the God who is present in narratable form.[126] Jenson is therefore arguing that the doctrine of the Trinity is meant to function as a condensed summary of a story that thereby amounts to a proper name.[127] The doctrine is the means by which we can pick out this one eternity amid all the other claimants to that title, in effect amounting to a 'maximally compressed' telling of the narrative about these three pick-out-ables who mutually constitute the single pick-out-able that is God.[128] Thus, what we mean by 'God' is nothing other than the infinity of the narratable occurrence of these Three identities beyond which you cannot venture. In short, 'The one God is the *life* lived between the Father and the Son and the Spirit',[129] meaning that trinitarian theology does the work of identification – i.e. naming with situational descriptors – by riding 'the story's waves'.[130]

In other words, Jenson is arguing something quite radical. He thinks that by tracing what happens with Jesus, we get 'the triune proper name of Christianity's particular God',[131] in that

> the 'trinitarian relations' by which in classic trinitarian doctrine the identities of the three are constituted – that the Father begets the Son and the Son is begotten, that the Father breathes the Spirit and the Spirit is breathed – are slogans for plot lines of this story. If we ask what may be the being of this God, as one God, we can therefore only answer that he is the life, the history, that occurs between these *personae* and that has this plot. He is not a something or even a someone who has a history; no one has this history except the three. This God simply *is* the life lived between Jesus and the one he called Father, in the Spirit who liberates them for each other.[132]

All of this means the doctrine of the Trinity is focused entirely on the incarnate Jesus, in that 'Christians do not have "a God", about whose ideas Jesus then perhaps contributes some information. They have the particular God of whom the man Jesus is one identity, and who therefore is triune in the first rather than the second place.'[133] This means in turn that '"God is good" is a Christian sentence only insofar as it is used precisely equivalently for "Jesus of Nazareth will triumph".'[134] But this means Jenson has drawn narrative – and the time needed to tell it – into the doctrine of God. And that is where he breaks from the pack.

Because Jenson has prioritized narrative, the temporal structure of events is intrinsic to what makes God to be God. This is why he is keen to supplement the classical debates, seeking to move beyond an account of origination to incorporate the structure of a beginning, middle and end. As a result, he accepts that the Father can only be considered as the can't-get-behind-able Beginning, from whom the Son and the Spirit proceed. But he dares to imagine that the Spirit is the can't-get-beyond-able End, who is the identity within God's life by which the Father is freed to be alive in relation to this Son, who is nothing other than what happens in our midst. In effect, the eternity that brackets time is in no sense timeless but is instead the full possession of time in which God is his own First and his own Last so that he can be this Son who is definitively present as our history. In short, God is a *life*. As a result, the next task is to explore why Jenson thinks we must keep on 'remind[ing] ourselves what all these word games are about': the life of Jesus of Nazareth and his Father with the Spirit.[135] To put it bluntly, it is all about Jesus.

Notes

1 Robert W. Jenson, *The Triune Identity: God According to the Gospel* (Philadelphia: Fortress, 1982; reprint, Eugene, OR: Wipf and Stock, 2002), ix.

2 Pretty much all of Jenson's works will touch upon this subject at some stage, but the primary sources are Robert W. Jenson, *Systematic Theology, Volume 1, The Triune God* (New York: OUP, 1997) and Jenson, *Triune Identity*.

3 Jenson, *Triune Identity*, x.

4 Jenson, *Systematic Theology*, Vol. 1, 60.

5 For example, Jenson often highlights the Second Council of Constantinople in 533, where he thinks his approach to Christology is dogmatized. See Jenson, *Systematic Theology*, Vol. 1, 133.

6 Jenson, *Systematic Theology*, Vol. 1, 139.

7 Robert W. Jenson, 'The Futurist Option in Speaking of God', *The Lutheran Quarterly* 21.1 (1969), 25.

8 Jenson, *Triune Identity*, 130.

9 For an example of Jenson's use of the image of the sawn branch, see Robert W. Jenson, 'The Triune God', in *Christian Dogmatics*, .ed. Carl E. Braaten and Robert W. Jenson (Philadelphia: Fortress, 1984), 102.

10 Robert W. Jenson, 'Lutheranism and the *Filioque*', in *Ecumenical Perspectives on the Filioque for the 21st Century*, ed. Myk Habets (London: T&T Clark, 2014), 164. As he puts it elsewhere, 'Homer and Plato write the first chapter in the locus on God.' Jenson, *Triune Identity*, 117.

11 Robert W. Jenson, 'For us . . . He Was Made Man', in *Nicene Christianity: The Future for a New Ecumenism*, ed. Christopher R. Seitz (Grand Rapids: Brazos, 2001), 84.

12 Robert W. Jenson, *A Large Catechism* (Delhi, NY: American Lutheran Publicity Bureau, 1991), 28.

13 Robert W. Jenson, *Unbaptized God: The Basic Flaw in Ecumenical Theology* (Minneapolis: Fortress, 1992), 119. Jenson's thinking on religion is set out in Robert W. Jenson, *A Religion Against Itself* (John Knox Press, 1967; reprint, Wipf and Stock, 1967).

14 As an aside, Jenson therefore thinks it is a mistake to say, for example, that 'old Israel had no talent for metaphysics'. The issue is always *which* metaphysics. Robert W. Jenson, *Systematic Theology, Volume 2, The Works of God* (New York: OUP, 1999), 157–8.

15 For example, Jenson makes the point that Aquinas 'regularly made "the philosopher" say the exact contrary of anything the historical Aristotle could have dreamed'. See Robert W. Jenson, 'Choose Ye This Day Whom Ye Will Serve . . .', in *Essays on the Trinity*, ed. Lincoln Harvey (Eugene, OR: Cascade, 2018), 16.

16 Robert W. Jenson, 'Jesus, Father, Spirit: The Logic of the Doctrine of the Trinity', *Dialog* 26.4 (1987), 245.

17 As he says, 'we may hardly so glory in hindsight as to suppose we should have done better [than the early apologists]'. Jenson, *Systematic Theology*, Vol. 1, 95.

18 Jenson, *Triune Identity*, 62.

19 Jenson thinks the Spirit is 'the whirlwind of [God's] *liveliness* that agitates whatever he turns towards'. Jenson, *Systematic Theology*, Vol. 1, 86.

20 Jenson argues that 'recent clamor for "contextual" theology is of course empty, there never having been any other kind.' Jenson, *Systematic Theology*, Vol. 1, ix.

21 As Jenson puts it, 'Christianity is a missionary faith: those who believe that Jesus is indeed risen are sent across history and geography to tell this gospel-news to the world'. Jenson, *Large Catechism*, 49.

22 Jenson, *Systematic Theology*, Vol. 1, 90.

23 For an example of Jenson working out the doctrine of the Trinity in a different context, see Robert W. Jenson, 'The Risen Prophet', in *God and Jesus: Theological Reflections for Christian-Muslim Dialog*, American Lutheran Church Division for World Mission and Interchurch Cooperation (Minneapolis: American Lutheran Church, 1986), 57–67.

24 That is because, 'the clash will always be at the same point: religion's normal reluctance to take time seriously for God'. Jenson, 'The Triune God', 115.

25 On this point, Steve Wright has helpfully drawn my attention to John Flett's critique of Jenson, in which Jenson's use of contingency is charged with bankrolling the priority of Western culture. Flett argues that Jenson's account of contingent historical development creates a *single* dominant narrative of the church, into which all of us must be enculturated, rather than celebrating pluralized *local* accounts. In effect, contingency leads to normativity, i.e. the prioritization of one local over others. This critique leads him to conclude that Jenson's missionary logic is effectively colonial in its method. See John G. Flett, *Apostolicity: The Ecumenical Question in World Christian Perspective* (Downers Grove: InterVarsity Press, 2016), 103–38. David W. Congdon similarly charges Jenson with 'the wholesale adoption of Israel's centripetal mission, the result of which is a rejection of crosscultural translation and

contextualization'. David W. Congdon, *The God Who Saves: A Dogmatic Sketch* (Eugene, OR: Cascade, 2016), 175–6.

26 Jenson, *Systematic Theology*, Vol. 1, 10.

27 Robert W. Jenson, 'Response: The Philosophy that Attends to Scripture', in the Symposium on Kenneth Oakes, *Karl Barth on Theology and Philosophy*.

28 Jenson, *Systematic Theology*, Vol. 1, 9–10.

29 See also the discussion in Jenson, *Systematic Theology*, Vol. 2, 163–4.

30 For example, see Jenson, *Systematic Theology*, Vol. 1, 7–9.

31 Robert W. Jenson, 'How Does Jesus Make a Difference?' in *Essentials of Christian Theology*, ed. William C. Placher (Louisville: WJK Press, 2003), 193.

32 Or to put the point negatively, Jenson thinks Western theology could one day come to an end. Jenson, 'Choose Ye This Day', 19.

33 This way of putting it restates earlier work of mine. See Lincoln Harvey, 'Introduction', in *Essays on the Trinity*, ed. Lincoln Harvey (Eugene, OR: Cascade, 2018), 1. Jenson makes the point in Jenson, 'The Triune God', 93.

34 As Jenson puts it in regard to concepts drawn from secular theory, 'Borrowings . . . may sometimes be convenient but must be done strictly ad hoc and with great circumspection and usually ... with considerable bending of the recruited concepts.' Jenson, *Systematic Theology*, Vol. 2, 172.

35 Jenson, *Systematic Theology*, Vol. 1, 139.

36 Robert W. Jenson, *Essays in Theology of Culture* (Grand Rapids: Eerdmans, 1995), 93.

37 Jenson, *Triune Identity*, 108.

38 See Jenson, *Triune Identity*, 1–18.

39 Jenson thinks this 'bankrupts' the concepts because the language was only ever about the biblical narrative. Jenson, *Systematic Theology*, Vol. 1, 112.

40 Jenson, 'For us . . .', 83–4; Jenson, *Triune Identity*, 64; Jenson, *Systematic Theology*, Vol. 1, 95–6.

41 For a summary of how the Greeks identified something, see Jenson, *Triune Identity*, 109.

42 Jenson, *Triune Identity*, 73.

43 For a summary of Jenson's understanding of why the Greeks identified something under the accidents, see Jenson, *Triune Identity*, 109.

44 For an account of Jenson's understanding of the original meaning of the technical concepts, see Jenson, *Triune Identity*, 104–5.

45 Jenson, *Systematic Theology*, Vol. 2, 39.

46 Jenson, *Triune Identity*, 104. See also the example of linguistic confusion in Boethius's work that Jenson provides, 115.

47 In what follows, I draw heavily from John McGuckin, *Saint Cyril of Alexandria and the Christological Controversy* (Crestwood, NY: St Vladimir's Seminary Press, 2004), 138–45. For an analysis of different ways to understand the concepts, see Michael Schulz, 'The Trinitarian Concept of Essence and Substance', in *Rethinking Trinitarian Theology*, Robert J. Wozniak and Giulio Maspero (London and New York: T&T Clark, 2012), 146–71.

48 McGuckin, *Saint Cyril*, 138.

49 For a summary of Jenson's understanding, see Jenson, *Triune Identity*, 101 n201.

50 This is John McGuckin's example. McGuckin, *Saint Cyril*, 139.

51 McGuckin, *Saint Cyril*, 139.

52 McGuckin, *Saint Cyril*, 138.

53 McGuckin, *Saint Cyril*, 138.
54 McGuckin, *Saint Cyril*, 140.
55 McGuckin, *Saint Cyril*, 141.
56 McGuckin, *Saint Cyril*, 144.
57 Again these words draw directly from McGuckin, *Saint Cyril*, 138.
58 Jenson, *Systematic Theology*, Vol. 1, 207.
59 Hence, the concept of *ousia* 'carried the feel of – to make a barbarism – "an is-er," that which "is-es"'. Jenson, *Triune Identity*, 101 n201.
60 Jenson, *Systematic Theology*, Vol. 1, 208. Emphasis added.
61 Martin Heidegger, *Being and Time*, translated by Joan Stambaugh (Albany, NY: State University of New York, 1996), 2.
62 Jenson, *Systematic Theology*, Vol. 1, 208–9.
63 Jenson, *Systematic Theology*, Vol. 1, 215.
64 Jenson, *Systematic Theology*, Vol. 1, 209.
65 Thanks to Donna Lazenby for this way of putting it.
66 For a statement of the way this works itself out, see Jenson, 'Jesus, Father, Spirit', 246.
67 Jenson, *Systematic Theology*, Vol. 1, 208–9.
68 Jenson, *Triune Identity*, 104, 163–4.
69 Jenson, *Systematic Theology*, Vol. 1, 94.
70 Jenson, *Triune Identity*, 25. Jenson knows Augustine spotted why that is so: change implies a 'was' and 'will be' and so is irresistibly temporal. Jenson, 'The Triune God', 141–2.
71 See Robert W. Jenson, 'Second Thoughts About Theologies of Hope', *Evangelical Quarterly* 72.4 (2000), 335–46.
72 Robert W. Jenson, 'What Kind of God Can Make a Covenant?' in *Covenant and Hope: Christian and Jewish Reflections*, ed. Robert W. Jenson and Eugene B. Korn (Grand Rapids: Eerdmans, 2012), 3.
73 For Jenson's analysis of the Greek concept of Being, see Jenson, *Triune Identity*, 58–61.
74 Jenson, 'What Kind of God'.
75 Jenson, *Systematic Theology*, Vol. 1, 94–5.
76 For an indication of Jenson's understanding of the religious outworking of the substance metaphysics in sharp distinction from Israel's God, see Robert W. Jenson, 'The God of the Gospel', *Baltimore Paper*, 11–13. See also comments in Jenson, *Systematic Theology*, Vol. 1, 47.
77 Jenson takes from Luther the idea that 'incurvature' is the 'formal structure common to all the possibilities of sin'. Jenson, *Systematic Theology*, Vol. 2, 139.
78 Hence, Jenson thinks the Greeks concluded that 'the human person . . . is either somehow devised for eternity or, if a purely temporal being, then one singularly ill-begotten for the situation, a bad ontological joke.' Jenson, *Systematic Theology*, Vol. 2, 56.
79 Jenson, 'What Kind of God', 5. To change the idiom slightly and hammer the point, 'A fiery or cloudy will-o'-the-wisp may have been an impressive standard for Moses' ragtag, but not if you were used to pyramids'. Robert W. Jenson, 'Election and Culture: From Babylon to Jerusalem', in *Public Theology in Cultural Engagement*, ed. Stephen R. Holmes (Milton Keynes: Paternoster, 2008), 52.
80 Robert W. Jenson, 'A Reply', *Scottish Journal of Theology* 52.1 (1999), 132.
81 Robert W. Jenson, *Lutheran Slogans: Use and Abuse* (Delhi, NY: American Lutheran Publicity Bureau, 2011), 8. Jenson is talking about modern American

variants of the mistake, but only because he can draw a straight line between the two.

82 Jenson, 'Jesus, Father, Spirit', 247. See also the list of similar rhetorical questions set out in Jenson, *Systematic Theology*, Vol. 1, 95.

83 Jenson, *Systematic Theology*, Vol. 1, 210–12.

84 Jenson, 'The Triune God', 138. See also, Jenson, *Triune Identity*, 108.

85 Negatively: 'Each of the old gods is one and only one. And the great sea of deity of which they are manifestations is defined as sheer oneness. There is no *room* in them for others. We can stand over and against one or more of the old gods, and be influenced or moved or causally affected by him or her or them. Or we can melt into deity and become whatever is characteristic of deity. But none of the old gods can bless us simply by taking us to himself.' Jenson, 'God of the Gospel', 18.

86 Robert W. Jenson, 'Basics and Christology', in *In Search of Christian Unity: Basic Consensus/Basic Differences*, ed. Joseph A. Burgess (Minneapolis: Fortress Press, 1991), 47.

87 Jenson, *Triune Identity*, 64.

88 Jenson, *Systematic Theology*, Vol. 1, 207. Note: Having attacked the concept of an intermediate Logos, Jenson can add: 'which is not to say anything against "the Greeks" as such or to decry their place in the history of Christian theology'. Colin Gunton and Robert W. Jenson, 'The *Logos Ensarkos* and Reason', in *Reason and the Reasons of Faith*, ed. Paul J. Griffiths and Reinhard Hütter (London: T&T Clark, 2005), 79.

89 As Jenson makes clear, 'The Cappadocians first sorted out the terminology', and Jenson attempts to build on their work throughout his constructive proposal. Jenson, *Systematic Theology*, Vol. 1, 105.

90 Jenson, *Systematic Theology*, Vol. 1, 90.

91 Jenson, *Triune Identity*, 103. In what follows, I have tried to capture Jenson's proposal, but do so while drawing from wider reading. Particular debts: Ángel Cordovilla Pérez, 'The Trinitarian Concept of Person', in *Rethinking Trinitarian Theology*, ed. Robert J. Wozniak and Giulio Maspero (London and New York: T&T Clark, 2012), 105–46, and Schulz, 'Essence and Substance', 146–71. For Jenson's account of the development of doctrine leading up to Nicaea, see Jenson, *Triune Identity*, 61–84.

92 For Jenson's reading of the concept 'homoousion', see Jenson, *Triune Identity*, 85–9.

93 See discussion of the Cappadocians' reworking of *ousia* in Jenson, *Triune Identity*, 111–14 and 162–3.

94 Jenson, *Systematic Theology*, Vol. 2, 39.

95 See discussion of the Cappadocians' reworking of *hypostasis* in Jenson, *Triune Identity*, 105–11.

96 Jenson, *Triune Identity*, 105. On this, see Pérez, 'Trinitarian Concept of Person', 108–13.

97 'Look toward', i.e.; 'What stands before us'. On the etymology, see Pérez, 'Trinitarian Concept of Person', 109–10.

98 Jenson, *Systematic Theology*, Vol. 1, 118–19.

99 Pérez, 'Trinitarian Concept of Person', 112–14.

100 Jenson, *Triune Identity*, 106.

101 As Jenson argues, 'I have lived with my wife for forty-five years, and she becomes more mysterious daily; but there is no problem about how I know her and her mystery. And I have lived with God at least since my baptism sixty-eight years

ago; it is no trope to say I know him, and what I know is the mystery of the hope that he is for himself and for me.' Jenson, 'Second Thoughts', 344.

102 On this, see John Zizioulas, 'The Trinity and Personhood: Appreciating the Cappadocian Contribution', in John Zizioulas, *Communion and Otherness: Further Studies in Personhood and the Church*, ed. Paul McPartlan (London: T&T Clark, 2006), 155–70.

103 Jenson, *Systematic Theology*, Vol. 2, 95–7.

104 Robert W. Jenson, 'Creator and Creature', *International Journal of Systematic Theology* 4 (2002), 219.

105 Jenson gets this from Aquinas. Robert W. Jenson, 'Some Riffs on Thomas Aquinas's *De Ente et Essentia*', in *Theological Theology: Essays in Honour of John Webster*, ed. R. David Nelson, Darren Sarisky and Justin Stratis (London: T&T Clark, 2015), 125–30.

106 On this point, see Zizioulas, 'Trinity and Personhood', 155–70.

107 Robert Jenson, *God After God: The God of the Past and the God of the Future as Seen in the Work of Karl Barth* (New York: Bobs-Merrill, 1969; reprint, Minneapolis: Fortress Press, 2012), 112.

108 Robert W. Jenson, *Story and Promise: A Brief Theology of the Gospel About Jesus* (Philadelphia: Fortress Press, 1973; reprint, Eugene, OR: Wipf & Stock 2014), 71. In another essay, Jenson offers a threefold analysis of our existence, arguing that the 'I' is the given, the 'self' is the persistence of that 'I' through narrative time, and the 'person' is the mysterious unity of the two. Robert W. Jenson, 'Jesus in the Trinity: Wolfhart Pannenberg's Christology and Doctrine of the Trinity', in *The Theology of Wolfhart Pannenberg: Twelve American Critiques, with an autobiographical essay and response*, ed. Carl E. Braaten and Philip Clayton (Minneapolis: Augsburg, 1988), 188–206.

109 Robert W. Jenson, *A Theology in Outline: Can These Bones Live?* transcribed, ed. and introduced by Adam Eitel (Oxford: OUP, 2016), 47.

110 Pérez, 'Trinitarian Concept of Person', 109.

111 Jenson, *Triune Identity*, 121. See also Jenson's discussion of the Cappadocians' reworking of *hypostasis* on 113.

112 In one place, Jenson notes that 'An "advanced" conception of God is very likely to be one of "pure substance," visually pictured as an infinitely extended pudding (to steal someone's devastating remark).' Robert W. Jenson, *Alpha and Omega: A Study in the Theology of Karl Barth* (New York: Thomas Nelson & Sons, 1963; reprint, Eugene, OR: Wipf and Stock, 2002), 74. I will use variations of this phrase, but here note the origin.

113 '[T]here *is*, for example, the Father only because "Father" and "begets" are inseparable'. Jenson, *Triune Identity*, 123.

114 Robert W. Jenson, 'Reversals: How My Mind Has Changed', *The Christian Century* (20 April 2010), 30.

115 Jenson, *Systematic Theology*, Vol. 1, 109.

116 Chris E. W. Green, in personal correspondence.

117 Tee Gatewood, 'A Nicene Christology? Robert Jenson and the Two Natures of Jesus Christ', *Pro Ecclesia* 18 (2009), 32.

118 Jenson, *Triune Identity*, 104.

119 Hypostasis is therefore a '*way* of having being'. Jenson, *Systematic Theology*, Vol. 1, 117.

120 Jenson, *Triune Identity*, 113.

121 Jenson, *Triune Identity*, 113.

122 Jenson, *Systematic Theology*, Vol. 2, 95–6.
123 Jenson, *Triune Identity*, 61.
124 Jenson, *Unbaptized God*, 119.
125 Jenson, *Triune Identity*, 127.
126 Jenson, *Triune Identity*, 113.
127 Jenson, *Triune Identity*, 21.
128 Hence Jenson thinks the name of God, 'is not an arbitrary name, like "Robert" for the author of these pages. A proper name is proper just insofar as it is used independently of aptitude to the one named, but it need not therefore lack such aptitude. "Father, Son, and Holy Spirit" is appropriate for naming the gospel's God because the phrase immediately summarizes the primal Christian interpretation of God.' Jenson, 'The Triune God', 96.
129 Jenson, 'God of the Gospel', 18.
130 Jenson, 'What Kind of God', 11–12.
131 Jenson, *Triune Identity*, x.
132 Jenson, 'Second Thoughts', 343.
133 Jenson, 'Wolfhart Pannenberg's Christology', 206.
134 Jenson, 'The Triune God', 190.
135 Jenson, *Triune Identity*, 106.

5

We Believe in One Lord, Jesus Christ

5.1 Not a standard 'Christology'

Jenson's trinitarian theology remains focused on Jesus of Nazareth at every step. The Nazarene is front and centre of pretty much everything he has to say. Somewhat surprisingly, this doesn't mean we should describe what he is doing as 'Christology', at least not if we are working with the textbook definition of that term. Jenson is no fan of run-of-the-mill Christology. He thinks the entire project is misconceived from the start.

Through the course of this chapter, we will take a close look at why Jenson believes standard Christology is a mistake, as well as begin to explore the alternative he offers. We will again tell a double history, because Jenson has both good and bad things to say about the way theologians have spoken about Jesus. He will diagnose an inherent pathology within the dogmatic tradition, but also discover some remedial support within the same tradition for his attempt to fix the problem.[1] As before, we will track the negative reading first before turning to look at the way his constructive proposal piggybacks on the church's conciliar teaching. By adopting this method, we will see how Jenson commandeers Cyril of Alexandria's central thesis – as he reads it[2] – as a counterpoint to the pseudo-Nestorianism he thinks has plagued Christian theology over the centuries, thereby positing Jesus of Nazareth as both our God and our brother in the singular life that he lives as the interface of creaturely time and God's eternity. As this will show, Christ's two natures need to be understood as dynamic 'communal' realities, by which 'Mary's boy and Pilate's victim' determines what it is to be God and what it is to be human in his lively communion with the relevant *hypostases*. With this definition in play, Jenson can justify his startling conclusion that 'the second person of the Trinity *is* a man – Jesus of Nazareth'.[3]

5.2 Same question, new focus and mainly the wrong answer

The first thing to grasp is relatively simple, albeit highly contentious. Jenson thinks that 'Christology' only develops into a distinct subdiscipline because theologians have attempted to mitigate the oddity of the gospel message.[4] In effect, they fail to hold their nerve and therefore backtrack from the trinitarian breakthrough in an attempt to pacify the 'unbaptized' God of the Greek philosophers.[5] Jenson thinks the results are hypertrophic.

As he reads the tradition, Jenson argues that the majority of theologians create their own labour by positing a conceptual conundrum that they must then try to solve.[6] We imagine there are two metaphysical 'counters', which must be cobbled together to create a conceptual picture of the existential constitution of Jesus of Nazareth.[7] In one hand, we take hold of a puddingy-type substance called the divine nature, and in the other the human nature, with the consequent assignment being to patch together the two.[8] Jenson thinks the two natures are thereby defined in abstraction from the gospel narrative, and so it quickly becomes obvious that they cannot both be predicated of the singular identifiable subject who the church claims is Lord; that is, 'Mary's child, the hanged man of Golgotha'.[9] To put the point otherwise, Jenson thinks our attempt to solve the conundrum is bankrupt from the start.

As Jenson sees it, the 'rearguard defence' of the Greek metaphysics – which has subsequently 'plagued the church' from its earliest days[10] – has produced little more than a series of 'marvellously ingenious and sophisticated, but in [Jenson's] judgment finally impotent, christological systematics',[11] with all the 'traditional christological anathemas occur[ing] within a *common* christological tradition which itself harbors the flaw we should seek and cure'.[12] In short, the way we set things up makes it impossible to understand the relation between a timeless deity and the contingencies of the gospel narrative. As a result, any discussion about Jesus quickly breaks down, with the resulting echo chamber bringing out the worst in us all. We use the blank canvas of a timeless eternity to uphold our favourite ideals, with God – like an 'immaterial mirror'[13] – becoming a conceptual mannequin, dressed up in whatever clothes we fancy, while the temporal Jesus is reduced to little more than 'a beach-boy guru', 'archetypal social worker' or whatever we judge to be best about humanity.[14] In other words, our projections run riot in the definitive space *between* the two natures.

With the singular Jesus dissected in this way, Jenson thinks the biblical exegete gets to work. Bits of the gospel narrative are attributed to whichever nature best fits what is happening, but only on the assumption that we already know which types of action must be done by God and which by humanity. With the biblical witness rent asunder, the gospel event will no longer scandalize us, because it isn't allowed to identify God with the narrated event as a whole. Instead, God is defined in abstraction from the story and so he ends up looking just like the God the Greek philosophers had expected. Put otherwise, the God of standard Christology does not surprise us, because we already know him from elsewhere.[15]

Jenson attacks this kind of Christology in countless essays and at length in his two-volume *Systematics*. His diagnosis is forensic in detail and vast in scope, and he will often name names as he picks out culpable parties – both human and conceptual – who distort our understanding of the God of the gospel. At every turn, Jenson demonstrates how our christological task is driven by its wrongly configured rationale, thereby pointing out all the conceptual dead-ends it creates, and thus showing that Christology – at best – is a colossal waste of time. Time and again, Jenson emphasizes how trinitarian theology was originally an attempt to explain to the Greeks – in terms familiar to the Greeks – how the Christian God is most basically what happens between Three equiprimordial identities, therein compressing the narrative of the dramatic act of Jesus, his Father and the Spirit they share into the form of a proper name.[16] In short, Christian theology is focused on Jesus, as he lived with us.

As Jenson sees it, the root of the christological problem is therefore to be found in the missionary encounter with the Greeks. The church's account of God's triune identity was met with a could-have-been-predicted response. The Greeks simply raised their eyebrows and proceeded to press their original question, enquiring as to how the trinitarian metaphysics could function within their own foolproof system. The issue thereby boiled down to a simple question: How can a man who is known by way of a temporal span – i.e. a life framed by the blood and guts of both its beginning and end – be eternally caught up in what makes God to be God?

To put the point otherwise, the Greeks refused to accept the trinitarian metaphysics. They therefore pressed the church further, enquiring as to whether there was a deeper reality 'standing under' the story of Jesus. The revised question could of course have been answered in a variety of ways, and Jenson will give his own response in due course. But the problem – as he reads it – is that the early theologians took fright, effectively losing their nerve and beating a retreat into the established metaphysics, which Jenson thinks most of them had never departed in the first place.[17] In short, the theologians were just as scandalized by the idea of a womby-tomby God as the philosophers, and so they attempted to mitigate the gospel's offence.[18]

Jenson thinks there was an obvious way to do this. The theologians needed to explain the internal constitution of the Nazarene in such a way that some kind of distance remained between him and the God the philosophers described. One technical concept proved vital in this regard, the *Logos*.[19] It was familiar to any ancient philosopher.[20] The Greeks believed the *Logos* 'bridged the gap' between the movements of the temporal world and immovable timeless *Being*.[21] From the human side of the equation, it is the sense of the world, the means by which it is ordered. Whereas – from eternity's side of the equation – it is the sense given to the world.[22] As a result, the *Logos* could be said to originate from God, without being God, while at the same time constituting the order by which the chances and changes of our fleeting world are regulated. To put that in Jenson's terms, the *Logos* is the eternity that gives meaning to time; that is to say, a 'God'.[23]

With the concept functioning in this way, Jenson thinks the early theologians wondered whether the *Logos* provided them with a holding station between God's timeless eternity and the gospel events.[24] In effect, the standard conception of the *Logos* provided them with an entity of blurry status, which was not quite God and not quite creature, somehow being suspended over the metaphysical abyss – 'bridging being's chasm'[25] – which the philosophers assumed to separate God from history, effectively 'existing a mini-step down' from God but an ontological step up from us, and thus as good as God 'from our perspective'.[26] And that was precisely its apologetic value. Because the *Logos* is not God *per se*, it could be said to inhabit the gospel narrative without causing offence. Apology accepted, as it were.[27]

With this possibility in mind, the early theologians spotted that *Sonship* and *Logos* are interchangeable titles in Scripture, in that both are attributed to Jesus at different points in the New Testament.[28] They therefore wondered whether the concepts of 'Sonship' and '*Logos*' are picking out two different realities, rather than being predicated of the single most basic subject, Jesus of Nazareth. However, the theologians were not daft. They knew that Israel's God tolerates no *almost*-Gods, with jealousy being one of his attributes, in that God ensures he alone is the God he wills to be, thereby refusing to tolerate any idol or share his identity with any imposter.[29] As a result, the theologians faced a straightforward question: is this *Logos* – which the Greeks have defined – finally the Creator or a creature?

Jenson knows this is a *pre*-Nicene question. Arius had triggered the original controversy by arguing that the Son/*Logos* was created *ex nihilo*, thus meaning 'there was a time when he was not'.[30] Arius had basically fudged the matter, introducing the idea that the Son/*Logos* was the 'perfect creature but not as one of the creatures'. However, Athanasius wouldn't let him off the hook. His objection centred on whether a creature can save other creatures or whether such a creature should in fact be worshipped and adored, with the Nicenes eventually settling that the Son/*Logos* must therefore be God, in that the Son's being is from the Father, thereby making him true God, because to be the Father is to be Father of this Son and only then is there the one God.[31] In other words, Nicaea – as we saw in the previous chapter – blocked off the escape by teaching that the eternal Father never possesses anything before, behind or beneath the eternally generative relation that is the Son in the Spirit they share.[32]

As a result, the church decided that God's being is the simple nexus of concrete relations by which the Father is *Father-ing*, the Son is *Son-ing*, the Spirit is *Spirating*, in the singular event of their mutual determination; or, in Jenson's own words, 'Father, Son and Spirit are distinct identities as and only as poles of the relations between them. The Father begets the Son and breathes the Spirit, and just and only so is the Father; and just and only so is the one God.'[33] This decision meant no single *hypostasis* could be called 'true God' in isolation from the others, because the Three are mutually 'of one being'. Just so, the Arian subordination of the Son to the Father was rendered anathema.[34]

And 'so far so good', as Jenson will often refrain.[35] However, he thinks reactionary forces were at work,[36] with the 'conceptual dissonance' between the timeless eternity and historical time – which had originally driven Arius to make his case – being 'pried open at a different place'.[37] The question was no longer to do with the status of the Son in relation to the Father, but instead centred on the relation of the Son to Jesus. As a result, the 'christological question has merely been Arius's question in a new location'.[38]

To show how this worked itself out, Jenson identifies a series of disastrous steps. First, Nicaea had laid down an unmovable premise, in that the Son is God fully. But theologians were left wondering whether this Son – if '100% God' – must still be defined by the existing Greek metaphysics, that is be the recipient of the full paraphernalia of omni-this, omni-that and omni-the-other which the philosophers had worked into their definition of *Being*.[39] If he is, it implied that the Son must remain at a distance from the wombs of women and the tombs men dig, which is why the timid theologians – according to Jenson – parked the concept of the *Logos* in the timeless eternity and proceeded to work out how it – and that is the right pronoun – might relate to Jesus' temporal life.[40] In other words, the trinitarian question about how Jesus is related to the Transcendence he calls Father and the Spirit they share mutates into a 'christological' question about how the divine Son – who is 'incapable of wombs and crosses'[41] – can be related to Jesus. In effect, the philosophical definition of deity simply took 'up residence in the new christological reflection, and there it was never overcome'.[42]

As Jenson sees it, any answer to the relocated question will always be self-defeating, because the doctrine of God has been leveraged from the primary story of Jesus, which – to recall – is what the doctrine was meant to 'maximally compress'. Therein, the identification of God slips its object, and we effectively saw off the branch we are sitting on.[43] This is 'a disastrous misstep',[44] because it is driven by a deep-seated aversion to anything that challenges the dominant Greek metaphysics, with the primary concern being 'to allow no thought to pass which might sully the deity of God'.[45] In effect, because Jesus of Nazareth has a mother and an executioner, we must assume he is qualified in his Sonship – *if* Sonship is of God – because we already know that 'full-fledged *God* could not [be found] emerging from a womb and hanging on a cross'.[46] And this – according to Jenson – is what created the need to posit the eternal existence of the *Logos asarkos*, the unfleshed Word. Theologians needed something that could pacify the Greeks, thereby positing that the unfleshed *Logos* possessed the timeless attributes that the substance metaphysics had legislated. Of course, the unfleshed *Logos* must be related to the historical Jesus, whose life, death and resurrection stand at the heart of the gospel narrative, and that is precisely why the subdiscipline of 'Christology' emerged. It is designed to work out the small print in our contractual obligation to the Greeks.

With this in mind, Jenson thinks mysterious mechanisms were soon introduced, by which the unfleshed *Logos* can be drawn into the orbit of the gospel event, without ever closing the 'gap' the Greek metaphysics had leveraged open. However, Jenson suspects a category error has taken place. The attempt to explain how the eternal *Logos* works within time 'was mostly wasted, because it was assumed that "eternal" meant "timeless", and when the question is set that way no answer is possible. It is all but obvious: a sheerly timeless God simply could not *act within* time. He could – again at incoherent best – only interfere with it from a distance.'[47] In short, recourse to 'mystery' papers over a metaphysical gap.

Jenson's conclusion is drastic. He argues that we don't need to conjure up this unfleshed entity – this 'metaphysical double'[48] – if we accept that Jesus is the Son he claimed to be and then do the difficult work of bending our conception of the most basic features of the triune reality around the 'single protagonist of the gospel story'.[49] As a result, fearing 'a Logos who somehow "was" not yet Jesus', Jenson intends 'to avoid such discourse',[50] not least because

> the *incompletion* of Christianity's primary theological task: *the interpretation of God* by what happened and will happen with Jesus Christ . . . [has led to] an interpretation of God only partly bent to the

gospel, [which means] dialectics are generated within the practice and understanding of faith which *compel* Christianity's repeated division into polar communities which can neither be reconciled nor leave one another alone.[51]

Jenson therefore rejects the metaphysical assumption driving the christological task. He refuses to work out the relation between two 'puddingy-type substances' – the divine and human natures – because that exercise is no more than our attempt to fix the pseudo-problem the timid theologians had created in subservience to the substance metaphysics. Thus, Jenson will approach things differently.[52] His project 'is not about crunching God and world together into the person of Christ, [but] about confessing their essential union in him and getting on with the rest of the story'.[53] To put that otherwise, Jenson 'works to put God "deep" in that flesh'.[54]

5.3 We believe in one Lord, not two

Before we trace Jenson's constructive proposal, we should note that he doesn't think he is doing anything new. Instead, he draws from a catalogue of supporting witness, piggybacking on the insights of countless theologians who he believes were on the right track, even if they do not always venture far enough along it. However, Jenson's supporting testimony is somewhat scarce, and his fellow witnesses are often sporadic in their testimony, and not always intentional in offering it.[55] But this is all the more evidence – according to Jenson – that the material is itself the work of the Spirit, who alone ensures the church's faithful witness to Jesus of Nazareth makes its way through time. We will return to this matter in a later chapter, where we will examine the way Jenson thinks our theological deliberations intersect with God's own deliberation about who he will always forever be for us. The point here, however, is simple. Jenson's voice is intoned with the accent of others.

In broad terms, Jenson's positive account goes something like this. The Christian gospel scandalizes us, because it posits the personal particularity of one man's narratable life as one of the *hypostases* who together make God what it is to be God. This means we must talk only about Jesus and the Transcendence he named Father – thereby making himself out to be the Son[56] – and the Spirit of the life they share. We have no warrant to leave the epicentre of the *hypostases'* joint work in our midst, but must hold our gaze on what happened between these Three in and around Jerusalem.

Keeping this point in mind, Jenson proceeds on the basis that the early church answered the philosophers' original question by confessing the personal name of God at Nicaea, with the doctrine of the Trinity thereby functioning as a condensed summary of the narrative by which the church picks out who it is referring to when we talk about the most basic nature of reality.[57] The Three *hypostases* – one of whom is Mary's boy and Pilate's victim – must be understood in relation one to another, constituting the dramatic act by which God tells God who he will forever be. The concepts of 'person' and 'nature' thereby function within this trinitarian framework as a snapshot of the story, and so that is how they should continue to be used in the 'christological' setting. The bottom line is simple: 'What Christology is – or ought to be – *about* is the Jesus who appears in the Gospels, as he is in fact the Son of God he was accused of claiming to be.'[58] Simply put, Jesus is the Son, born of Mary, executed under Pontius Pilate and raised from the dead.

To make the same point a different way, Jenson thinks the Nicene Creed tells us what we need to know about Jesus. The second article of the Creed begins with a statement of belief in 'one Lord Jesus Christ' and thereafter plots this one's unity in being with the Father, before proceeding to summarize the historical trajectory of this one and the same who 'for us and our salvation came down from heaven and was incarnate of the Virgin Mary'.[59] Jenson wants his readers to note that the second article never introduces a new subject for what is being predicated, but instead sticks with 'one Lord Jesus Christ' as its singular focus. In consequence, everything contained in the second article is being attributed to this one identifiable *hypostasis*: it is the same Jesus who is eternally begotten of the Father *and* born of Mary. Jenson thereby concludes that we must 'Say nothing that in any way suggests that he is not fully one of us or that he is not fully one of the Trinity.'[60]

As Jenson works out the implications of this premise, he questions whether the 'distinction between "for himself" and "for others" [is] a meaningful distinction with the God of the gospel, as it indeed was with the gods of those to whom the gospel came on its way to us'.[61] That is to say, Jenson wonders whether God does himself with us, so to speak, in such a way that the temporal missions are identified with the eternal processions in their metaphysical coincidence. Jenson accepts, however, that most readers will instinctively take the creedal sequence and map it onto the dominant metaphysics, usually by inserting a rupture between eternity and time in the word 'became'. The first part of the second article is taken to be about some entity – an eternal *Logos*, likely timeless, certainly unfleshed – and the second bit is about that same something after something has happened to it, namely '*became man*'. As a result, we imagine two successive states, with two resulting subjects to which we can apportion what is most appropriate to either of them. But – as we have seen – Jenson thinks this approach is being driven by the substance metaphysics, rather than the gospel narrative. The move is therefore unwarranted, and mainly because 'the Bible violates our notion of time more or less on every page'.[62]

Jenson knows his readers will likely rush to John's prologue at this point, therein finding the biblical evidence we need to legitimize the unfleshed state of the Word prior to its enfleshment.[63] But Jenson will regularly counter this move, showing how John's speech about Jesus is a lot odder than we imagine, not least in the way the apostle presents the enfleshed Jesus pre-existing Abraham.[64] This Johannine verse thereby 'forbids a crudely serial-chronological interpretation of the prologue',[65] and so, like it or not – and he thinks we don't! – the second article of the Creed is good exegesis: we believe in one Lord Jesus Christ, and everything thought to happen in eternity and time is about this 'one and the same'. Put otherwise, 'God happens for God in the same way that God happens for us'.[66]

In other words, Jenson doesn't want us to make sense of the 'became' sequentially. He will even 'go so far . . . as to deny that what eternally precedes "flesh" is any actual unincarnate state of the Logos',[67] instead noting, in one discussion about Old Testament prophecy, how 'the word customarily translated "came" does not mean quite what the English might suggest. The verb . . . does not necessarily specify arrival at one place *from* some place else. By itself, it is closer to "happens to/at . . ."'.[68] As a result, with an alternative metaphysic in place, Jenson thinks we have every right to posit an eternal 'happening' that has two terms, in that this single person finds their meaningful end with the Father and with us in one act. In effect, the concept 'became' denotes the brute actuality of the hypostatic union, by which two vectors of mutuality are personally lived out and lived in, so to speak, by this same man in a simultaneous '*explo*sion of love' and '*im*plosion of freedom' by which the temporal birthing and eternal begetting coincide in the selfsame subject.[69] Put simply, Jesus of Nazareth is God and man, with both being defined by the singular act that the word 'became' encapsulates.

Now, the details of Jenson's understanding of 'became' will occupy us right through to the end of the book, so this first reference only flags up what we will be tackling later. But here it is helpful to note that he thinks Cyril of Alexandria will be cheering him on. Jenson will often celebrate Cyril's role in the Nestorian controversy, usually by first rehearsing how Nestorius's conjunction of two persons was a tempting – and persisting – alternative to what eventually became the orthodox position at Chalcedon.[70] Cyril's primary concern was to focus on the 'one protagonist'[71] in the drama the gospel recounts, where Jesus is presented as a man who claimed to be God's Son, and never in a way that allows us to apportion different aspects of his singular life to two different agents. Cyril thereby has a different starting point to Nestorius, and so he doesn't need to work with ancient assumptions about what a God can do and what a man can do. Instead Cyril – according to Jenson – begins with the prima facie textual witness to this one 'as he is in fact the Son of God he was accused of claiming to be',[72] and thereby argues that Jesus does what is appropriate to both natures at one and the same time, i.e. *theandrically*. Everything is predicated of the Godman, meaning that this one person 'is unmixed and unadulterated creature and Creator'.[73]

With this the case, Jenson learns from Cyril:

> The first and fundamental christological teaching should then be: When you talk of Christ, always remember that you are talking about a single figure, the one protagonist of the Gospels' narrative, of whom the gospel message claims that he is risen. Say nothing that in any way suggests that any one of 'Jesus' or 'the Christ' or 'the man from Nazareth' or 'the Son of God' or 'the Christ-principle,' or whatever other christological name, title, or description, inherited or made up, refers to a different entity from any other.[74]

As a result, Jenson describes himself as a hyper-Cyrillean,[75] believing this description places him on the right side of the dogmatic settlement. However, the qualification 'hyper' will prove to be important, mainly because Jenson recognizes that Cyril's success was in some sense qualified. The bishop's impact on the Chalcedonian Definition was undermined by Pope Leo's appended *Tome*,[76] in which the Pope attempted to sort out the controversy (albeit decades earlier). Leo argued that two agents can be seen to be at work within the gospel story, with 'each nature doing its own work, in cooperation with the other'.[77] Therefore, birth, death and the contingent happenings in between should be allotted to the human nature, with the Godly bits left to the agency of the *Logos*.[78] However, Jenson wants us to remember how the concepts of 'person' and 'nature' function in the doctrine of the Trinity, where – in contrast to Pope Leo's account – it is the persons, not the nature, who do things (i.e. the mutual doing of the divine nature). He therefore thinks Leo's *Tome* amounts to a sleight of hand, because the function of the concepts has been switched. The concept of 'person' is thereby rendered all but redundant, and the results are not good.[79]

As Jenson sees it, Leo's argument – at best! – causes confusion by blurring the straight line between the trinitarian and christological concepts, with the formal Chalcedonian Definition thereby failing 'to describe a continuity of agency throughout the life of the one person Jesus Christ'.[80] But even worse than that, the use of Leo's *Tome* to interpret the Definition 'runs the risk of replicating a cosmic dualism at the heart of the confession',[81] effectively undermining the hypostatic union and leaving us all intents and purposes Nestorian. With two most basic realities in play, God and humanity are not essentially united in Christ. They each get their moments, but do not coincide personally. Just so, 'the vacuity of Chalcedon's formulas' becomes a disaster.[82] The church can proceed to think about Jesus in abstraction from its own trinitarian metaphysics.

5.4 One single person, two communal natures

Jenson attempts to reconstruct the christological task on the terms set by the Nicene settlement, offering 'a form of teaching that seeks to get behind the missteps which make the tradition so tortured'.[83] To this end, he begins with the unusual claim that the second Person of the Trinity is the man Jesus of Nazareth, with everything listed in the second article of the Creed being predicated of this single *hypostasis*. Of course, this means Jenson quickly begins to say some strange things about God. He is born of Mary, for example, and dies under Pilate, as well as doing all the other things we find in the story of the Nazarene.

Jenson knows these kinds of statements – such as 'God dies' – are already in wide use. All theologians know the gospel requires us to say something similar, even if these statements need to be whitewashed with 'mystery' and 'paradox' at some stage. But Jenson is much bolder, countering that 'mere paradox will not suffice for the long run'.[84] He therefore dares to believe that the statements are unequivocally true, because they are about one single *hypostasis*; there is one most basic reality who is at once both God and man.[85]

Jenson accepts that 'We may still apprehend paradox in his position', although he quickly adds that it is 'not that the presumed impassible Logos suffers, *but that the suffering Son is the Logos of the presumed impassible Father*'.[86] He recognizes that it is difficult to work out how it can really be true that God is born and dies, although he thinks the doctrine of the 'communication of attributes' can help us understand why we must say that he does. The 'communication of attributes' is the way theologians draw together what would usually be predicated of the two natures in their difference, with what it is to be divine and what it is to be human being attributed to one single person, namely the most basic *hypostasis*. Because one person lives what it is to be God and what it is to be human simultaneously, everything he does can be said to be done by both, which is to say, *theandrically*. Jenson therefore takes this teaching on board, arguing:

> We should in consequence entertain a strong version of what has been called *communicatio idiomatum*, 'the fellowship of attributes,' the way in which in the being and work of the one *hypostasis*, each nature brings not only what is proper to it but also what is proper to the other, so that by Christ – and by him alone – divine things are done humanly and human things divinely. 'Jesus rules' and 'God the Son is crucified' are not just notionally or verbally true, but state facts about the one concrete person of Christ, and have the appropriate form for so doing.[87]

However, the question is, how does that work?

Tee Gatewood spots how 'Jenson proceeds to answer this question by suggesting that Christ's two natures are communal realities'.[88] That is to say, the concepts of divine and human are being used as 'labels for communities' – as Jenson puts it[89] – meaning that Jesus 'is one of the three whose mutuality is the divine life, who live the history that God is',[90] and, at precisely the same time, participates in 'a second set of mutually determining relationships' as one of us.[91] In other words:

> To have 'human nature' in the christologically relevant sense is not to instantiate an essence shared by all humans – though doubtless there are characteristics without which we would not call an entity human – but is rather to have a role in the one community through time of those who together make that history in which Jesus, and Napoleon, and the writer and readers of this essay, and the writer's great-aunt all participate. To have the 'divine nature' is not to instantiate an essence shared by all putative gods – though doubtless there are characteristics without which we would not think of something as divine – but is rather to be one of the three whose mutuality is the life that creates all that is not one of those three, the life that therefore is God.[92]

As this suggests, Jenson is claiming that this most basic *hypostasis* – the person who is Jesus – is simultaneously uniquely one of the Three who together make God what it is to be God *and* one of the many who together make up what it is to be human; and, if we are counting 'most basics', that amounts to saying that one most basic is two most basics, which of course is odd. To make sense of Jenson's claim, however, the *en/an hypostatic* debate might prove helpful.[93]

This technical debate centres on the question as to what sort of human nature God the Son assumes. Theologians recognize that if the assumed nature is thought to be already personal, so to speak, then the Son's assumption of that nature would leave us with two 'persons', meaning we are back with Nestorius. But theologians also know it cannot be right to say the human nature assumed by the Son is impersonal, because this would be sailing too close to the Apollinarian rocks, suggesting there is something missing which God occupies in this instance. As a result, theologians agree something different must be said: the human nature assumed by the Son is not personal other than in the assumption by the second Person of the mutuality that is God.[94] But again, how does that make sense?

At this point, I think Wittgenstein's teaching on the difference between 'seeing that' and 'seeing as' can be helpfully deployed, although with an important qualification.[95] Wittgenstein used the duck/rabbit image to show that different languages offer different depictions of the world, and that it is impossible to judge between these incommensurable pictures. To make his case, he noted how the single image can be perceived both as a duck – with its bill protruding from its round head – and also as a rabbit, with the bill suddenly appearing as a set of ears. The lines never move, but our minds enable us to see both the duck's bill and the rabbit's ears in the exact same image. In some respects, Jenson is arguing that something like this happens when we look at Jesus, in that this singular subject is both divine and human, although there is an important difference to note. In Wittgenstein's illustration, the image is seen either as a duck or a rabbit, but you never see both at the same time and so they cannot be compared. Not so with Jesus, says Jenson. The one we behold is God and man simultaneously as the one theandric *hypostasis*. As a result, there is no incommensurability between the natures, because Jesus is the singular Godman who is what it is to be both God and man. In short, we see that God and man are one, because that is what this most basic reality most basically is.

To put this another way, Jenson is arguing that the person is the 'ontologically robust marker' of both natures,[96] in that the 'one subject is demanded by the *reality* of the case'.[97] This means that whatever Jesus does – whether taking a nap or suckling the breast, or walking on water or raising Lazarus, or making the world or being laid in a tomb – is being done by/to the single protagonist who is the Godman.[98] And that brings with it some drastic implications. God is doing humanly, so to speak, and – strange to think – the human is doing Godly.

To help us begin to see what this means, Jenson often reworks technical debates to show how one person can be the *doing* of two natures. He thinks many of these debates have been read through the Leonine lens of two active natures, so he knows his revisionary approach to these various conundrums will strike us peculiar. For example, he tracks the complexities of Maximus the Confessor's arguments in the *dyothelite* controversy.[99] The original argument had been about the number of wills in operation in Jesus, with some theologians arguing that there can only be one will at work, thereby making God to be the sovereign agent in the Nazarene's life. Maximus – according to Jenson – reads the Gospels more closely, recognizing that there is clearly a human deliberation taking place in Gethsemane. As a result, Maximus attempts to align this human willing to the divine willing, which means – if anyone is counting 'wills' – there are two at work, hence the *dyothelite* name. However, Jenson thinks Maximus spotted that only one person is doing these two willings as that singular person, and the only way to make sense of this claim was to recognize that will is a function of nature.[100] If this is accepted, Jesus' human will can be understood in the same way as ours, in that it is lived out in existential relation to other people. However, what makes the human will of Jesus different is that it is completely aligned to the divine will, thereby rendering him sinless, unlike us. But Jenson thinks the divine will must similarly be defined as the single mutual will of the Father, Spirit and this Son, with the drastic consequence that the human willing is thereby seen to be a participation in the mutual willing that is God's by nature. In other words, the human will of the Godman is simultaneously the divine will, which is to say there is one person with one decision – to accept this cup, etc. – but this personal decision plays out in two directions, so to speak.[101] The human decision is God's too, singularly. 'It is "one and the same" who lives both of these communal stories.'[102]

Now, Jenson knows his reading of the two wills in Christ pushes the contingency of the human deliberation – taken in a particular garden at a particular time – up into the being of God. He thereby sees that

> once it is clear that there truly is only one individual person who is Christ, who lives as one of the Trinity and one of us, and that he is personal precisely as one of us, then to say that he as creature is our saviour – or that he as creature exercises any divine power – is simply to say that he plays his role in the triune life and does not need to abstract from his human actuality to do so.[103]

Jenson accepts that the consequences of this move are immense. It implies that if the man Jesus had said 'no' – with a 'My will, not your will, be done' – then God's singular mutual will, which is at one with his nature, would have collapsed into 'a mutually betraying pantheon',[104] by which God would somehow have undone himself – and therefore us his creatures – in the cataclysmic process.[105] Put otherwise, God might have destroyed himself if the man Jesus had chosen otherwise. The human decision is genuinely vital to God.

Of course, Jenson knows the possibility of God undoing himself beggars belief. It amounts to the extraordinary claim that God is 'the one absolute contingency'.[106] This strange idea will become the centre of our attention soon enough, when we examine the way in which God freely determines himself from eternity to eternity. However, before we get to that point, there remains one last thing to note. Jenson doesn't think the 'person' in the *theandric* reality is a pudding-type thing, which can somehow be abstracted from time to create the image of a new punctiliar 'substance', which stands under the accidents of this particular life. Instead, the 'person' needs to be understood as the coherence of the episodic temporal span that the gospel specifies, being finally identifiable only because this life comes to an end. In other words, the *hypostasis* is the coherence of this plot, which remains narratable in essence while being definitive in form, in that it is fixed as the temporal passage between conception and death. In short, the pick-out-able life of the Nazarene – in its entirety – is the *hypostasis* of the second Person of the Trinity. There is therefore no 'unincarnate *Logos* lurking somehow before or behind or beyond Jesus the Son. There is no such thing, to be known or unknown'.[107] Simply put, the Son is, 'a stretch of this world's history'.[108]

With this being so, Jenson sees that God in himself must be the event in which the precise same plot is the eternal mutuality by which he bespeaks himself. Or, to put that more starkly, Jenson sees that if God the Son is this span, then God in himself is somehow temporal in structure, in being the 'froming' and 'toing', the 'Whence' and 'Whither' of the story the gospel depicts.[109] Thus, with 'person' understood as a narratable quality, the *hypostasis* of the Son is nothing other than his obedience to the Father and for the Spirit, being no more than those mutual relations, which means 'there is no way to refer to God the Son that does not refer to the man Jesus, and no way to refer to Jesus that does not refer to God the Son'.[110] They are the same plot.

However, with the issue set up in this way, Jenson knows the obedience of God the Son – depicted in the Gospels – is also towards *yet another*. The Son's obedience to the Father and for the Spirit is directed towards his death, which is his unconditionality for us.[111] The hypostatic trajectory of the path the Son takes – and *is* – is therefore the manner in which God does himself in such a way that it includes us as well.[112] Put otherwise, the gospel shows that the nature of God is eternally God-with-us, because Jesus 'acts in the unity of his person to unite humanity with God'.[113]

No doubt, this is beginning to look like a very odd doctrine of God, because we are somehow to be included. But Jenson thinks it will only look odd from a Greek perspective, which is why he thinks the oddity of his proposal is entirely to our shame. The conceptual revolution – that is the trinitarian metaphysic – should have determined our understanding of 'persons' and 'nature' by the story of Jesus, thereby allowing us to grasp that we ourselves are somehow incorporated into the mutuality that is God because of what happened over the Easter weekend in our presence. However, that is not what most of us think. As a result, the question, as Jenson himself asks, is 'where do we go from here?'[114] And the answer is Karl Barth's doctrine of election.

Notes

1 Jenson thinks those who defend the eventually orthodox positions are 'a minority until the very end'. Robert W. Jenson, *Systematic Theology, Volume 1, The Triune God* (New York: OUP, 1997), 104.

2 See Jenson, *Systematic Theology*, Vol. 1, 128–33.

3 Robert W. Jenson, *Ezekiel* (London: SCM Press, 2009), 42–3.

4 For an overview, see Jenson, *Systematic Theology*, Vol. 1, 125–33.

5 Robert W. Jenson, *Song of Songs: A Biblical Commentary for Teaching and Preaching* (Louisville: John Knox Press, 2005), 13.

6 Jenson, *Systematic Theology*, Vol. 1, 126.

7 Jenson, *Systematic Theology*, Vol. 1, 133.

8 Again, with this adjective, I borrow from Robert W. Jenson, *Alpha and Omega: A Study in the Theology of Karl Barth* (New York: Thomas Nelson & Sons, 1963; reprint, Eugene, OR: Wipf and Stock, 2002), 74.

9 Jenson, *Systematic Theology*, Vol. 1, 145.

10 Robert W. Jenson, 'What Kind of God Can Make a Covenant?' in *Covenant and Hope: Christian and Jewish Reflections*, ed. Robert W. Jenson and Eugene B. Korn (Grand Rapids: Eerdmans, 2012), 9.

11 Robert W. Jenson, 'How Does Jesus Make a Difference?' in *Essentials of Christian Theology*, ed. William C. Placher (Louisville: Westminster John Knox Press, 2003), 199.

12 Robert W. Jenson, 'Basics and Christology', in *In Search of Christian Unity: Basic Consensus/Basic Differences*, ed. Joseph A. Burgess (Minneapolis: Fortress Press, 1991), 47.

13 Robert W. Jenson, 'What if It Were True?' *Neue Zeitschrift für Systematische Theologie und Religionsphilosophie* 43.1 (2001), 11.

14 On this, see for example, Robert W. Jenson, 'Jesus in the Trinity', *Pro Ecclesia* 8 (1999), 309, 318.

15 And hence, 'why the church's preaching and catechesis are mostly so dull'. Jenson, 'What if', 11.

16 See for example, Robert W. Jenson, *The Triune Identity: God According to the Gospel* (Philadelphia: Fortress, 1982; reprint, Eugene, OR: Wipf and Stock, 2002), 125.

17 Jenson, *Systematic Theology*, Vol. 1, 104. Or, put more positively: the problem in the West was that 'the doctrine of the Trinity came . . . as a finished product. Thus it was more something to be explained, than itself an explanation . . . [the resulting] terms had been through none of the Eastern conceptual wars'. Robert W. Jenson, 'The Triune God', in *Christian Dogmatics*, ed. Carl E. Braaten and Robert W. Jenson (Philadelphia: Fortress, 1984), 141.

18 Jenson, *Systematic Theology*, Vol. 1, 49–50.

19 On this, see Jenson, *Triune Identity*, 66–72. In what follows, I am indebted to Jenson, 'Jesus in the Trinity', and also to Tee Gatewood, 'A Nicene Christology? Robert Jenson and the Two Natures of Jesus Christ', *Pro Ecclesia* 18 (2009), 28–49.

20 See Jenson, *Systematic Theology*, Vol. 1, 96–7.
21 For Jenson's wording, see Jenson, 'Jesus in the Trinity', 311.
22 Jenson, 'Jesus in the Trinity', 311.
23 Jenson, 'Jesus in the Trinity', 311.
24 Jenson, 'Jesus in the Trinity', 311.
25 Jenson, *Systematic Theology*, Vol. 1, 97.
26 Jenson, 'Jesus in the Trinity', 311.
27 Jenson, *Systematic Theology*, Vol. 1, 97–8.
28 Jenson, 'Jesus in the Trinity', 311.
29 Jenson, *Systematic Theology*, Vol. 1, 47.

30 Jenson, 'Jesus in the Trinity', 311–12. See also his account of 'The Arian Crisis' in Jenson, *Triune Identity*, 78–84, and Jenson, *Systematic Theology*, Vol. 1, 100–1.

31 As Jenson states, 'Across this beautiful spectrum the biblical radical distinction of Creator from creature could only make an ugly slash somewhere.' Jenson, 'Triune God', 124.

32 See Jenson, *Triune Identity*, 84.

33 Robert W. Jenson, 'The Hidden and Triune God', *International Journal of Systematic Theology* 2.1 (2000), 7.

34 For an example of Jenson's reading of Nicaea and Constantinople, see Jenson, *Triune Identity*, 84–92.

35 For use, see for example, Robert W. Jenson, *Canon and Creed* (Louisville: Westminster John Knox Press, 2010), 28.

36 Jenson regularly names Augustine as the main culprit, seeing his failure to grasp the distinction between *ousia* and *hypostasis* as leading to 'the presence of a Jonah in the Western trinitarian ship'. Robert W. Jenson, 'Lutheranism and the *Filioque*', in *Ecumenical Perspectives on the Filioque for the 21st Century*, ed. Myk Habets (London: T&T Clark, 2014), 161.

37 Jenson, *Systematic Theology*, Vol. 1, 126.

38 Robert W. Jenson, *Unbaptized God: The Basic Flaw in Ecumenical Theology* (Minneapolis: Fortress, 1992), 121.

39 Jenson, 'Jesus in the Trinity', 312.
40 Jenson, 'Jesus in the Trinity', 312.
41 Jenson, 'Basics and Christology', 48.
42 Jenson, 'Basics and Christology', 49.

43 As he puts it in a critique of one theologian's work, 'I disapprove his sliding away (as I see it) from the doctrine, "'Jesus is the Logos' is an identity-statement." I fear he opens the door to speculation untethered from the historical Incarnation.' Robert W. Jenson, 'On the Ascension', in *Loving God With Our Minds: The Pastor as Theologian*, ed. Michael Welker and Cynthia A. Jarvis (Grand Rapids: Eerdmans, 2004), 331.

44 Jenson, 'How Does Jesus', 198.
45 Jenson, 'Basics and Christology', 48.
46 Jenson, 'Basics and Christology', 48.
47 Jenson, 'What Kind of God', 7.
48 Jenson, *Triune Identity*, 146.
49 Jenson, 'How Does Jesus', 199.

50 Robert W. Jenson, 'Afterword', in *Trinitarian Soundings in Systematic Theology*, ed. Paul Louis Metzger (London: T&T Clark, 2005), 220.

51 Jenson, 'Basics and Christology', 46–7.

52 Again, see Jenson, 'Jesus in the Trinity'.

53 Paul Cumin, *Christ at the Crux: The Mediation of God and Creation in Christological Perspective* (Eugene, OR: Pickwick, 2014), 132.

54 Eric W. Gritsch and Robert W. Jenson, *Lutheranism: The Theological Movement and Its Confessional Writings* (Philadelphia: Fortress, 1976), 106.

55 Jenson therefore thinks, 'such an enterprise . . . is a minority report in the present church'. Jenson, 'Triune God', 84.

56 Robert W. Jenson, *Systematic Theology, Volume 2, The Works of God* (New York: OUP, 1999), 184.

57 See Jenson, *Triune Identity*, 1–18.

58 Jenson, *Systematic Theology*, Vol. 1, 134, and an account of the sleight of hand on Vol. 1, 132–3.

59 It is of note that Jenson spots how the second article runs in parallel to Israel's confession in Deuteronomy 26.5–9. Jenson, *Systematic Theology*, Vol. 1, 43.

60 Jenson, 'How Does Jesus', 201.

61 Jenson, 'How Does Jesus', 195.

62 Robert W. Jenson, 'Conceptus . . . De Spiritu Sancto', *Pro Ecclesia* 15.1 (2006), 106.

63 See the section on the pre-existence of Christ in Jenson, *Systematic Theology*, Vol. 1, 138–44.

64 Jenson, *Systematic Theology*, Vol. 1, 139. For a critique of Jenson's use of Irenaeus, see Emmitt Cornelius, 'St Irenaeus and Robert W. Jenson on Jesus in the Trinity', *Journal of the Evangelical Theological Society* 55 (2012), 111–24.

65 Colin Gunton and Robert W. Jenson, 'The *Logos Ensarkos* and Reason', in *Reason and the Reasons of Faith*, ed. Paul J. Griffiths and Reinhard Hütter (London: T&T Clark, 2005), 80.

66 Chris Green's way of putting it, shared in personal correspondence.

67 Gunton and Jenson, '*Logos Ensarkos*', 81. Elsewhere, Jenson states, 'no one has ever suggested a plausible answer [to what "became" means]; the arbitrary metaphysical posit of a "*Logos asarkos*" persists mostly because people cannot think of a better idea'. Jenson, 'Conceptus . . .', 106.

68 Jenson, *Ezekiel*, 28.

69 Robert W. Jenson, 'Karl Barth on the Being of God', in *Thomas Aquinas and Karl Barth: An Unofficial Catholic-Protestant Dialogue*, ed. Bruce L. McCormack and Thomas Joseph White (Grand Rapids: Eerdmans, 2013), 51.

70 Jenson, *Systematic Theology*, Vol. 1, 127–33.

71 Jenson, 'Jesus in the Trinity', 314.

72 Jenson, *Systematic Theology*, Vol. 1, 134.

73 Gunton and Jenson, '*Logos Ensarkos*', 82.

74 Jenson, 'How Does Jesus', 201.

75 Jenson describes this as 'my hyper-Cyrillean (i.e., old Lutheran) positions'. Jenson, 'On the Ascension', 331.

76 See Jenson, *Systematic Theology*, Vol. 1, 130–3.

77 Jenson here cites 'the key passage of the Tome', in Jenson, 'Basics and Christology', 51.

78 'According to Leo, one entity, "the divine nature" does the glory bits and another entity, "the human nature," does the suffering bits, each "with" the other.' Robert W. Jenson, 'What if', 9.

79 Jenson, *Triune Identity*, 125.

80 Gatewood, 'Nicene Christology', 35.

81 Gatewood, 'Nicene Christology', 35.
82 Jenson, 'Basics and Christology', 49.
83 Jenson, 'How Does Jesus', 201.
84 Robert W. Jenson, 'Jesus, Father, Spirit: The Logic of the Doctrine of the Trinity', *Dialog* 26.4 (1987), 246.
85 So, for example, see Jenson, *Systematic Theology*, Vol. 1, 129.
86 Jenson, *Systematic Theology*, Vol. 1, 137.
87 Jenson, 'How Does Jesus', 200.
88 Gatewood, 'Nicene Christology', 31.
89 Jenson, 'How Does Jesus', 202.
90 Jenson, *Systematic Theology*, Vol. 1, 138.
91 Gatewood, 'Nicene Christology', 32.
92 Jenson, 'How Does Jesus', 202–3.
93 On this, see Eugene R. Schlesinger, 'Trinity, Incarnation and Time: A Restatement of the Doctrine of God in Conversation with Robert Jenson', *Scottish Journal of Theology* 69 (2016), 201–2.
94 McGuckin helpfully summarizes the technical debate: the *an/en* distinction means the Son, 'did not displace a human foetus that had a human hypostatic reality of its own, because there was never an instant when this human foetus existed independently of his personal creative act'. John McGuckin, *Saint Cyril of Alexandria and the Christological Controversy* (Crestwood, NY: St Vladimir's Seminary Press, 2004), 215.
95 See Marie McGinn, *The Routledge Guidebook to Wittgenstein's Philosophical Investigations* (London: Routledge, 2013), 311–17. Hunsinger makes use of this image when analysing Jenson's proposal, but without the important qualification I will add. George Hunsinger, 'Robert Jenson's Systematic Theology: A Review Essay', *Scottish Journal of Theology* 55 (2002), 161–200.
96 Jenson, *Systematic Theology*, Vol. 1, 129.
97 Jenson, *Systematic Theology*, Vol. 1, 130.
98 Jenson, *Systematic Theology*, Vol. 1, 129–30.
99 Jenson, *Systematic Theology*, Vol. 1, 134–8.
100 Jenson, 'Jesus in the Trinity', 316–17.
101 Jenson, 'Jesus in the Trinity', 317.
102 Jenson, *Systematic Theology*, Vol. 1, 138.
103 Jenson, *Systematic Theology*, Vol. 1, 144–5.
104 Jenson, *Systematic Theology*, Vol. 1, 65.
105 Jenson, *Systematic Theology*, Vol. 1, 48.
106 Robert W. Jenson, 'For us . . . He Was Made Man', in *Nicene Christianity: The Future for a New Ecumenism*, ed. Christopher R. Seitz (Grand Rapids: Brazos, 2001), 77.
107 Jenson, *Systematic Theology*, Vol. 1, 142.
108 Jenson, *Systematic Theology*, Vol. 1, 201.
109 As Jenson has it, 'the triune God is not a sheer point of presence; he is a life among persons.' Jenson, *Systematic Theology*, Vol. 2, 35.
110 Jenson, *Ezekiel*, 43.
111 Jenson, *Triune Identity*, 22.
112 Jenson, *Triune Identity*, 23.
113 Gatewood, 'Nicene Christology', 35.
114 Jenson, *Systematic Theology*, Vol. 1, 133.

PART THREE

Jenson's Doctrine of God

6

Adopting and Adapting Barth's Doctrine of Election

6.1 An initial warning

We are now heading towards the business end of the book, i.e. approaching an articulation of Jenson's doctrine of God. In many respects that is all we have been dealing with from the start. Time and again, we have witnessed the way Jenson seeks to identify the nature of God as he examines exactly what happens with Jesus, thereby remaining entirely focused on the gospel narrative as he details his vision of a speakable eternity. That is pretty much his signature move. As a result, we would be foolish to think his gaze will turn away now, as if he would ponder an unconnected plane of reality as he begins to talk about what makes God to be God. With his hyper-Cyrillean Christology in place, there is no metaphysical 'gap' to cross as he explores the eternal relation between the Son, his Father and their Spirit. Instead he is entirely preoccupied with the concrete actuality of this one God among us, who raised Jesus from the dead into the never-ending future of his specific infinity in which we are called to participate. No unfleshed Word, no God in abstraction. Things remain entirely grounded.

Of course, this should go without saying by now, although the point is of such importance that it bears repeating. It is all too easy for us to assume that Jenson must have vacated the historical realm when he talks about God in himself, especially when he begins to deploy a series of technical concepts such as begetting, spirating, perichoresis and the like. We already know how these concepts function in trinitarian discourse, believing them to signify eternal states within God himself, with the concepts thereby assuming a certain timeless quality, which thus makes them impossibly difficult to grasp and makes them best posited in sharp distinction from what happens to Mary's boy and Pilate's victim. Nicaea, for example, made clear that we do not know what the generative act of *begetting* means, other than it being different from being *made*. But Jenson thinks otherwise. When he uses a term like 'eternal begetting', he is still only talking about the temporal trajectory of the Son as he moves from conception in Mary's womb through ministerial life unto death on the cross, and then again beyond resurrection. In effect, the eternal relation is simply the time-bound steps, thereby being specifiable by 'riding the plot waves' of the story we tell about the enfleshed Son.[1] In other words, Jenson refuses to abstract the technical concepts from the wombytomby reality of Jesus' narratable life. The eternal 'begetting' and temporal 'birthing' are but one single act – albeit with two terms – that is the twofold event of God with the creature. As a result, we must be careful not to draw too heavily from what we already know when we investigate how these concepts function within Jenson's doctrine of God. We would likely smuggle in the wrong metaphysics.

As this is beginning to make clear, Jenson will not be pondering an 'immanent' life of God somehow a step removed from God's 'economic' work with us.[2] God's being is only ever his decisive work towards, with and upon us, in that the immanent Trinity is the economic Trinity eschatologically.[3] Jenson will therefore claim that God is all he will ever be in the End, and – somewhat remarkably – that End includes us. Of course, Jenson thinks this conclusion is entirely warranted, primarily because he thinks this is what the trinitarian concepts had only ever been about. The existing metaphysical terms had been redefined by the church, thereby rendering them conceptual auxiliaries to the primary story, which is the narrative of God plotting himself with us in Jesus Christ. Thus, there isn't anything – not even nothing! – beyond this story as it stands. And with that being the case, Jenson will want to analyse how this particular way of historical being is genuinely eternal being, i.e. the God we name as Father, Son and Holy Spirit; or – to put that in classical terms – it is the *taxis* of God that he will delineate. However, when he does, we must remember that 'This God's eternity is itself a temporal event: the resurrection of Christ'.[4] We never leave the Easter event.

We can now sense that some serious work needs to be done if we are to understand how the structure of Jenson's revisionary metaphysics works itself out in the doctrine of God. To begin that task, we will first venture into the theology of Karl Barth, albeit not too far and with clear intent.[5] As Jenson sees it, 'The content of Barth's great post-dialectical work, the *Church Dogmatics*, is, in fact, an enormous and genial essay of "christological ontology"',[6] which means it can help us '*get over* the self-evidences about God which antecedent religion has deposited in the structures of our apprehension'.[7] As a result, Jenson's work pivots on his commandeering of Barth's proposal, which provides him with an alternative metaphysics that he adopts *and then adapts* in the process of identifying the place of the always enfleshed Jesus in the eternal life of God.[8]

6.2 Heading in a different direction along the same path

Jenson's constructive proposal never deviates from Barth's revisionary doctrine of election, although he certainly presses beyond the place Barth himself reached in the later volumes of his *Dogmatics*. Any reader of Barth knows the material consequences of Barth's desire to link revelation and ontology only become clear in the second part of the second volume, where we find him arguing – arguably! – that Jesus Christ must be the eternal self-determination of God if he truly reveals God to man, therein making Jesus the one personal act of decision from eternity in time that makes God what it is to be God. In other words, Barth thinks Jesus is really God revealing God to us, and so everything – i.e. God and creature – must somehow coincide in that one person, who is thereby rendered definitive of our conception of God from eternity and how things stand in relation to him in time.

Without wanting to get caught up in the ongoing 'Barth Wars', it seems clear to me that Jenson is one of the first theologians to run with Barth's proposal – as Jenson reads it – and thereby develop his own account of God's eternal being in conversation with Barth's metaphysics.[9] Jenson certainly journeys beyond anything we find directly in Barth's teaching, within which it is clear – again, to me at least – that Barth will often apply the handbrake, so to speak, in an attempt to control his own acceleration beyond the norms of established discourse, thereby taking away with one hand what he has just given with the other. Whether or not Barth does this deliberately is in some sense by-the-by, and best left to scholars like Hunsinger and McCormack to work out in their ongoing disputes. But it reads to me – to twist the metaphor – that Barth gets caught in his own headlights, in that he is unable to take on board the consequences of his own theological proposal. Jenson, however, has no such hesitance. The accelerator is floored. The handbrake is off.[10]

As this is beginning to suggest, Jenson will try to keep in step with Barth's thinking, but – to adopt the current idiom of Barth scholarship – only in the McCormackian sense of moving beyond its conclusions.[11] Of course, there are many twists and turns in the journey Jenson takes, with his work differing markedly from Barth in many respects.[12] In fact, it is fair to say that Jenson wants to travel further along the path that Barth took, but in the opposite direction, thereby criticizing the way Barth arguably frontloads everything that happens in time by prioritizing a previous eternal decision.[13] The difference between these two theologians – as I read them – is to be found in the way Barth's theology gravitates towards the beginning, in which God eternally decides all he will ever be, whereas Jenson turns towards the end for his premise, by which God's being is the final outcome of his work with us. But – and here is the convergence – both theologians head in the opposite direction by focusing entirely on the presence of Jesus of Nazareth with us. They are both radically Christocentric.

To put the point otherwise, Jenson is wary of positing an always-already-established decisive beginning, which he thinks is in danger of remaining timeless in essence, and so posits an always-already opening up towards a decisive future by which God becomes all he will already ever be within time. Or – to play with words a little – Jenson effectively posits a *what-is-ahead-of-us-stance* in distinction from Barth's protological *what-was-always-before-us-stance*, which is to say that Jenson's thinking is even more historical than Barth's, because it is driven by futurity, i.e. a temporal divine eschatology that reaches a climax and then decrees 'encore'.[14]

However, whatever convergences and disagreements lie between these two thinkers, the point here is simple enough. Jenson's thinking is profoundly shaped by his reading of Barth, and of that there can be little doubt.[15] His doctoral thesis – later published as *Alpha and Omega*[16] – concentrated on Barth's pioneering work, and it is worth noting that Barth greatly appreciated Jenson's dissertation, describing the young American as the only theologian to date who had grasped his proposal adequately.[17] By shaping the formative years of Jenson's career in this way, Barth was to become a major influence on the most basic decisions Jenson made, even if other theologians would also have their say. In one article, for example, Jenson can write that 'we can appropriate another of Karl Barth's maxims, *which has been an axiom for me since I encountered it fifty years ago* . . .'[18] with the word 'axiom' indicating how Barth is ever-present, even when that isn't always made explicit. In short, Jenson didn't fall far from the first tree he climbed.[19]

But it is also worth noting – albeit as an aside – that Jenson wrote directly on Barth's doctrine of God during the last few years of his life, producing an essay which is extremely helpful.[20] For a start, the essay provides an insight into the practical mechanics of Jenson's methodology, including as it does some autobiographical reference to the way in which it was written. Jenson describes how he was reclining in his chair with his eyes shut as he thought things through, with Blanche – his wife – even asking whether he had fallen asleep as Jenson pondered what he had just discovered in Barth. A sense of pleasure imbues the piece, with Jenson very much at home in every sense of the word, leisurely enjoying the theological labour of working with Barth and the joy of thinking about God in the comfort of his own home. Theological delight comes through loud and clear.

Andrew J. Stobart has made the point that Jenson will usually read someone's work for contingent reasons – for example, Blanche encourages him, or a conference invites him – and then proceed to gather his findings into summary format, with the resulting constellation of his research being used as his definitive exegesis ever after, meaning that Jenson's first encounter with a theologian feeds forward in whatever form his first reading of that theologian took, forming long running – and very concise – summary conclusions on which Jenson frequently builds; Jenson doesn't keep turning the soil, as it were, but instead trusts the ability of his own historic mind.[21] I think Stobart is right, and it is one of the reasons why Jenson is regularly criticized for his reading of historical figures. Contemporary scholarship will often move on, digging deeper into the life and thought of a particular theologian, and thereby undermining what scholars had concluded yesteryear. This is notable with regard to Jenson's reading of Augustine and the Fathers, for instance, which is now regularly critiqued, although in some respects this is by-the-by for Jenson.[22] He wasn't interested in scholarly accuracy for its own sake, but instead wanted to discover what needs to be said to be saying the gospel today. In that sense, footnotes are secondary, because Jenson's subject is always God, and him proclaimed.[23]

What is most interesting about the essay on Barth, however, is that Jenson does revisit his past musings, thereby approaching Barth like an old acquaintance. We thereby get to see how Jenson's settled mind is initially baffled by the fact that Barth – who Jenson thought he already knew – could possibly be saying what he now sees him to be saying.[24] Jenson therefore 'beats a further retreat' to the primary texts to read afresh what Barth writes, and with the relevant volumes dusted down from the shelf, he proceeds to retrace Barth's account of God's nature through the course of the *Dogmatics*. As always, where Jenson's interpretation of his interlocutor ends and his own constructive proposals begin is not entirely evident, which is partly the point I'm making: the difference between Barth and Jenson is only ever within a close family resemblance.[25]

What is most helpful, however, is that the essay concludes with some startling Jensonian propositions, rather than Barth-neat, so to speak. These sentences pretty much capture Jenson's doctrine of God in just a few words. He concludes that 'God's being is an *im*plosion of freedom' and 'an *ex*plosion of love', and that the hinge between the two is the doctrine of election.[26] Our next task is to work out what these phrases mean, and to do that we turn our attention to Jenson's reading of Barth's revisionary account of election.

6.3 Jenson's reading of Barth's doctrine of election

Barth's doctrine of election should not intimidate us, although it often does.[27] It needs to be seen for what it is, namely, an account of God's *being*, namely, what makes God to be the God he is. As such, the doctrine of election is only ever doing the same work – albeit in a different manner – as the substance metaphysics. As a result, we are in some sense on familiar ground.

Of course, commonality needn't make the doctrine of election any easier to understand. Metaphysical proposals should intimidate us, because they force us to think deeply about the most basic features of the world we inhabit. But if we begin by noting that Barth is only doing what every theologian must at some stage do, then we should be less daunted by the prospect of what lies ahead. No matter how odd this gets, Barth is doing something normal: offering a proposed metaphysics.[28]

Nevertheless, this preamble has alerted us to the demanding nature of the work ahead. However, the difficulty of our task can make us assume that everyday words start playing tricks when they are drawn into metaphysical service, making us wonder – in this instance – whether 'election' might mean something different to what the word usually signifies. Of course, shifts in meaning do take place when words are drawn into theological discourse, with Jenson's account of the development of trinitarian doctrine showing how familiar concepts were radically – yet subtly – altered by their novel use in the theological setting.[29] However, we also saw how the everyday meaning of concepts such as *substantia* and *hypostasis* was never irrelevant. We need to know what the concepts originally meant in order to see what was novel about the Nicene proposal. In short, the technical concepts continued to trade on former meanings.

I make this point because we can often assume 'election' means something entirely new in Barth's work, because of the subject of which it is predicated, i.e. God. But that assumption would only follow if we had already assumed that anything predicated of God must signify something different to what it means in the historical realm, which – and here is the main point – is a conclusion that rests on metaphysical assumptions not yet decided. The assumption thereby begs the question we are seeking to answer, or – to put the same point more positively – we can only decipher the relation between words and God once the work of identifying God has been done, because the relation between God and words will depend entirely on what sort of God we are dealing with. And this should come as no surprise. Our earlier discussion about Jenson's theology of prayer noted how our understanding of language is linked to our understanding of God, and if we forget this connection here the circle will become vicious – which is precisely what makes run-of-the-mill words intimidating. But, as I understand it, the concept of 'election' doesn't change much once it has been theologized.

PART THREE | JENSON'S DOCTRINE OF GOD

In some respects, this is what is at stake in the first volume of Barth's *Dogmatics*. Barth begins with the assumption that God is known in his address to us, and that the successful reception of that address shows how this God – in the event of revelation – can commandeer everyday concepts and set them to his own use, i.e. revelation happens, and it is a 'success word'.[30] Barth's brilliance lies in the way he allows the actuality of our knowledge of God to inform our conception of God's being, i.e. the assumed success of revelation drives the consequent proposal about the structure of God's life, because – via a 'backwards glance' from our encounter with God[31] – we can see that God *is* the revealer, the revelation and the revealedness. In other words, by assuming that God's revelatory act reveals God to us, Barth can argue that God's being must be aligned positively with this act, and so God's being must be eventful because his dynamic act expresses it accurately.

Now, the link between Barth's epistemology and ontology raises all sorts of issues to which we must return, but the point here is simple enough: we mustn't assume the concept of 'election' has some sort of esoteric meaning. Just so – if I'm right about this – it will be worth reflecting on the concept's everyday use before turning to discover how it functions in the context of Barth's theology.

If I were to announce to a colleague that an election has been called, or ask them to remind me who won the last election, I am confident they would have a good idea what I was speaking about. A cluster of associated ideas would immediately spring to mind, thereby informing the meaning of the word by situating it within the political realm, i.e. government and the like. If we were then asked to define what sort of event a political election is, we could easily draw up a list of characteristics by analysing what we have experienced, even if we might quibble over some of the details. We might discuss how elections are periodic, for instance, in that they happen every four years or so. This would allow us to agree that elections are in some sense timely, amounting to specific episodes that happen at a particular time, rather than denoting a continuous state of affairs.[32] We might then discuss the way elections are both public and private, in that an election involves each voter making a private choice, which is personally executed in the ballot box – hidden and in secret, as it were – but which thereby informs the way we live as a public. In effect, voters get to choose between rival candidates and their competing parties privately, thereby making a personal decision for either one candidate or another to determine our common life. Of course, we might also note how an election involves deliberating between various options, before being executed in a decisive choice by which we rule some candidates out as we vote one in,[33] and this aspect might lead us to conclude that the voter's choice is an act of freedom, unless of course a tyrannical dictator has rigged the election – though as is often the case, this exception only proves the rule. Thus conceived as an act of freedom, we might link the concept to the question of sovereignty, seeing an election as the means by which voters wield power over their rulers, in that the common mind decides – and thereby legitimizes – who will have the right to govern over the coming years. This is why we would want to say the private act is irreducibly public, and not only in the negative sense that there would be no need for anyone to vote for themselves in an electorate of one, but in the sense that an election determines the future of the people together. This point is important, and we should note it for later, because it is clear that a country can be very different after an election depending on who gets elected. If the people vote for a nationalist government, or a socialist government, or a green government, and so on, then the people will become a different kind of people. In that respect the concept of 'election' denotes an act of self-determination; it determines who we are going to be going forward. Finally – and perhaps unsurprisingly – because we are talking about freedom, order, particularly, decision and possibilities, we should note that an election is in some sense contingent, in that there is nothing necessary about them, if only because history – both ancient and modern – demonstrates how the world can get along without them. In short, power can be exercised in different ways.

As I read it, none of the above is controversial. Therefore, by reflecting on the everyday use of the word, we can see the way 'election' signifies an authoritative sovereign act that privately/publicly determines the future by an executive decision as to who will rule *and* how they will rule; in other words, it determines the character of the people going forward. With this definition in mind, we have a solid foothold into what 'election' means in Barth's theology, because all these ideas will run through his proposal like a thread.

6.4 Jesus Christ: electing God and elected man

Barth says that what makes God to be God is an act of election, and this is 'the sum of the Gospel'.[34] However, in making this unusual claim, the meaning of the term remains pretty much the same as in everyday life. Of course, there are differences, which we will come to shortly, not least in the way in which God's act coincides with his being in such a way that person and act are identical so that God 'behappens himself', as Jenson puts it, by choosing himself in an act of self-determining in which his will is perfectly executed.[35] But for now we need only see that Barth – by commandeering the concept of election into metaphysical service – is able to differentiate his work from the metaphysical norm, because 'election' enables him to offer a lively account of what makes God to be God, which stands in stark contrast to the substance metaphysics we have already examined.[36]

As Barth works the concept of election into shape, the key premise is that there is no unknown God, because God is who he is in his revelation; what you see in Jesus Christ is what you get.[37] As this suggests, Barth's systematic link between revelation and ontology is pivotal, and it centres on Jesus Christ as God's Word; Jesus is really God addressing us and saying 'God' definitively so that we hear God.[38] Barth doesn't spend time justifying this move in advance of making it, because this Word – as the divine Word – stands in no need of introduction.[39] Barth thereby refuses to work from the possibility of this occurrence to its actuality, but instead approaches his task from the opposite direction. God has spoken his Word and we have heard, so what do we now say?

In other words, Barth is primarily interested in the content of that eternal Word, rather than whether or not it has been spoken. He wants to decipher the meaning of God's address to us, rather than working out whether it could have happened. What follows – i.e. the entire metaphysical project that is the *Church Dogmatics* – simply trades on his belief that God's act is a success, that this means his being must somehow be in his successful act, and that his being must therefore in some sense be active in that it possesses a certain dynamic character in his expression to us. Or, as Jenson neatly summarizes, Barth's

> first proposition is therefore that God is in himself no different than He is in His revelation. But in the life and works of Jesus Christ we have to do, not with static 'being,' but with an event, with happenings. It follows that God's being is also an event, a *deed,* and not the static peace of pure 'isness' which theologians have often described.[40]

The consequent task is to specify what sort of 'deed' God is, and so Barth will proceed to read from the economy of God's work into the immanent life of his being, with the logic running from countless directions to pick out the various attributes of the specific being God is in his act towards us.[41] For example, Barth sees that God's act towards us is free, and so concludes that God's being is pure freedom. He sees that God's act is decisive, and so his being is therefore a pure decision, and so on; and the outcome is key: what the entirety of God's act towards us looks like – when grasped as a structural whole – and therefore what God actually is, is an election. That is to say, an act of decisive choice that determines a people.[42]

At this point, the everyday sense of 'election' will help us cash out Barth's doctrine. Barth is saying that God is a timely authoritative act of freedom, which is the decisive choice both for and against possibilities, which is thereby God's personal act of self-determination to be the particular God that he is going forward; God elects to be this one and not that one, thereby establishing his character, and thus determining our future – a future in which we are included as conversation partners with God. Of course, this summary races ahead somewhat, because the previous sentence has ventured into the outcome of God's self-election, i.e. what is decided as a result. Nonetheless, the metaphysical structure of that outcome remains easy enough to grasp. The underlying question is '*What* is God?' and Barth is simply arguing that God's act shows us that what makes God to be God is the act of his own decision, or better: God is simply the act of that decisive choice, and that absolute act is the irrepressible choice in his own life to be God-with-us, namely, Jesus Christ, and him crucified and risen.[43]

In other words, 'The act of election, which is the event of the Godman's pre-existence, is an event in the eternal trinitarian life of God.'[44] Therefore, God's act of self-determining – his aseity, in classical terms – is the eternal act of a pure decision to be a particular God, with the transcendence of that act – i.e. its active purposeful playing out, its faithfulness to his own determinative will – being what Barth means by the covenantal nature of election.[45] In short, God elects God, and thereby there is God, because he is the decision which is the event of his own being. Thus, cashed out in full: God is the event of electing himself to be '*for* the rest of reality'.[46]

Now this is somewhat odd, although, as Jenson says, 'infinite being is [always] an odd sort of being'.[47] However, it is in fact not that strange. Barth has simply taken what he finds scattered across the dogmatic tradition and reconfigured it in line with the fundamental premise that God's being is in his successful act towards us in Jesus Christ.[48] For example, Barth identifies the way in which 'election' in Scripture is a historical act, in that God chooses Jacob not Esau, Israel not Babylon, one person, one people – and not the others – for 'an earthly mission'.[49] He also sees how the meaning gets changed in the West, with the focus – after Augustine – shifting from the historical vocation of a chosen people to the heavenly/hellish destination of every person, with the doctrine becoming more abstract in the process as it is separated from the historical communal realm by being given a teleological twist to make it have to do with where individual people end up; in other words, it becomes an 'eternal vision [about] a heavenly destination'.[50] Recognizing how the doctrine thereby becomes a matter of our eternal state rather than our historical calling, Barth sees how this leads into Calvin's famous treatment of the doctrine in Book III of the *Institutes*, and most notably his account of 'double predestination',[51] where the church reformer attempts to use the doctrine to rally the faithful by assuring the elect of their salvation to prevent them lapsing into works righteousness.[52] Calvin concluded that it is impossible to fall from grace, because God has always-already determined which of us are in (and which of us are out) in an inscrutable act of primordial decision by which our future destination is decided in the beginning by God's sovereign act of election. In short, an 'inexplicable fate' befalls us, because of the act of God's eternal hidden will.[53]

However, Barth saw how there is a twist in this tale. Calvin's attempt to find 'a cure for anxiety only reinforced the disease', because he argued that it was a hidden unknown God who elects, and that meant we couldn't know where we stand in the double predestination unless we display the consequent righteousness.[54] Hence, we all get back to work to prove we are 'in'. To counter this outcome, Barth argues that God's decree cannot be secret – that is, abstracted from the historical mission of particular people which the Bible presents – and so must in some sense be taken in Jesus Christ, who doesn't come after the hidden decision, as some sort of outworking, but is himself the decision being made for God and his people.[55] Otherwise put, there isn't another Word by which God decrees what's what, other than the one Word who is addressed to us, namely, Jesus, and him crucified.[56]

As a result of this move, Barth is doing something new, but he is using existing materials to do it. He simply takes all three dogmatic soundings – the historical, teleological and predestined nature of election – and spins and inverts them and thereby turns them inside out in his revisionary proposal that all three coincide in the public life and death of Jesus of Nazareth. In other words, his 'pathfinding' doctrine of election is the unity of the historical and the eternal united in the double predestination – election and rejection – of Jesus Christ who is the very public God doing God-with-us-and-for-us as the act that makes God to be God.[57] Or, to put that in his own words, Barth sees that 'Jesus Christ is the electing God',[58] God's self-constitutive 'yes' to us, and 'Jesus Christ is elected man',[59] our constitutive 'yes' to God, which is to say that Jesus is both the choosing and chosen one at the same time, because he is God himself venturing into the 'far country' so we can come home.[60]

As Jenson summarizes Barth, the entire 'dialectic of election and rejection . . . [is] the inner dialectic of the one person's, Jesus Christ's, story'.[61] As a result, there is no need for us to be anxious, because God travelled publicly into the dereliction of the 'far country' in order to say yes to us. Barth's central point, in other words, is that you can't bypass this electing God to some hidden double predestination because both happen in Jesus, with Barth thereby reconfiguring the existing doctrine by closing the gap between ontology and revelation and making us attentive to God's singular Word, who is Jesus. And so, as Jenson argues, 'At the end of it all we arrive at this: Jesus Christ, as lived and acted in Palestine, is the content of the eternal covenant.'[62]

To put the point otherwise, Jenson sees that only a God who is other, yet simultaneously present in genuine dwelling, could make a covenant by which a shared future for both parties in the covenant opens up. But for this to be God's covenant, without collapsing him into the event of its execution, it requires a 'covenantal' structure in God's own life, by which he can dwell with us while Lording it from beyond, so to speak. 'That is to say, his own life somehow has an antecedent covenantal structure', and that means a spoken Word, and a shared future of the parties, by which there is a Third – the Spirit of the covenant.[63] What is most important to note, however, is that Jenson spots how this leaves Barth with a question: is the historical act of God in Jesus Christ – which we are witnesses to in the event of revelation – replicating an already-decided eternal act or is it simply that act in and of itself?[64]

'It would seem that Barth can be read either way,' Jenson notes, or at least that is what the current 'Barth Wars' suggest.[65] However, what seems equally clear is that whichever way we cut it, the freedom of God is the issue; either way, he chooses.[66] Jenson thinks this can only leave us wondering whether God is so free that he is Lord over his own Being, or – to put that negatively – 'It is a great abiding failure of theology that freedom is not treated as – in its own way – constitutive in God and so in being'.[67] Of course, in some respects, Jenson knows that Barth answers that question with a resounding 'yes', in that God is sovereign over the ways of his being. As Jenson spots, this requires him offering a radical redefinition of eternity, in that it must be given a 'historical' character. That is because, as Jenson reads it, 'history is self-transcendence', in that it is a movement from what something is to what it is not, which in itself requires the present of 'that-which-I-am-not', in that 'an isolated being is necessarily a static ahistorical being'.[68] This insight is then aligned to the structuring of the triune life, in that the 'modes of being' move one to the other to be each other in their self-transcending communal history that is their freedom. But this is thereby seen to be a temporal structure of moving from what was, to what is, to what is to come, each of which Barth then sets within his account of the purity of God's historical eternity, in that the poles of 'time' do not fall away, as they do for us, but instead cohere as the full possession of the life this God freely lives in doing himself from eternity to eternity.[69] But even if this complex point is granted, the mechanics of it, so to speak, remain uncertain.

To put it otherwise, the question exercising Jenson is, *where does God's free act of decision happen*? No doubt an answer depends on what we mean by 'freedom', with at least two readings being possible. We can imagine a freedom *from*, in that God does himself in isolation. But at the same time, we can imagine a freedom *for*, in that God does himself with us.[70] Either way, the covenant – which is God's faithfulness – is the first of God's works, and we are not parties to it. Nonetheless, the question still remains as to whether this elective covenant is a work 'in' and 'upon' God himself (with creation as the external form for the theatre of God's out-doing of himself) or whether the time of creation is that act of internal self-determining.[71] Barth, it would seem, finds his proposal hovering uncomfortably in the dialectic between time and eternity. Or so thinks Jenson.

Now, this sketch does not come close to exhausting Barth's teaching in any way. It simply gestures towards it, so that we can catch sight of the actualistic ontology that becomes the presupposition of Jenson's own work. But we have begun to see the question Barth faced, and that Jenson will answer in his own way. Where does the eternal covenant that is God's freedom happen? In some respects, Jenson thinks Barth simply papers over the issue, noting that 'For the most part Barth is content to describe the relation with an "and". God has acted on our behalf from eternity *and then* in the centre of temporal history.'[72] But he adds, 'Very well – but it is just the meaning of this "and" that we want to discover.'[73] Jenson will therefore look to adopt and adapt Barth's doctrine of election with the aim of clarifying this 'and', thereby situating the act of decision slap bang in the middle of the history of the Father, Son and Spirit with us. That is to say, the covenant decision is acted out – and acted in, so to speak – right here in our presence. Or better put, God *is* because of God's act with us. That is to say, the eternal election happens in our midst, or, more accurately, in the environs of Jerusalem as he gives himself to us. God doesn't choose this life in abstraction from it; he *lives* it as his choice. In short, Jesus of Nazareth's journey into the far country is eternally definitive.[74]

6.5 Jenson's grounding of election

So, to Jenson. At the outset of his postgraduate studies, Jenson is steered towards Barth's theology.[75] He thereby discovers the way Barth pushes together divine revelation and divine ontology in the first volume of his *Dogmatics*, thus utilizing the structure of our knowledge of God to underwrite an account of the configuration of God's eternal life.[76] Jenson thereby appreciates the way Barth makes the unusual move of laying out the ways of God's being directly across the structure of revealer, revelation and revealedness to posit – via a 'backwards glance' – that only the triune God could be knowable in the way that this God is in fact known.[77] Jenson thus learns that God's act and God's being must go hand in hand, which is another way of saying God is identified *by* and *with* the revelatory event of his Word to us.[78]

Through the course of his studies, Jenson then spots how the material consequences of Barth's move only emerge downstream, when the relation between eternity and time comes into focus as Barth explores the relation between the incarnate Son and the eternal nature of God.[79] Having drawn act and being together so closely, Jenson knows it can only be a matter of time before Barth has to decide whether Jesus of Nazareth is the eternal Word or instead a gracious analogue to that Word, with whatever length – or type[80] – interval we posit in between. In effect, Barth must specify the way Jesus' time is related to God's eternity.[81]

Jenson knows Barth is grappling with a run-of-the-mill conundrum here. Every theologian must wrestle with the question of Jesus and the Trinity at some stage, because their entire project will be trading on the assumption that God's being is in his act towards us, in that God is not tricking us in the way he relates to us in Christ. This means theologians must explore the way God's being is in some sense bound up with the gospel event, which is precisely the issue Jenson thinks the church was wrestling with in the run up to Nicaea, by way of which a type of 'happening' was pushed up into the eternity of God's being. God was thereby deemed to be somehow an eternal begetting and procession by which his nature is the endless generative event of mutual communion in the differentiation of the singular threefold act that God does in our midst. But Jenson knows that the 'somehow' is everything.[82]

Jenson recognizes that the relation between time and eternity was never spelt out officially, and he spots how this deficit has allowed theologians to read whatever metaphysics they like into the trinitarian formula, meaning in turn that anyone can dodge the issue of the relation between the gospel's account of this one man's life, death and resurrection and God's being in itself.[83] This – according to Jenson – has meant Nicaea's revolutionary ontology was quickly undermined, because theologians can take the path of least resistance, thereby continuing to use the substance metaphysics, which means that God's being is considered in abstraction from the gospel narrative. To put that otherwise, theologians are free to forget precisely who the original discussion was about, Mary's boy and Pilate's victim, with the result that the divine nature can remain as static as ever, because it is not defined by the apostles' teaching that Jesus of Nazareth has been raised from the dead and now lives in the infinity of God's life.

In Jenson's judgement, the failure to define the relation between eternity and time leaves God's 'being' somehow distinct from his historical act, rather than being identified with it, with Jenson concluding that mere lip-service is then paid to the dynamic event-like reality of 'begetting' and 'procession', with God's essence remaining essentially unmoved.[84]

We are then left with an incarnate Son who is somehow related to an unfleshed Word, but again that 'somehow' is everything.[85] But, as Jenson reads Barth, he begins to see how Barth's doctrine of election has 'thrown the furniture around',[86] and thereby allows the question of the relation between temporal happenings and eternal states to be asked once again. In short, is Jesus of Nazareth the eternal Word the Father speaks, and no other?

As Jenson works his way through the second volume of Barth's *Dogmatics*, he begins to see that Barth may have found a way to say that God's being is in no way abstracted from the gospel event, being neither a close or distant analogue of the career of this particular Nazarene. Of course, the key to unlocking the puzzle is Barth's doctrine of election, which Jenson knows to pivot entirely on the freedom of God to choose who he will always forever be.[87] Jenson therefore begins to explore the way in which he can use Barth's metaphysical framework to conceptualize God's freedom so the act of God's self-determination happens in temporal form, in that God can choose the decisive way of his eternal existence from beginning to end, thereby allowing us to say that Jesus is the eternally spoken Word. As Jenson understands it, were Barth 'to hedge the "is" in any way, he would end up saying: God is *very like* Jesus. We are Christ's, *if* we do such and such . . . [and then] he would be repeating standard dishwater Protestantism and would have fallen back to a position well before the *Commentary on Romans*.'[88] As a result, Jenson thinks, 'now Barth has said it, let us take courage and proclaim Jesus Christ, without ambiguity, as the one for whom all things are made and done'.[89]

Jenson therefore begins to work out how God can be so free that he eternally chooses to be Mary's boy and Pilate's victim, in effect allowing the relation between the temporal missions and eternal processions to be approached with an eye on their coincidence.[90] That is to say, 'In *our* history God makes His *eternal* decision'.[91] As he then sets out to explain how time and eternity can be identified in this way, he begins with the assumption that we are dealing with the 'one protagonist' that the gospel presents, and then begins to create the necessary metaphysical structure by which the temporal birthing and eternal begetting can be conceived as a single act by which Mary is genuinely the Mother of God 'without needing to be a goddess to achieve this'.[92] Jenson's brilliance is in offering us a framework in which this odd statement makes sense, although he knows he has little choice if we are to avoid driving a wedge between Jesus and the Son. As Gaghan puts it, Jenson

> bridges the chasm between the works of God *ad extra* and God's identity *ad intra* by contending that 'God is so identified *by* the risen Jesus

and his community as to be identified *with* them.' If this were not so and God is other than the way he appears in history, Jenson's entire theological enterprise would disintegrate as God's involvement in history is the epistemic foundation from which all theological claims derive.[93]

As a result, Jenson wants to 'speak more unequivocally than Barth of the life of Jesus Christ in our history, of His life in created time and space', but to do so in a way in which this life is the pure act of God's self-determining decision.[94] In short, Jenson thinks God happens with us, and only if we go with this radical conclusion will we be 'free of the nagging worry – which sometimes we feel in Barth's case – that we may after all be speaking of a different history from that which took place in Palestine and now takes place in our churches'.[95] Our task, therefore, is to see how Jenson grounds his doctrine of eternal election in what happens with Jesus. In short, we must explore what it means to say God *became* man. As a result, we finally turn 'to the business', as Jenson once said.[96]

Notes

1 Put otherwise, Jenson thinks, 'The relations are either *temporal* relations or empty verbiage.' Robert W. Jenson, *The Triune Identity: God According to the Gospel* (Philadelphia: Fortress, 1982; reprint, Eugene, OR: Wipf and Stock, 2002), 126.

2 Robert W. Jenson, *Systematic Theology, Volume 1, The Triune God* (New York: OUP, 1997), 114.

3 Jenson, *Triune Identity*, 140. See also Robert W. Jenson, 'The Triune God', in *Christian Dogmatics*, ed. Carl E. Braaten and Robert W. Jenson (Philadelphia: Fortress, 1984), 154.

4 Robert W. Jenson, *Essays in Theology of Culture* (Grand Rapids: Eerdmans, 1995), 92.

5 This chapter will likely frustrate Barth scholars. However, Barth's theology is not what's at stake here, as I am more interested in showing his impact on Jenson's thought. We are therefore dealing with my reading of *the impact* of Jenson's own reading of Barth on Jenson's thinking, rather than Barth himself. It's the Barth we see *through* Jenson.

6 Robert W. Jenson, 'Jesus, Father, Spirit: The Logic of the Doctrine of the Trinity', *Dialog* 26.4 (1987), 249.

7 Robert W. Jenson, 'Basics and Christology', in *In Search of Christian Unity: Basic Consensus/Basic Differences*, ed. Joseph A. Burgess (Minneapolis: Fortress Press, 1991), 47.

8 Barth's impact on Jenson is plain throughout his work. As Jenson puts it, 'I am convinced that Barth's thought is a watershed in the history of theology, that discussion must now be pursued for or against Barth, and that a theological

PART THREE | JENSON'S DOCTRINE OF GOD

position must now be dated before or after Barth. Ignorance of the central core of Barth's thought dooms any contemporary theologian to obsolescence even before he begins to speak.' Robert W. Jenson, *Alpha and Omega: A Study in the Theology of Karl Barth* (New York: Thomas Nelson & Sons, 1963; reprint, Eugene, OR: Wipf and Stock, 2002), 19.

9 The current 'Barth Wars' centre on the question of how best to read Barth. The issue boils down to whether apparent inconsistencies within Barth's work are intentional or whether instead Barth only finds his true voice in the later stages of his career, thereby moving on from his earlier thinking (even if he can't admit to doing so). For a helpful summary of the current state of play, see Philip Cary, 'The Barth Wars; A Review of Reading Barth with Charity', *First Things*, April 2015. For some of the key texts, see George Hunsinger, *Reading Barth with Charity: A Hermeneutical Proposal* (Grand Rapids: Baker Academic, 2015); Bruce L. McCormack, 'Election and the Trinity: Theses in Response to George Hunsinger', *Scottish Journal of Theology* 63 (2010), 203–24; Bruce L. McCormack, 'Grace and Being: The Role of God's Gracious Election in Karl Barth's Theological Ontology', in *The Cambridge Companion to Karl Barth*, ed. John Webster (Cambridge: Cambridge University Press, 2000), 92–110; and Bruce L. McCormack, 'Let's Speak Plainly: A Response to Paul Molnar', *Theology Today* 67 (2010), 57–65.

10 On reading these final sentences, Chris Green added, 'the windows are down and the music is up'.

11 Bruce L. McCormack notes how Jenson – in his 'own inimitable way' – had pre-empted pretty much everything McCormack was later to argue about Barth. See Bruce L. McCormack, 'In Memoriam: Robert Jenson (1930–2017)', *International Journal of Systematic Theology* 20.1 (2018), 7. Thanks to Matt Key for this reference.

12 For an example of the way Jenson disagrees with Barth, see Robert W. Jenson, 'You Wonder Where the Spirit Went', *Pro Ecclesia* 2.3 (1993), 296–304.

13 See his critique of Barth's prioritizing of the 'primal reality' of Jesus, not 'final reality', in Jenson, *Triune Identity*, 180.

14 Jenson often makes clear – to use one example – that Barth's 'influence has been persuasive through this entire study, and that must here be explicitly acknowledged. But his contribution to required new trinitarian *analysis* is not so great as might be expected, nor does he carry us to full liberation from a past-determined interpretation of God. There is room for further reflection.' Jenson, *Triune Identity*, 138.

15 That is because, as Jenson puts it, Barth's *Dogmatics* is 'an enormous attempt to interpret all reality by the fact of Christ; indeed it can be read as the first truly major system of metaphysics since the collapse of Hegelianism. One need not adopt all Barth's characteristic theologoumena to take this massive work as model and challenge in this respect.' Jenson, *Systematic Theology*, Vol. 1, 21.

16 See Jenson, *Alpha and Omega*.

17 Karl Barth, 'No Angels of Darkness and Light', *Christian Century* (20 January 1960), 75, cited in D. Stephen Long, 'Responses to Reviewers: Identifying What Matters Most', *Pro Ecclesia* 24.2 (2015), 157. As Jenson recounts, 'Barth invited me to his study, and after some conversation said, "Aber Herr Jenson – Sie haben mich verstanden," "But Mr. Jenson – you have understood me." A bit later an interviewer for the Christian Century asked Barth if anyone had grasped the real center of his thinking. Barth answered that there was "one, a young American." Subsequently I was identified by name in the journal as the

one – not by me.' Robert W. Jenson, 'D. Stephen Long's *Saving Karl Barth*: An Agent's Perspective', *Pro Ecclesia* 24.2 (2015), 132.

18 Robert W. Jenson, 'What Kind of God Can Make a Covenant?' in *Covenant and Hope: Christian and Jewish Reflections*, ed. Robert W. Jenson and Eugene B. Korn (Grand Rapids: Eerdmans, 2012), 9.

19 As a result, Jenson's final words in the published version of his doctoral research on Barth read like an executive summary of Jenson's own career: 'For all Barth's works want only to point to Him, the Alpha and Omega.' Jenson, *Alpha and Omega*, 171.

20 Robert W. Jenson, 'Karl Barth on the Being of God', in *Thomas Aquinas and Karl Barth: An Unofficial Catholic-Protestant Dialogue*, ed. Bruce L. McCormack and Thomas Joseph White (Grand Rapids: Eerdmans, 2013), 43–51.

21 Andrew J. Stobart, 'A Constructive Analysis of the Place and Role of the Doctrine of Jesus' Resurrection Within the Theologies of Rowan Williams and Robert Jenson', PhD Thesis, University of Aberdeen, 2011, 160-1.

22 Jenson is not always mentioned by name, but is often associated with anti-Augustine polemics. However, Scott Swain does directly critique Jenson's reading, offering counterpoints to Jenson's anti-Augustine statements. As Swain puts it, Jenson's 'reading has been largely refuted in recent scholarly literature'. Scott R. Swain, *The God of the Gospel: Robert Jenson's Trinitarian Theology* (Downers Grover: IVP, 2013), 130-1, esp n47.

23 As Chris Green puts it, Jenson is more like an artist than a scientist, and therefore would probably have been wise to qualify his confident use of 'Augustine said . . .' etc., by adding phrases like a 'On one reading of Augustine . . .' Chris E. W. Green, in correspondence and used with permission.

24 Jenson, 'Karl Barth', 43-4.

25 Jenson, 'Karl Barth', 45.

26 Jenson, 'Karl Barth', 51. Unusual emphasis in original.

27 Barth's doctrine of election can be found in Karl Barth, *Church Dogmatics* II.2 *The Doctrine of God* (Edinburgh: T&T Clark, 1957), chapter VII.

28 With this noted, an aside: part of the problem, as Jenson rightly notes, is that Barth 'devotes an astonishing 563 pages of the *Church Dogmatics* to election'. In other words, it is the quantity, not the distinct use of the concept, that makes it so hard to fathom. Jenson, *Alpha and Omega*, 141.

29 As we have already caught sight of – and will soon see – the everyday concept of 'became' changes radically when Jenson uses it.

30 This is Gilbert Ryle's phrase, cited in Colin E. Gunton, *A Brief Theology of Revelation* (London: T&T Clark, 1995), 113.

31 Bruce McCormack, *Karl Barth's Critically Realistic Dialectical Theology: Its Genesis and Development 1909–1936* (Oxford: Clarendon Press, 1995), 425.

32 Of course, a direct democracy might make it constant, but that exception only proves the rule.

33 You cannot vote both 'yes' and 'no' in a referendum, for instance, though transferable votes may muddy the waters here, but not beyond use.

34 Barth, *Church Dogmatics* II.2, 3.

35 Having used the phrase 'behappens himself', Jenson adds: 'It seems to me that someone who wished to say what Barth says, might simply say that and fall silent'. Jenson, 'Karl Barth', 47.

36 The rationale for making election primary in Christian thinking centres on the existence of Israel, 'understood as a *choice*'. Jenson, *Triune Identity*, 36.

37 Jenson does write on the hiddenness of God, with primary reference to Luther's work. See Robert W. Jenson, 'The Hidden and Triune God', *International Journal of Systematic Theology* 2.1 (2000), 5–12. The primary point, as he sees it, is that 'God is hidden precisely by his ineluctable nearness to us'. Jenson, *Triune Identity*, 27. See also, Robert W. Jenson, *Systematic Theology, Volume 2, The Works of God* (New York: OUP, 1999), 161–2.

38 Karl Barth, *Church Dogmatics* I.1 *The Doctrine of the Word of God*, 2nd edition (Edinburgh: T&T Clark, 1975), especially chapters I and II.

39 Barth, *Church Dogmatics* I.1, especially paragraph 6.

40 Jenson, *Alpha and Omega*, 69.

41 See Karl Barth, *Church Dogmatics* II.1 *The Doctrine of God* (Edinburgh: T&T Clark, 1957), on 'The Perfections of the Divine Loving' and 'The Perfections of the Divine Freedom.'

42 Jenson, 'Karl Barth', 49–50.

43 Barth, *Church Dogmatics* II.2, especially paragraph 33 on 'The Election of Jesus Christ'.

44 Jenson, *Alpha and Omega*, 74.

45 See summary in Jenson, *Alpha and Omega*, 54.

46 Jenson, 'Karl Barth', 51.

47 Jenson, *Triune Identity*, 163.

48 In this section, my work uses notes taken during Colin Gunton's Barth lectures, which I attended as a postgraduate at King's College, London. The lectures have been published posthumously as Colin E. Gunton, *The Barth Lectures*, ed. P. H. Brazier (London: T&T Clark, 2007), with quotes taken from Brazier's transcript.

49 Gunton, *Barth Lectures*, 110–11. Jenson makes the point about the particularity of election in Jenson, *Alpha and Omega*, 144.

50 Gunton, *Barth Lectures*, 111–12.

51 For Jenson's treatment of this doctrine in conversation with Barth, see Jenson, *Systematic Theology*, Vol. 2, 174–5.

52 Gunton, *Barth Lectures*, 112–13.

53 Gunton, *Barth Lectures*, 112.

54 Gunton, *Barth Lectures*, 112. Jenson sees how Barth's analysis shatters the concept of Christ 'mirroring' an original decision, as 'the mirror will be impossible to trust completely'. Jenson, *Alpha and Omega*, 144.

55 Jenson, *Alpha and Omega*, 143.

56 Jenson, *Alpha and Omega*, 143.

57 Jenson, *Systematic Theology*, Vol. 2, 175–6.

58 Barth, *Church Dogmatics* II.2, 103.

59 Barth, *Church Dogmatics* II.2, 116.

60 This is the key image in Barth's account of reconciliation. Karl Barth, *Church Dogmatics* IV.1 *The Doctrine of Reconciliation* (Edinburgh: T&T Clark, 1956), 157–210.

61 Jenson, *Systematic Theology*, Vol. 2, 176.

62 Jenson, *Alpha and Omega*, 51. See also the fuller discussion, 66–74.

63 Jenson, 'What Kind of God', 8.

64 See, for example, Jenson's discussion of a 'third' reality distinct from the eternal Son and the man, i.e. 'the reality of the choice in which the Son chooses to be *and* is one with man'. Jenson, *Alpha and Omega*, 67–8 (67).

65 Jenson, 'Karl Barth', 49.

66 Jenson, 'Karl Barth', 50–1.

67 Robert W. Jenson, 'Lutheranism and the *Filioque*', in *Ecumenical Perspectives on the Filioque for the 21st Century*, ed. Myk Habets (London: T&T Clark, 2014), 165.

68 Jenson, *Alpha and Omega*, 75.

69 Jenson, *Alpha and Omega*, 75–6.

70 See Jenson on freedom as enrapture in Robert W. Jenson, 'An Ontology of Freedom in the *De Servo Arbitrio* of Luther', *Modern Theology* 10.3 (1994), 247–52.

71 Jenson discusses Barth's proposal that 'the covenant is the *inner basis* of creation' in Jenson, *Alpha and Omega*, 94–6.

72 Jenson, *Alpha and Omega*, 84.

73 Jenson, *Alpha and Omega*, 85. Jenson knows Barth spells things out more clearly than a mere 'and', detailing the way the concepts of 'implementation' and 'revelation' explain the link between the eternal decision and what happens in time as 'Christ's *prophetic* office' (85–6). Jenson is therefore aware Barth's account is more complex than my summary makes out, understanding that God's eternal decision *is* the decision *that* the decision be lived out amid witnesses. This means a two-step view of Barth's account of God's movement from eternity to time 'would be entirely erroneous', because the 'first' decision *is* the decision for the 'second'. Jenson, *Alpha and Omega*, 90–2.

74 Jenson's concluding comments on Barth reveal the way he reads him, in that the implications of Barth's proposal are clear: 'If what happened in Christ is really God's will for us, if it is not secondary to a prior, abstract, and largely unknown will of God, then it indeed follows that God's decision to be merciful falls not "above" but *in* the life of Jesus Christ. His life is this decision.' Jenson, *Alpha and Omega*, 146. Jenson's final reflections in the book show the way in which he decides right at the beginning of his career that it is 'the history of the Crucified and Risen' that is itself the act of election (156).

75 Jenson therefore calls Barth, 'the archetype, inspiration, and major achiever' of recent attempts to set the doctrine of God on the gospel's terms. Jenson, 'Jesus, Father, Spirit', 249.

76 'The entire doctrine of the Trinity, [Barth] says, is but specification of which God it is that *can* so reveal himself as in fact happens with Christ.' Jenson, *Triune Identity*, 137.

77 Jenson, *Triune Identity*, 137.

78 'The divine being *is* that very lordship that occurs in God's act of triune revelation.' Jenson, *Triune Identity*, 138.

79 See Jenson wrestling with this issue in Jenson, *Alpha and Omega*, 84–93.

80 This qualification indicates the difference between the analogy of being and the analogy of faith, with analogy amounting to the family resemblance between the two.

81 See Jenson's discussion of *eternal history* as *primal history*. Jenson, *Alpha and Omega*, 74–8.

82 Of course, the 'somehow' was intrinsic to the debate, in that the difference between spirating and begetting was never spelt out. Jenson, *Systematic Theology*, Vol. 1, 102.

83 In his words, the church 'overcame pagan antiquity's revulsion at the obtrusively temporal facts of gestation and childbirth . . . [but] the disinclination has continued underground'. Jenson, *Systematic Theology*, Vol. 1, 49–50.

84 Jenson lays a lot of blame for this at the feet of Augustine, notably the bishop's self-confessed failure to grasp the distinction between *ousia* and *hypostasis* in Cappadocian theology. See, for example, Jenson, *Systematic Theology*, Vol. 1, 110–11.

85 See, for example, the double stress Jenson places on 'somehow' in Jenson, *Systematic Theology*, Vol. 1, 127.

86 The image is O'Conner's: 'I distrust folks who have ugly things to say about Karl Barth. I like old Barth. He throws the furniture around'. See Stephen N. Williams, *The Election of Grace: A Riddle without a Resolution?* (Grand Rapids: Eerdmans, 2015), 179.

87 As Jenson sees it, election must be the key to this, otherwise the God of Exodus and Resurrection is no more than 'a double illusion'. Jenson, *Systematic Theology*, Vol. 1, 53.

88 Robert W, Jenson, *God After God: The God of the Past and the God of the Future As Seen in the Work of Karl Barth* (Minneapolis: Fortress, 2010), 74.

89 Jenson, *Alpha and Omega*, 169.

90 Jenson, *Systematic Theology*, Vol. 1, 140–1.

91 Jenson, *Alpha and Omega*, 163.

92 Robert W. Jenson, 'For us . . . He Was Made Man', in *Nicene Christianity: The Future for a New Ecumenism*, ed. Christopher R. Seitz (Grand Rapids: Brazos, 2001), 83–4.

93 Josh Gaghan, 'Reason, Metaphysics, and their Relationship in the Theologies of Jenson and Aquinas', *New Blackfriars* 99.1082 (2018), 533.

94 Jenson, *Alpha and Omega*, 163.

95 Jenson, *Alpha and Omega*, 170.

96 Robert W. Jenson, 'A Lutheran Among Friendly Pentecostals', *Journal of Pentecostal Theology* 20 (2011), 48–53 (49).

7

One Dramatic Act, Two Terms

7.1 Avoiding confusion: God does the difference

Jenson's signature move is to stick with Mary's boy and Pilate's victim. He is therefore prepared to rethink the most basic features of our reality, so that they all spring from his unshakeable belief that the God of Israel raised Jesus from the dead. With this being so, time and eternity are soon aligned, because Jenson thinks the life of this finite Nazarene – who now lives with death behind him – is in some sense infinite. Thus, he wants to show how 'this particular human individual with all his peculiarities . . . *is* the second identity of God'.[1]

Of course, Jenson knows his account of the infinity of Jesus can look problematic. God's being – what makes God to be God – looks to have been historicized, because of the way Jenson identifies the trajectory of this one man's temporal life with the Son's eternal begotten-ness. At first glance, this would appear to confuse the Creator with the creature, so that it looks like God could only ever be the God that he is on the basis of the creation's prior existence. In short, God is not free. Instead, he needs us.

I think we must reckon with this issue before we get any further into Jenson's constructive proposal. If Jesus is truly God 'without qualification',[2] then it would certainly suggest the creaturely reality of Nazareth – and its population, and so on – is somehow necessary for God to be the God that he is. And that is anathema for the Christian. We believe God created the world in total freedom, summoning us 'out of nothing' into his company, and with no intrinsic or extrinsic force compelling him in the process. As a result, creation is in no way necessary for God, and so it certainly looks to be problematic when Jenson – to take but one example – claims, 'the one God is an *event;* history occurs not only in him *but as his being.*'[3]

I flag this up before we get into the nitty-gritty of Jenson's proposal, because Jenson often makes it look like God is caught up in the historical process of his own theogony, his own birth. That is why his system has been described as a form of '"dialectical historicism" with a trinitarian and teleological contour', in that the struggle between God and creatures in the drama of Christ appears to produce God only consequently at the end.[4] But Jenson disagrees. He thinks the charge is fundamentally misconceived, because his proposal is being read through the lens of the dominant metaphysics that he is trying to evangelize. In other words, his novel proposal should not be judged on the basis of a conception of reality we have already adopted, which is why we must take seriously Jenson's attempt to maintain the sheer difference between God and creation, even if he describes the difference in a highly unusual manner and with varying degrees of success.

Jenson accepts that the qualitative difference between God and creation is 'the first axiom'.[5] However, he thinks much more needs to be said about how this axiom should be understood. As he sees it, the difference is something *done* by God in the act of his being, by which the Father jealously ensures Jesus of Nazareth alone is the eternal Son of God.[6] This act-pivoting approach means some of the conceptual categories we usually work with get blurred, in that it is not the case that there are two realities – God and creation – fixed in their sheer difference and thereby possessing a heap of characteristics that are attributable to them in abstraction from the drama of Christ (as if it is simply a matter of lining up God and creation, and then ascribing omni-this, that and the other to one side of the pairing, and beginnings and endings to the other). Instead, Jenson thinks it is better to imagine God and creation within the singular act of the selfsame God, being two terms of that one act, but without thereby implying that the Father is ever confused about who his one and only Son is, and which are his adopted children. Therefore, even if the family resemblance between the Son and the creatures is extremely close within the eventual life of the Spirit they share, the active difference between Jesus and creation is finally a matter of their ongoing relation to the Father – and relation is everything when it comes to God and his ways. Therein lies the difference.

To put the matter otherwise, Jenson thinks God's freedom in relation to the creature is the possibility exemplified in Gethsemane, where the Son could have said 'no' to us and thereby seek to curve in towards his Father alone, thus being a different God in abstraction from us.[7] Or, to put that more positively, God's freedom is the Son's faithfulness to the creature within the one act God is, whereby he upholds the creature in the freedom of our distinct communion with his Father in the Spirit as his siblings.[8] And that is to say,

> The 'infinite qualitative difference' between God and us indeed obtains, but it is not a barrier between God and us; on the contrary, as this

difference is enacted in the death and resurrection of Christ, it constitutes God's identification with us.[9]

In other words, Jenson thinks God can, 'distinguish himself from others not by excluding them but by including them',[10] and that means the difference between God and creation is absolute, even if the birthing and begetting of the Son coincide, because the Father relates to this Son uniquely, *so that* we may be found in him.[11] In short, God is so different he can do the difference in the act of transcending the difference to make us one in Christ.

As this opening section makes clear, Jenson will keep sight of the difference between God and creation at all times and work hard to avoid their confusion. He may understand the matter in an idiosyncratic way, but the distinction is there nonetheless. As a result, we cannot dismiss his proposal on the grounds of confusing Creator and creature but must enquire instead as to how it works out in Jenson's constructive proposal. And, as expected, the *hypostasis* of the Son is central to that.

7.2 The two directions of the Son

To recall: Jenson thinks our primary task is to identify the real God from the 'putative' gods, and so the results of that work should never be decided in advance. We do not begin the theological task knowing the outcome of our work, because we do not possess a photofit by which we can measure the various candidates on offer. As a result, a conclusion is obvious. We cannot stop God being a lot stranger than we might at first imagine.

With this possibility in mind, Jenson thinks the Christian must begin somewhere if they are to get on with the task of identifying which God is the true God, and so he decides to launch from the gospel-premise that 'the God of Israel raised his servant Jesus from the dead'.[12] The act of resurrection thereby provides us with a focus, from which we must draw conceptual materials to work out the structure of the eternity by which we are enveloped in time. In other words, God must be identified *by* and *with* what happens in the garden tomb, rather than this unique event amounting to little more than a flickering image of an alternative reality, long since established on the far side of a metaphysical chasm.[13]

Of course, we have seen how Jenson learns from Barth that epistemology and ontology must run hand in hand, so that God's being must be identified *with*, and not only *by*, his act with us. However, Jenson thinks this is why we must finally reject Barth's idea that God's act of election happens in some atemporal eternity, being only subsequently extended into time. Instead, Jenson wants to ensure our identification of God remains centred on the story we tell of Jesus, and he finds no warrant in that story to evacuate it for a more primary one about a timeless covenant. That move would simply leverage open a space between God's act in himself and his act towards us, and to such an extent that we would have two acts, meaning that God in himself remains at a distance, with all sorts of mysterious 'extensions' being required to bridge the resulting gap.

To avoid this outcome, Jenson dares to think God happens with us. That is to say, he agrees with Barth that the event of God's decision to be Jesus constitutes the very being of God.[14] But, with that premise in place, Jenson refuses to believe that anything can prevent the historical act of resurrection being the eternal covenant itself.[15] As a result, he begins to revise Barth's doctrine of election, not so much in its structure – which he adopts pretty much unchanged – but more in the sense of *where* the act of election happens.[16] With no warrant in the gospel narrative for distinguishing the Father's Son from Mary's boy – other than the pressure of an entire rival metaphysics – the only way forward is to draw the covenantal act of election into the nexus of the historical relations which together constitute the story of the gospel.[17] And that is what Jenson does, and with startling results.

Jenson begins to explore the way in which we can identify the being of God *by* and *with* the precise plot of Jesus' life, thereby 'riding the waves of the story' to construct a vision of God as the eternal decision by which he establishes who he always forever will be. He thereby posits the Father as the un-get-behind-able most basic reality, who is nothing other than the verbal expression of his own sheerly contingent identity, which is the inescapable Presence of the thereby expressed Son. This Son is Jesus, and it is precisely this selfsame Jesus who – by the act of God's own can't-get-beyond-able future – is raised to be the infinite reality of who God will decisively be. What is most remarkable, therefore, is how the plot of the gospel – the narratable event of the life, death and resurrection of Jesus – is understood to be God essentially turning to himself through himself to possess himself as the act of his own being, with the twist centring on the fact that God decides that us lot will be thrown in as well. In short, God does God-with-the-creature, because Mary's boy and Pilate's victim is his infinite address.[18]

Now, this is clearly a complex matter, so we need to run at it from several directions. First, we can see that Jenson's God is absolutely *public*. His eternal decision is the speaking of the Son's journey from the womb to the grave by which the last word – 'it is finished' – is the termination of the Son's distinct identity as 'utterly-directed-towards-that-which-God-is-not'. In other words, the individuating terminal of the Son's hypostatic being on a Roman gallows amounts to the posing of a question to his Father, who is himself nothing other than the originating pole of this selfsame trajectory, in which the entire reality of God's eternal life pivots on *'whether you will be the Father of me, your Son, who lives so fully for these others – even unto death – that my identity is nothing other than the prioritizing of these others unconditionally, so that it weds who I am for you to these creatures who are killing me.?'* The resurrection is the Father's resounding 'Yes'. He wants to be 'stuck' with us too.[19]

By drawing the covenantal act into the gospel narrative in this way, Jenson argues that the crucifixion determines *which* sort of God there will be, with the resurrection establishing *that* this God is. Or, as Jenson puts it:

> *Who* and *what* is the God of Scripture is settled by the life and death of Jesus. The Father determines what it means to be God by looking to the one identified by this particular life and this particular death. *That* this God is in fact God is settled by Jesus' resurrection.[20]

Jenson's conclusion is again trading on his belief that there is only one *hypostasis* in Jesus, whose singular identity is irreducibly tied up with God and with man. But – and here is the second point – it is vital we grasp how Jenson is reworking the concept of *hypostasis* in this account.[21] The Son's *hypostasis* is not static, in the sense of being a 'puddingy-type substance', which stands under the accidental contingencies of his temporal life.[22] Instead, the *hypostasis* is the 'vectored' relation, so to speak, of this singular life in relation to the other *hypostases*, both divine and human.[23] In other words, Jenson thinks the Son's *hypostasis* is divine in mutual relation to his Father, but also – by developing his relational ontology along creaturely lines – posits the simultaneity of another axis, so to speak, by which the identity of this selfsame Son is established in mutuality with the created order, thereby drawing all things into communion with his Father at the exact same time in determinative fashion. In short, the Son lives two directions, so to speak, and thereby defines God and creature.

This is a vital point, and we will focus on it primarily in the next chapter where we will discover how the Son's double horizon is similar to the way in which the Father generates both the Son and the Spirit *singularly*. Here, however, we need only note the way Jenson thinks the witness of Scripture 'confuses simple vertical-horizontal coordinates past rescue'.[24] With that in mind, he proceeds to sharpen his proposal, emphasizing again and again that there is only one identity in Jesus, with this one – who is Jesus of Nazareth – doing both God and man at the same time. In effect, the Son's *hypostasis* is unstoppably for the other, but this is at once his absolute obedience to his Father's command – which is what he is – and the outward vector of that selflessness towards the creature in the unconditionality of his death on a cross. To put that otherwise, Jesus is the Man for Others *eternally*, which is his relation to his Father. Jesus is the Man for Others *temporally*, which is his relation to us. *And* Jesus is the personal unity of the two. That is the hypostatic union considered dynamically.

Now this is obviously piling another complex idea onto a series of complex ideas, although it is worth remembering that the hypostatic union will be the point where any explanation runs aground. There isn't a series of logical steps towards understanding the way by which God becomes man (while still being God), which is why Jenson thinks we must be careful about how we understand the concept of 'becoming'. It is far too easy for our existing metaphysics to get to work unnoticed, thereby assuming what happens in Mary's womb is the coming together of two separate – and previously existing – realities in a discrete moment, which is thereby the miracle of an instant act of union, which is then somehow established in independence of what then follows. But Jenson questions whether we can assume the hypostatic union is simply an inexplicably punctiliar act outside history, by which God enters history to unite himself with creaturely nature.[25] Instead, there is no reason why the act of 'becoming' cannot be a lot stranger than that. Why can't it be the extended span of Jesus' life, death and resurrection that constitute the hypostatic union? In short, the whole is the singular act of becoming.

In other words, Jenson's metaphysics allows him to handle the hypostatic union in a novel way. Because the 'substance' of both natures is not static, and thereby isolatable in that sense, Jenson can handle the span – the trajectory – of this singular life, from the womb to the tomb, in his account of what amounts to God's *hypostatic* union with our humanity. He is not looking for anything 'standing under' the accidents of this temporal span, but instead wants to trace the vectors of the plot line we recount to make sense of what's happening. As a result, the Son's *hypostasis* – which is his specific being as the concrete actuality of Jesus' life – is established along the horizontal trajectory of vectored communion. And by horizontal, I mean *horizon*. The entire life of the Nazarene is the act of assumption that terminates definitively in death, whereby the Son's identity as both God and man is sealed.

To put the point otherwise, Jenson thinks it is the end – the *telos* – that makes anything the thing that it is. He therefore wonders whether the Son's *hypostasis* needs to be seen as the coherence of a series of contingent episodes so that the Son is simply the life that he lives to his end, *for us*. In short, we need to see the Son's 'very individuality is his unhindered way to others',²⁶ so that 'He is risen into the future that God has *for creatures*'.²⁷ And that future is God.

Of course, much more needs to be said about all this as well. But we can see that whereas Barth argued Jesus *is* the electing God and the elected man, Jenson instead wants to flesh that out historically, preferring to say that 'One of the Trinity is a Palestinian Jew who came eating and drinking etc.' That is because he thinks Barth's '*is*' – in 'Jesus Christ is the electing God' – can be read in different ways, with the possibility remaining that the perceived *hypostasis* is absolutely punctiliar, and into which the timeless stasis of the substance metaphysics can then be read. Jenson, in contrast, thinks the Son is utterly alive, so the concept of *hypostasis* needs to be developed into the dynamic actuality of explicitly 'eating and drinking' along the way. That is to say, the Son is nothing other than the life he in fact lives, in obedience to his Father for us. Or to put that otherwise: the eternal procession is a relation without a term and the incarnation is that precise relation *with a term*, namely, the life Jesus lives from conception unto death. The question, of course, is – once again! – how on earth does that work?

7.3 The speed of God's being

Jenson is attempting to solve the puzzle of the relation between the being of God and the works of God by shifting the axis of the usual equation, refusing to think in the punctiliar terms of the substance metaphysics – with one lying alongside the other – but instead thinking in a more linear fashion. He will argue that the Son is simultaneously related to his Father eternally and to us in time, although this double horizon will get a twist. Jenson will claim the immanent Trinity is the economic Trinity eschatologically, in that God does God in the End, thereby forever being God-with-us.²⁸

In other words, Jenson thinks the two vectors of 'vertical' and 'horizontal' are flattened out, so to speak, so that the difference is not in direction but in pace.²⁹ He argues that God is so utterly alive that we cannot keep up with him, in that God is always prior to us, sheerly unbegotten, and ahead of us, as the future posed to us, but moving in the same arrowed direction as the present we live in his journey with us.³⁰ Of course, this will again sound weird, but in many respects Jenson's account is simply pivoting on the belief that God is a 'pure act'. This clearly puts him in good company, in that *actus purus* is a classical concept by which theologians posit that God suffers no potentiality, in that his existence and essence coincide so that he is always forever what he is in his irresistible freedom.³¹ But Jenson has drawn this act of self-determination into creaturely history, so that he has opened up some temporal space, so to speak, in the eternal act of God's self-existence, by which God can be said to do God as the time he makes to quicken us. What makes the act-that-God-is pure is that *act* and *doer* are one, but not in the sense of strict identity, in which the one swallows up any difference between the Three agencies – usually by leading to an account of simplicity in which the attributes all cash out into each other and God ends up claustrophobically one, in the sense that there is no space for difference between the Persons – but instead in the *perichoresis* that is their dramatic coherence from End to Beginning. In other words, it is the absolute coherence of the singular plot of these Three that renders it pure, in that there is no deviation within the singular movement of God *being* the story he tells himself.

This is another unusual claim. However, Jenson knows controversy comes with the territory. It is always hard for us to imagine how an act *and* the doer of that act can be absolutely one. We tend to imagine there has to be a someone to do anything, so it is impossible to imagine how God is the act of doing himself personally, so that the act that he does coincides with who he is, in that he 'behappens himself', as Jenson puts it.[32] What is important to note, however, is that the structure of the act – that God is – can be conceived in different ways, depending on which metaphysics is driving the conceptual apparatus. That is to say, we can all agree that God's act is pure, but differ in our account of how it is so.

By introducing the concept of pace into the discussion, Jenson hopes to avoid the static nature of a pure act by positing the speed of the act in which God is – and *is* in two directions. In other words, he thinks God happens quicker than any metric – any mode of measurement – other than himself, because first and foremost there is only himself, with all else that exists being temporal pursuits of the event that he is. And the event that he is, is timely.[33] In other words, Jenson thinks the metric God *is* can only be the structure of the relations between the Whence, Whither and specious Present of the life that Jesus lives from his Father to their Spirit. It is the irresistible and unstoppable pace of the movement from Beginning to End that is pure, meaning there is no resistance to the frequency of God's desire to be like *this*.[34] Jenson therefore argues that God, from our perspective, is

> an event that cannot be transcended, which is inescapable in all temporal dimensions. He is never something that has happened and so is over and done with. Yet neither is he only our present, but has always already happened. And again he is purely future, the not-yet we await. Because there is no way past the temporality of God's action, there is no static 'essence' of God behind God's act ... God *is* the event of what happens with Jesus.[35]

In effect, Jenson is claiming that both horizons correlate, but happen at a different speed. God goes ahead of us, as it were, to draw the creature in his wake, thereby making him the God that he is. Once again odd, but not impossible.

To put the point yet another way, the question exercising Jenson is again to do with location: where does God do the pure act of himself? Of course, Jenson knows it is 'an ancient maxim [that] "God is his own space"', and so it can only make sense to say that he does himself in the simplicity of his own being, which he does. But Jenson thinks this cannot rule out the 'roominess' of that space, so to speak.[36] *That* God is the possession of his own extension is clear, being where he comes from and gets to, as well as the journey in between. This must be something along the lines of what *begetting* and *spirating* mean, in that there is a genuine coming forth, a going towards, a movement, which is what makes God a happening, even if it is a movement within the life that God himself is and therefore necessarily motionless because it is measured by the metric that he *is*. But that is precisely where Jenson's revision of eternity as a temporal infinity kicks in: the spacious act of God doing God *is* his eternity, but not in the abstract sense of an idealized realm, but in the temporal infinity of the specific life, death and resurrection of Jesus in which God makes room for the other, the creature.[37]

Of course, Jenson accepts we can never keep up with God in his act of decision, because he is quicker than any created metric – which may explain why we are so keen to create a static conception of a motionless eternity[38] – but Jenson still thinks, 'God takes time in his time for us', within the act of his temporal infinity, with that accommodation being his act of creation.[39] In short, creation, 'is a mutual implosion of the agencies of Father, Son, and Spirit that opens time within God's eternity'.[40]

Admittedly, Jenson's concept of the *actus purus* is going to be difficult to think.[41] Because Jenson is arguing that God's eternal act of making God to be God is precisely his transcendence through the act of dying for us in the fullness of time, he is saying – again to shift the idiom – that what happens over the Easter weekend *is* the aseity of God. Classically, God is always thought to be *a se*, in that he causes himself, rather than resulting from anything prior to his own actuality, with a raft of concepts springing directly from that claim, in that God is therefore without potential, simple, unchangeable and resolutely one. But Jenson knows the concept of self-causing again remains undetermined in meaning, until it is situated within a metaphysical structure of being (or divorced from all of them in mysterious apophatic isolation). Therefore, by attending to the gospel narrative, Jenson decides to stress the active nature of the act God is, in that his entire project rests on the supposition that God's being is in his act and his act is active, so his activity cannot be alien to his being.

By making this move, Jenson sees that God's being must therefore have a temporal quality to it, in that it is narratable as a series of episodes – *'There! That's God!'* etc. – by which the doctrine of the Trinity becomes the name that is a condensed summary of the story of what actually happened as God does God – and what happened is that 'the God of Israel raised Jesus from the dead'.[42] What is most remarkable, therefore, is that Jenson dares to think that God *is* the act of that happening. He causes himself in slow motion, so to speak, and he does so in the tomb.

In other words, Jenson argues that God – by making himself present to us in this way – is known to be the dramatic coherence of the story of these Three *personae dramatis*. God simply is whatever makes these episodes cohere as a singularity in which Beginning, Middle and End make a genuine unity in storied form. But he sees that this can only mean, 'The God of crucifixion and resurrection is one with himself in a moment of supreme dramatic self-transcendence',[43] and that unity – to put it bluntly – is 'an *historical* unity'.[44]

To press the point, Jenson argues that God is as 'palpable as a train wreck and kiss', which – by the standard definition of 'palpable' – means he is sensible, which is to say he is a tangible actuality, rather than some pure abstraction.[45] And that is where the rubber finally hits the road. Jenson is arguing that the pure act God *is* has a particular character, rather than being utterly generic to the point of abstract banality; God does something definite when he does himself from eternity. And that brings us back to the doctrine of election: *election is the plot of the story that the doctrine of the Trinity is a condensed summary of*, in that 'the Lord's resolve to meet and overcome death and the constitution of his self-identity in dramatic coherence are but one truth about him'.[46] In short, to do himself, God is the eternal speaking who is Jesus, and him once crucified and raised for our salvation. But how on earth does that cash out as the doctrine of aseity?

7.4 The resurrection is the being of God

Jenson has already developed a cluster of concepts to make his case. We have seen the way the identification of God by name and narrative depends on the 'completion' of the one who is thereby identified. The good news is that the one who is raised into infinity – and by which our definition of God is thereby anchored – is precisely the one who ate with tax collectors and sinners and died for the ungodly, etc. That is to say, this man is truly for others, because he was so unto death. Therefore, the story we tell about Jesus, with its specific determination derived from the narrative completion of a specific finitude, means the plot line coheres to give us a name that is the condensing of this very same story, namely, the doctrine of the Trinity. But because Jenson has revised the metaphysics, this account of God's being needn't pivot on a punctiliar point, abstracted and rendered static in substance beneath the occurrence. Instead, it can be allowed to be nothing other than the lifespan of this one unto death, and then again.

To put that otherwise, Jenson is arguing that Jesus becomes the Son, because his divine *hypostasis* is identifiable – like anything else – only when the span is complete. If not, God remains like an unfinished sentence, into which meaning can be projected or denied. In Jenson's own words:

> Since the Lord's self-identity is constituted in dramatic coherence, it is established not from the beginning but from the end, not at birth but at death, not in persistence but in anticipation.[47]

Now, it is worth noting that here – as elsewhere! – Jenson can be misunderstood. On first hearing, any thought of the Son becoming who he is at the end, sounds adoptionistic, i.e. heretical.[48] But that would only be the case if we are reading Jenson without undergoing the metaphysical conversion he is instigating. We must remember that he thinks God's act of decision takes time, in that God has a life, and this allows Jenson to make the case that the eternal Word has genuine content. The Father is the speaking of all that Jesus is.[49] What makes the content of this life eternal is that it simply is the only Word that God has always spoken and will never supersede, because it is his being expressed. Thereby, the span of the Son's life is rendered Alpha and Omega, in that it is the roomy determination of God's being, but – to be a *particular* being – it must paradoxically come to an end. In effect, the Son dies as the act of determining who he is from the beginning of his ways; that is, the Father's only begotten Son.

In other words, Jenson thinks God knows himself in the mutual converse that is Father, Son and Spirit, but that eternal conversation has content; the eternal Word is not empty. God knows himself – and therefore in his simplicity is himself as the act of that knowing – but only by turning to this Son. When God identifies God – asks 'who am I?' – the Father is the turning towards this crucified Jew, who *is* his eternal Word that he forever speaks.[50] But that Son is not a static *hypostasis*, but instead the narratable trajectory of this singular span from conception in the womb to death on the cross, with all the contingent twists and turns in between, by which the meaning of God is determined as a *being-for*.[51] In short, 'Love appears as the path of being', and vice versa.[52] The Son is God's reaching outwards as himself.

Therefore, what makes this Word absolute, according to Jenson, is simply that God's eternity is in no sense a compression of time – the compression of a singularity without duration – but is its own extension as the full possession of this one who is his own Beginning, Present and End, within which there is a certain *'roominess'*.[53] In other words, 'Jesus the Christ is the Word of God . . . as he is the content of the proclamation whose power is the Spirit and whose source is the Father',[54] with the drastic point being that the Father always speaks the fullness of this incarnate Son. That is to say, it is only in relation to Mary's boy that he *is* God, or, as Jenson puts it:

> The Word eternally spoken by the Father is the perfect self-utterance of the Father. Therefore, this Word must itself be a speaker – and so not properly an 'itself' but a 'himself.' It follows that the discourse of Father and Son is intrinsically *embodied*, that is, it is an address between mutually *available* someones, who can pick each other out and so respond to each other . . . the someone available to the Father is Jesus, available by his human embodiment.[55]

In short – and as Rowan Williams summarizes – 'God's self-definition is to be *this* filial person in history'.[56] And the history of this person is the posing of the question of God and the creatures.

In making this claim, Jenson is arguing that the eternal covenant – to put it in Barth's terms – happens right here in our midst, as the call and response of the questioning and answering of the crucifixion and resurrection, by which God is the decision to have this particular Son.[57] In that act of decision, however, this Son is defined both in relation to his Father and to us – his brothers and sisters – so that the Father finally can't have this Son – and he does want this Son, who is genuinely all that the Father can ever be – without the rest of us being thrown in. Jenson has therefore found a way to commandeer the classical concept of *actus purus*, but bend it to his revisionary use: God is one *pure act*, but it is an act with two terms. That is to say, doer and act are the same, in that God behappens himself in an '*im*plosion of freedom', but that is at one and the same time an '*ex*plosion of love' by which God is the venturing towards the creature to die for us.[58] Of course, Jenson thinks 'election' is the conceptual hinge between these two, but not in the abstract; God's act of electing God and man is the event of raising this dead Nazarene. In short, it happens in our midst.

In other words, the aseity of God – to use the classical term for self-causing – is the event of Easter. Or, to adopt the idiom of the Greeks, the substance of God is resurrection, understood as an active verb. It is the surprising taking up of this Son, whatever the cost, that constitutes

God's being, so that 'The resurrection of Jesus was the executing of the triune God's unity with himself'.[59] And just so: 'If we bend the old language a little, instead of replacing it, we may say that the resurrection is this God's *ousia*.'[60]

Now that is a remarkable claim. Jenson is arguing that whatever happened in that tomb is God identified 'by' and 'with' this pure act, which thereby amounts to God's *aseity*. That is why he thinks, 'To attend to the Resurrection and to attend to this particular putative God, to take either as the object of our reflection, are the same.'[61] In other words, there in the tomb, God defines himself as the merciful God, in that he is the dramatic act of this decision to raise this Son who is for us unconditionally. And with that being so, Jenson concludes that the singular nature of God is nothing other than the perichoretic mutuality in which the derelict Son is raised by the Father's command into the life of the Spirit with us. Or, as he puts it:

> The Spirit who raises the Son is the Spirit of the Father, and had already rested on this Son. The unity of the crucified Son with the risen Son is posited in the essential unity between this Father and this Spirit. The identity of the crucified Jesus and the risen Jesus is nothing other than the oneness of God.[62]

To put the point yet another way, Jenson is saying that whatever mechanics, so to speak, are denoted by the verb *'to resurrect this one'* is the being of God *a se*. It implies that 'the *risen* Son is, in his present-tense actuality, the identity within time of the Father's originating and the Spirit's liberating', and that is all God ever is.[63] Thus, 'the way in which the triune God is eternal, is by the events of Jesus' death and resurrection'.[64] As a result, Jenson can state in the starkest of terms that

> [T]he human person Jesus is 'one of the Trinity' [and] that compels me to say that if Jesus had not risen the Christian God would not be, rather than the other way around.[65]

As always with Jenson, that single sentence is worth pondering.[66] It encapsulates the revisionary nature of his proposal and does so with precision.

7.5 Impossible thinking

Now, I have stressed the oddity of all this time and again, although it is important to recognize that any proposal will strike us odd at this precise point. Because we are talking about God's *aseity*, words will surely fail us, in that we won't be able to break down the mechanics of what it means – in Jenson's case – for the eternal Father to be the raising of this Son through the liberating work of the Spirit.[67] In other words, *aseity* is another place where explanations run aground, and so we can only tell the story, name the name and sing the praises of the God thereby identified. Jenson himself is clear about this. He confesses that we still don't know God's being in any exhaustive sense, although he is adamant that this is not because God's being is situated at a metaphysical distance from us, shrouded the far side of a metaphysical chasm. Instead, God does himself in our midst – 'right in our faces', as it were[68] – while we are hammering nails, guarding tombs and sleeping on our watch, effectively turning our backs on what is happening as it happens over the first Easter weekend. But happen it does, and right here in our presence.[69]

Jenson thereby accepts that our witness to God's *aseity* will always prove inadequate, but only in the sense that we are learning to tell a story that is too quick for us even if it happened in slow motion over a series of days. Our words, however, are no different to the bread and wine that is offered at the Eucharist. The material offering similarly appears an inadequate means to communicate the being of God to us, but nonetheless that is how God chooses for them to work. And just as the loaf and the cup somehow become miraculously adequate, so too can our words, so long as God does his work with them. In effect, our words are one of the means by which God can slow himself down for us to reveal himself to us. Or – as Jenson puts it – 'God is indeed the ineffable mystery. But not because there is little to say about him, but because there is everything to say about him.'[70]

With this being so, Jenson claims the gospel is about reality in its entirety. If it were to be 'fully spoken', 'it would be a word about every item of reality that already is: every person, every atomic particle, every galaxy, every animal. And it would be an evocation of futurity, a creation of new language, infinite in its openness.'[71] Or to put that yet another way, speaking about the God of the gospel – as with any person, even those created – will always 'astonish us . . . [in that] we will glimpse depths we have not plumbed [before]'.[72] As a result, we cannot fully articulate the excitement that is God springing as a Person from the grave, because this event knows no end, other than the termination that it already transcends, and so speech about it will never cease even if what we say has genuine content. In short, we are talking about an eternal Word, but are nonetheless accurately talking about him *in* him and *through* him. That is to say, our envelopment within the being of God makes it too immediate for our words to capture entirely, because it constitutes everything within its own relations. But God is nonetheless known.

7.6 The perichoresis of God

Of course, the foregoing discussion has raised a number of significant points, and they will occupy our thoughts through to the end of the book. The first centres on the question as to how best to understand the dynamic unity of God in the event of resurrection. *Perichoresis* lies at the heart of Jenson's answer.[73]

The concept of *perichoresis* is usually employed in an attempt to delineate the way in which God's being is a dynamic interrelation, i.e. a self-formation, which is the coherence of the intensity of the distinct act of these Three persons to make one God. As such, *perichoresis* – just like 'person' and 'nature' – is again most basic, and so it cannot be broken down into more primary building blocks to understand how it works.[74] Of course, we can analyse the concept to a certain degree, perhaps looking to draw out its technical meaning by noting, for example, that the verb *perichorein* was initially introduced into christological discussions by Gregory Nazianzus to signify the communication of attributes from the natures to the person of Christ.[75] It was then drawn into discussions about the Trinity via John Damascene's *De Fide Orthodoxa*,[76] where the concept no longer signified an exchange of attributes, but began to signify a notion of reciprocal indwelling, thereby providing a technical answer to the question of how the Three are related as One. *Perichoresis* thus indicates the way the Three mutually indwell one another, cohering in the space that is God's own so that the eternal *begetting* and *spirating* happen in the one God in their personal distinction. And with this being so, theologians will often play with the etymology of the term, positing a 'dancing around' (choreography) and 'making room' (hospitality), both of which seek to gesture towards the notion that the *hypostases* 'see with each other's eyes', as S. T. Davis put it,[77] thereby capturing the way 'there is no isolation, no insulation, no secretiveness, no fear of being transparent to another' within the life of God.[78] In effect, the boundaries between the persons are open, so that generative terms such as begetting are just as much 'in' the Son as 'outside' him.[79] (And vice versa – and somewhat contrary to thought – the Son is also 'in' the Father as his own generator, so to speak.) In short, God does the distinctions that constitute his being as one.

Of course, this is just the kind of weird mutuality that Jenson needs, because the concept of *perichoresis* essentially flattens out the concepts of 'before' and 'after' in causation.[80] Because it bends causality around the concept of eternity, Jenson can therefore commandeer it to explain what happens over the Easter weekend, using the notion of a dynamic eternal communion of persons to account for the narratable movement of the resurrection of this one life. However, *perichoresis* is not being conceived as a circling around here, but instead the transcendence of a backward trajectory from the future as we move towards it, by which God *is* the self-determining act that is his self-definition as the past, present and future cohere as the one God meets himself in this threefold event. The act of resurrection thereby remains essentially historical, in that it is the *perichoresis* of these Three over the Easter weekend, but – to put it starkly – the concept denotes the speed by which the Spirit has always-already overcome the alienation of Son from the Father to be the place of their lively love. In short, the Spirit of his future rests on Jesus as he struggles.

To unpack this point, Jenson again draws from his reading of the narrative of Scripture. He thinks 'the proclamation of God's singularity is not in Israel the outcome of a metaphysical analysis but the slogan for a drama',[81] which is why he wants us to recall our earlier analysis of what makes a good story. We saw that to *storify*, as it were, is essentially to cohere, which is the act of transcendence by which episodic events make a singularity after the fact of their telling. The way in which a story is retroactively determined is thereby drawn into Jenson's metaphysics, with the concept of *perichoresis* functioning as a shorthand summary of the dramatic unity of the temporal act of God doing God in his resurrection from the dead. In essence, the Father speaks, the Son responds, but it is the Spirit who is always final as the future liberation of that converse from the start, with the Spirit thereby freeing the Father to be for this Son who is for others, with Jenson thereby concluding that God is finally Spirit, in that he is the end of the story he tells by which the episodic plot coheres as this life. In short, God is the possession of his own lively Future.

To put this otherwise, Jenson thinks God's aseity is the perichoresis by which he *storifies* himself in the narrative cohesion of that which he tells himself as the Father speaks Jesus and Jesus responds. Or to put that yet another way, perichoresis is 'active faithfulness to community',[82] by which the Conversation of God's life eternally coheres in person in the garden tomb.

7.7 The excruciating cost of being this contingent God

We can now see that Jenson has drawn God's self-determination into our history, thereby insisting that there is no prior deliberation behind the historical event of Easter. As a result, this means his account of the crucifixion is not underwritten by a deeper story as to why Jesus had to die. The crucifixion is simply what it actually takes for God to be the event of being ruptured open for others. But why is that so?

As Jenson understands it, the doctrine of the Trinity anchors our focus on a series of episodes, which reach their apparent conclusion on the cross. This is the dramatic climax upon which the story turns, with resurrection being the decisive conclusion in which God takes Godself up into the future that he has always determined himself to be – and therefore is – as his own Spirit. The historical movement away and towards this event – the patient sending and the expectant resting, as it were – are essentially plot lines, which are consistent enough to be named as vectors which are their own terms as Beginning, Middle and End of the story that happens in the tomb. The point here, however, is that the middle is a muddle, in that it is the act of including us, the excruciating pain of opening oneself to wed oneself to what is not oneself.

To make sense of this, Jenson draws from his reading of Jonathan Edwards, arguing that we are so 'close' to Jesus 'to be truly one personal being with him in the triune life'.[83] But this requires the crucifixion to make it so, which means the crucifixion 'is the pain of truly loving us'. As a result, though we are personally united with God by the death of the second Person of the Trinity, Jenson's account stops this from being considered a cost-free theoretical unity by stressing the actual cost which God bears that it might be so, i.e. it is not magical or natural, but instead a historically determinative act of God defining himself as God-with-us, which God finds excruciating because we are sinners. Therefore, this one event is to be understood as the way God decides to be the God who dies for the ungodly,[84] and serves no economy beyond its own actuality of establishing who God will forever be.[85]

What this means – and this point marks the beginning of the countdown to the next chapter – is that we are defined by the subsisting relation between the Father and this Son, who is 'Father, forgive them', so that by the historically actual grace of this event, the Father cannot have his Son without the rest of us being thrown in.[86] That alone is why there is no separation of God and man, but it is the unconditionality of the Son's *hypostasis* that leads to him dying for us. Now this will again be tricky to grasp, although, as Jenson says in one place, 'logic has nothing to say in the face of fact'.[87] Jenson's point is that there is no secret hidden God deciding anything about our heavenly or hellish destinations outside of our earshot, so to speak, because he is what happens here. Nor is there some God always-already established, who is at a distance from this event and somehow immune to the act as he resets the scales of his justice. Instead, crucifixion is God's deliberative self-election to be a particular God. And God has decided that he is the Man for Others, who are his enemies, so that the trajectory of unconditionality leads him into our murderous embrace. And that is why we can be confident that God is the forgiver of sinners, because the dead Jesus now lives, so there is nothing to fear. This can't be grasped, beyond being celebrated in the act of worship.

To put the point otherwise, Jenson thinks the identity of the infinite one is nothing other than dying for the ungodly, and so there is no need for us to be afraid, because this *is* God. We are thereby situated within the act of his mercy as we are plotted in relation to the internal relations by which he constitutes himself as this Nazarene. There is no secret economy behind this act by which we can make sense of it, other than the actuality of God-doing-God-for-the-ungodly. Or as John Webster put it, 'God's life is the evangelical drama, and the economy of reconciliation is, we might say, groundless.'[88]

As Jenson's account of the atonement again indicates, Easter is the *aseity* of God, and the point of *aseity* is that there is no more basic cause. God just is *this*, without needing to be so by any other metric than his own decisive freedom. As this suggests, contingency is key here. Jenson's interpretation of the crucifixion means God 'could have been otherwise', and in at least two ways. First, in the freedom of God, the Father could eternally speak another Word, who isn't the crucified-for-the-ungodly, but of that Word we cannot even imagine, and neither can God. We can only deal with the actuality of the act that he is, by which the Father eternally speaks the precise way of the Son into the Spirit of the far country. In other words, God is contingent to himself, in that his freedom is not some isolated solitude. Of course, freedom is widely recognized to be inherently relational, and thereby impossible in strict isolation, in that a self-possessed singularity situated as its own universe could never be described as free. Jenson is therefore right to argue that we ourselves must be free for another, rather than possessing some Archimedean point of neutral decision from which we can choose to choose, as it were. He thinks this is why we are therefore always enraptured either to God or to Satan, being bound to one or the other in strict relation, but God, in contrast, can choose to choose because the Trinity enraptures himself, possessing himself in the freedom of his self-relation. Thus, the only free will is the self-determination of the triune life to be the God that he chooses. *That* is God's own freedom, unique and splendid, and it is our freedom too as he liberates us from enslavement.[89]

Second, the way Jenson has set things up means that the actuality of God's decision retains a sense of contingency in its actual timely occurrence. That is to say, we could have ended up with a 'mutually betraying pantheon' if Jesus hadn't taken the cup. In other words, God 'behappens himself' as that pure contingency in which God does who he chooses to be, by which person and act are the mutual temporal converse of that spacious deliberation to include us. But in making this case, Jenson is not saying – as Heidegger did – that 'Higher than actuality stands *possibility*.'[90] He is instead arguing that the 'the one absolute contingency' – who is God – is the one necessity of his actuality, within which there remains possibility in its contingent actuality along the way.[91] In short, Good Friday could have undone God in the chaos of 'a mutually betraying pantheon', but the good news is that Sunday is the dramatic transcendence to establish self-identity in that integrative resurrection.[92] Here again, there can be no explanation beyond its contingent actuality, because 'love notoriously gives no reasons'.[93] He is to be worshipped, not explained.

Now, this is an issue to which we will return in the next chapter. However, we can already see that Jenson thinks we live and move and have our being in the decision that is God, by which this God is identified with us in that movement. And that is to say that God lives and moves and has his being in the perichoretic mutuality that is the Father, Jesus and the Spirit towards us. And the key terms here are lives and moves, because Jenson is arguing that God is the sweep of a flight, rather than a stationary point, always and forever opening up into the surprising future of our inclusion, which is never inconsistent with who he always is as the speaker of this Word, but instead a free improvisation on the themes of self-giving love. Or in Jenson's terms – as we will see – this God is 'a fugue'. That is to say, a repetition that opens up, to allow a counterpoint, which is itself a song of harmonic praise to the God who decides only to be himself in the sharing of himself – and that is the ground of our being, because it is the ground of God's own.

In other words, Jenson is claiming that God is no static substance, but instead the dance of freedom in which, 'the life of God is just, as it were, one big excitement, a kind of explosion of excitement . . . the excitement of giving something you've always wanted to give'.[94] That is to say, Jesus. And that means, our God is simply the sound of Easter, the joyful *Exultet* of rising from the grave.

Notes

1 Robert W. Jenson, 'What if It Were True?' *Neue Zeitschrift für Systematische Theologie und Religionsphilosophie* 43.1 (2001), 10.

2 The phrase comes from an essay title, Robert W. Jenson, 'With No Qualifications: the Christological Maximalism of the Christian East', in *Ancient and Postmodern Christianity: Paleo-Orthodoxy in the 21st Century*, ed. Kenneth Tanner and Christopher A. Hall (Downers Grove: InterVarsity Press, 2002), 13.

3 Robert W. Jenson, *Systematic Theology, Volume 1, The Triune God* (New York: OUP, 1997), 221. Second emphasis added.

4 George Hunsinger, 'Robert Jenson's Systematic Theology: A Review Essay', *Scottish Journal of Theology* 55 (2002), 173.

PART THREE | JENSON'S DOCTRINE OF GOD

5 Robert W. Jenson, *Systematic Theology, Volume 2, The Works of God* (New York: OUP, 1999), 37.

6 Robert W. Jenson, 'Creator and Creature', *International Journal of Systematic Theology* 4 (2002), 216–21.

7 See comments on how difference is established in the precise drama of God with creatures, so the difference is between 'primeval' relations and a created relation that 'comes *into* this life'. Jenson, *Systematic Theology*, Vol. 1, 226.

8 Jenson, *Systematic Theology*, Vol. 2, 48.

9 Jenson, *Systematic Theology*, Vol. 1, 170. Jenson's reading of Barth helpfully draws out the positive point from a different angle, in that 'The presence before God of his Son *as a creature* was what motivated him to create. We have seen that creation was an act of God's love. Now we can understand the inner reality of this. God loves His Son; in that His Son is eternally a creature, God loves the creature and in loving it wills its existence.' Robert W. Jenson, *Alpha and Omega: A Study in the Theology of Karl Barth* (Thomas Nelson and Sons, 1963; reprint, Eugene, OR: Wipf and Stock, 2002), 94.

10 Jenson, *Systematic Theology*, Vol. 1, 226.

11 This train of thought exemplifies Jenson's refusal to work with what he calls a 'two-valued logic', i.e. the binary character of framing things as either/or. For example, on the question of impassibility, Jenson's God 'is not a sort of hyperstoic, but neither is he at any temporal agent's mercy. He is, however, at the mercy of himself – which is the great difference between him and the impassible deity of the religions.' Robert W. Jenson, 'What Kind of God Can Make a Covenant?' in *Covenant and Hope: Christian and Jewish Reflections*, ed. Robert W. Jenson and Eugene B. Korn (Grand Rapids: Eerdmans, 2012), 11. On this matter, see also the way Jenson explores the musical features of 'meter bars' and 'hyperbars' to show how God is not limited by our conception of possibility and impassibility. Robert W. Jenson, 'Ipse Pater non est impassibilis', in *Divine Impassibility and the Mystery of Human Suffering*, ed. James F. Keating and Thomas Joseph White, O.P. (Grand Rapids: Eerdmans, 2009), 117–26.

12 Jenson, *Systematic Theology*, Vol. 1, 4.

13 His critique of Origen is precisely on this point: Jenson, *Systematic Theology*, Vol. 1, 98–9.

14 Jenson's reading of Barth's understanding of the event of God's decision to *be* Jesus Christ is succinctly stated in Jenson, *Systematic Theology*, Vol. 1, 140.

15 Again, to be fair, Jenson's concluding comments on Barth's theology reveal the way Jenson reads Barth, in that the implications of Barth's proposal are clear: 'If what happened in Christ is really God's will for us, if it is not secondary to a prior, abstract, and largely unknown will of God, then it indeed follows that God's decision to be merciful falls not "above" but *in* the life of Jesus Christ. His life is this decision.' Jenson, *Alpha and Omega*, 146.

16 See Jenson, *Alpha and Omega*, 162.

17 As Jenson sees it, it is only 'within trinitarian thought's captivity to an alien definition of deity . . . [that] we have had to say that Jesus is the dwelling and manifestation of his own preexistent Double'. Robert W. Jenson, *The Triune Identity: God According to the Gospel* (Philadelphia: Fortress, 1982; reprint, Eugene, OR: Wipf and Stock, 2002), 141.

18 Robert W. Jenson, 'How Does Jesus Make a Difference?' in *Essentials of Christian Theology*, ed. William C. Placher (Louisville: Westminster John Knox Press, 2003), 205.

19 Robert W. Jenson and Solveig Lucia Gold, *Conversations with Poppi about God* (Grand Rapids: Brazos Press, 2006), 20.

20 Jenson, 'How Does Jesus', 205.

21 For an analysis of Jenson's use of *hypostasis* in relation to natures, see Tee Gatewood, 'A Nicene Christology? Robert Jenson and the Two Natures of Jesus Christ', *Pro Ecclesia* 18 (2009), 28–49.

22 Jenson, *Alpha and Omega*, 74.

23 Jenson uses this adjective to capture the sense of an arrow within mutuality. See, for example, Jenson, *Systematic Theology*, Vol. 2, 347.

24 Robert W. Jenson, 'On the Ascension', in *Loving God With Our Minds: The Pastor as Theologian*, ed. Michael Welker and Cynthia A. Jarvis (Grand Rapids: Eerdmans, 2004), 336.

25 See, for example, his analysis of the problem of imagining God's *timeless* relation to the incarnation in Jenson, *Triune Identity*, 140.

26 Jenson, *Triune Identity*, 171.

27 Jenson, *Systematic Theology*, Vol. 1, 198. Emphasis added.

28 Robert W. Jenson, 'The Triune God', in *Christian Dogmatics*, ed. Carl E. Braaten and Robert W. Jenson (Philadelphia: Fortress, 1984), 154.

29 Jenson, *Systematic Theology*, Vol. 1, 233.

30 Robert W. Jenson, 'Jesus, Father, Spirit: The Logic of the Doctrine of the Trinity', *Dialog* 26.4 (1987), 247.

31 See his discussion of Barth's use of this concept and how it links to event and freedom in Jenson, *Alpha and Omega*, 69.

32 Robert W. Jenson, 'Karl Barth on the Being of God', in *Thomas Aquinas and Karl Barth: An Unofficial Catholic-Protestant Dialogue*, ed. Bruce L. McCormack and Thomas Joseph White (Grand Rapids: Eerdmans, 2013), 47.

33 Jenson, *Systematic Theology*, Vol. 1, 216.

34 Jenson, *Systematic Theology*, Vol. 1, 218–19.

35 Robert W. Jenson, *God After God: The God of the Past and the God of the Future as Seen in the Work of Karl Barth* (Minneapolis: Fortress Press, 1969/2010), 125.

36 Jenson, *Systematic Theology*, Vol. 2, 47.

37 See Jenson, *Systematic Theology*, Vol. 1, 216–17.

38 Jenson, 'Jesus, Father, Spirit', 247. Thanks to Donna Lazenby for linking this to a slow vision of a false eternity.

39 Jenson, *Systematic Theology*, Vol. 2, 35.

40 Jenson, *Systematic Theology*, Vol. 2, 25.

41 Of course, Jenson enjoyed setting his mind to such difficult tasks, see, for example, Robert W. Jenson, *On Thinking the Human: Resolutions of Difficult Notions* (Grand Rapids: Eerdmans, 2003).

42 Jenson, *Triune Identity*, 1–18.

43 Jenson, *Systematic Theology*, Vol. 1, 65.

44 Jenson, *Alpha and Omega*, 164.

45 Jenson, *Systematic Theology*, Vol. 1, 214. As Jenson immediately proceeds to explain, 'the being of God . . . is not something actualized but the event of actualization'.

46 Jenson, *Systematic Theology*, Vol. 1, 66.

47 Jenson, *Systematic Theology*, Vol. 1, 66.

48 One of the charges levelled in Hunsinger, 'Robert Jenson's Systematic Theology'.

49 See summary in Jenson, *Systematic Theology*, Vol. 2, 270.
50 Jenson, *Systematic Theology*, Vol. 2, 270.
51 Jenson, *Systematic Theology*, Vol. 1, 200.
52 The phrase is Walter Kasper's, cited in Ángel Cordovilla Pérez, 'The Trinitarian Concept of Person', in *Rethinking Trinitarian Theology*, ed. Robert J. Wozniak and Giulio Maspero (London and New York: T&T Clark, 2012), 106.
53 Jenson, *Systematic Theology*, Vol. 2, 25.
54 Jenson, *Systematic Theology*, Vol. 1, 171.
55 Colin Gunton and Robert W. Jenson, 'The *Logos Ensarkos* and Reason', in *Reason and the Reasons of Faith*, ed. Paul J. Griffiths and Reinhard Hütter (London: T&T Clark, 2005), 83.
56 Rowan Williams, *Christ The Heart of Creation* (London: Bloomsbury Continuum, 2018), 158.
57 As Jenson sees it, because he is arguing that 'God's eternal will . . . is achieved by God within temporal history . . . It is this one drastic sentence which separates us from Barth.' Jenson, *Alpha and Omega*, 165.
58 Jenson, 'Karl Barth', 51.
59 Robert W. Jenson, *Unbaptized God: The Basic Flaw in Ecumenical Theology* (Minneapolis: Fortress, 1992), 140.
60 Jenson, *Triune Identity*, 168.
61 Jenson, *Systematic Theology*, Vol. 1, 12.
62 Jenson, *Systematic Theology*, Vol. 1, 200.
63 Jenson, *Unbaptized God*, 140. Emphasis added.
64 Jenson, *Systematic Theology*, Vol. 1, 219.
65 Robert W. Jenson, 'Jesus in the Trinity: Wolfhart Pannenberg's Christology and Doctrine of the Trinity', in *The Theology of Wolfhart Pannenberg: Twelve American Critiques, with an autobiographical essay and response*, ed. Carl E. Braaten and Philip Clayton (Minneapolis: Augsburg, 1988), 199.
66 On one occasion, he suggests his readers spend time pondering his own summary of Barth's work. Robert W. Jenson, *A Theology in Outline: Can These Bones Live?* transcribed, ed. and introduced by Adam Eitel (Oxford: OUP, 2016), 59.
67 As he puts it, quoting Aquinas, 'Therefore Christ's resurrection itself could not directly be seen by humans . . .' Jenson, *Systematic Theology*, Vol. 1, 194.
68 Jenson, *Systematic Theology*, Vol. 1, 233.
69 Josh Gaghan, 'Reason, Metaphysics, and their Relationship in the Theologies of Jenson and Aquinas', *New Blackfriars* 99.1082 (2018), 534.
70 Robert W. Jenson, 'The God of the Gospel', *Baltimore Paper*, 19.
71 Robert W. Jenson, *Story and Promise: A Brief Theology of the Gospel About Jesus* (Philadelphia: Fortress Press, 1973; reprint, Eugene, OR: Wipf & Stock 2014), 76-7.
72 Jenson, 'What if', 12.
73 I'm again drawing from wider reading, notably Emmanuel Durand O.P., 'Perichoresis: A Key Concept for Balancing Trinitarian Theology', in *Rethinking Trinitarian Theology*, ed. Robert J. Wozniak and Giulio Maspero (London and New York: T&T Clark, 2012), 177-92.
74 Durand, 'Perichoresis', 177. Durand distances himself from this way of seeing it, later arguing that it is not 'primary', but neither is it a 'corollary' (181).
75 Durand, 'Perichoresis', 179.
76 Durand, 'Perichoresis,' 179.

77 Despite popular opinion, the stem is not the same as that from which we derive choreography. However, 'dancing around' is now widely used and therefore part of its contemporary meaning. The quoted words are S. T. Davis's, and cited in Thomas H. McCall, *Which Trinity? Whose Monotheism? Philosophical and Systematic Theologians on the Metaphysics of Trinitarian Theology* (Grand Rapids: Eerdmans, 2010), 24. I am in great debt to McCall's work.

78 The words again very closely paraphrase Thomas H. McCall, reordered here for better flow in its context. McCall, *Which Trinity*, 24.

79 The quoted words are Cornelius Plantinga's, cited in McCall, *Which Trinity*, 14. The ideas here are also taken from Durand, 'Perichoresis', 182–3.

80 Durand, 'Perichoresis', 183–4.

81 Jenson, *Systematic Theology*, Vol. 1, 75.

82 Robert W. Jenson, 'Justification as a Triune Event', *Modern Theology* 11.4 (October 1995), 426.

83 Jenson, *Systematic Theology*, Vol. 1, 191.

84 Jenson, 'Karl Barth', 51.

85 Succinctly to the point: 'And that not without cost'. Jenson, *Alpha and Omega*, 165.

86 Jenson, *Systematic Theology*, Vol. 1, 191.

87 Jenson, *Alpha and Omega*, 101–2.

88 John Webster, *God Without Measure: Working Papers in Christian Theology, Volume 1, God and the Works of God* (London: Bloomsbury T&T Clark, 2016), 151.

89 'It can be said that God too is contingent, indeed absolute Contingency, but in the triune perichoresis it is himself to whom he is contingent'. Jenson, *On Thinking*, 69 n20. On the concept of freedom, and how it is too often misconceived in abstraction from relation and therefore not as an enrapture, see Robert W. Jenson, 'An Ontology of Freedom in the *De Servo Arbitrio* of Luther', *Modern Theology* 10.3 (1994), 247–52.

90 Martin Heidegger, *Being and Time*, translated by Joan Stambaugh (Albany: State University of New York, 1996), 34.

91 Robert W. Jenson, 'For us . . . He Was Made Man', in *Nicene Christianity: The Future for a New Ecumenism*, ed. Christopher R. Seitz (Grand Rapids: Brazos, 2001), 77.

92 Jenson, *Systematic Theology*, Vol. 1, 65.

93 Robert W. Jenson, 'Election and Culture: From Babylon to Jerusalem', in *Public Theology in Cultural Engagement*, ed. Stephen R. Holmes (Milton Keynes: Paternoster, 2008), 51.

94 Jenson and Gold, *Conversations*, 15.

8

Easter First, Creation After

8.1 Like Father, like Son

We have come a long way, but more work needs to be done to get to grips with Jenson's proposal. That being said, we should have a pretty good idea what Jenson is up to by now, in that he wants to allow the story of Jesus of Nazareth – the life, death and resurrection of Mary's boy and Pilate's victim – to determine his account of God's eternal decision to be the God that he is. That is pretty much his signature move.

What is striking about Jenson's proposal, however, is the way that the Nazarene's place in the Trinity is not staggered, so to speak, but instead sheerly immediate. With this turn of phrase, I want to indicate Jenson's rejection of the idea that the fleshy Son is somehow related to a pre-existent unfleshed reality, by which the historical life of Jesus is appended by way of a mysterious movement of the *Logos asarkos* from eternity into time.[1] Of course, that is not how the gospel is usually understood. The doctrine of the incarnation tends to posit a mysterious extension – or some such act of grace – by which God's economic act is derived from his eternal nature, but without coinciding exactly with it. No doubt I could finesse that statement in all sorts of ways, but the point here is that Jenson – in stark contrast – thinks that the gospel centres entirely on the identity of Jesus as the Son, so that the particular life that Jesus lives is the second *hypostasis* of the Three who mutually do the single godliness of God. In other words, there is no *Logos asarkos* who then – by some mysterious movement – becomes man, because there is no gap, so to speak, for the unfleshed Word to move across. Jesus is the Father's Word, always enfleshed.[2]

To make his thesis work, Jenson dismisses the idea that the *hypostasis* is a punctiliar point. To conceive of it like that would suggest there is something more basic to the Son than the Son's life with us, buried as it would be beneath the accidental contingencies of the path Jesus in fact treads. In short, we would still be situating him within the substance metaphysics. Jenson instead argues that the second *hypostasis* of the Trinity must be the temporal span of the Lord's life, which is itself the narrative coherence of the Son's episodic way from conception through to death.[3] That is to say, the Word – who the Father eternally speaks – is everything that happens with Jesus, or to put that into more technical terms: the entire life of this one man is the subsisting relation, which is its own term. The *hypostasis* is the dynamic whole.[4]

To put the point otherwise, Jenson thinks the eternal relation is what starts in Mary's womb and terminates on Pilate's cross, and then springs into the infinite life of the Spirit. The Son's *hypostasis* is no more than this specific life, so there is nothing behind, or beneath, or even before the contingencies of this man's dynamic existence within the nexus of relations by which he is held before us by his Father and the Spirit they share.[5] Of course, this implies there is something alongside him, so to speak, other than his Father and their Spirit; namely his mother, an executioner, the people of Israel and all the rest of us who gather with 'torches and staves' to betray him.[6] Gatewood thereby spots what is at stake here, because Jenson's understanding of *hypostasis* implies,

> This person is God with God and at one and the same time the brother of James, the first cousin once-removed of Elizabeth, and a descendant of David [and this] implies that the Logos does not assume some*thing,* instead he deigns to pitch his tent among his sisters and brothers. He freely chooses to have his being in communion with the fallen race of Adam as a person with human persons.[7]

Gatewood's point is simple, though with drastic consequence. If Jenson thinks Jesus simply is the Son – in that he lives as one in communion with the transcendent beginning he names as Father, while being shaped by the transcendent future that opens before him as Spirit – the pain he suffers at the hands of sinful creatures is constitutive of his identity just as much as his trust of the Father is, albeit in a different way. In short, this single *hypostasis* is the life lived in two directions, so to speak, because, 'The man who is one of our potential mob and the second of the triune dancers are the same one'.[8]

Jenson is clear on this. 'Within the one person of Christ both natures are *determined* each by the other. They are mutually preoccupied'.[9] This means the life of Jesus must be understood as the way in which the always Beginning Father and never Ending Spirit cohere as one – so that there is God – but in such a way that this God is therefore a God who simply is what Jesus matter-of-factly does.[10] That is to say, what God finally is, is nothing other than this one man's life, death and resurrection, by which he determines to be only God-with-us. In other words, there is no God simply in and of himself. He is always forever *Emmanuel.*

With that point highlighted, we bump up against the strangest element of Jenson's proposal. The Son's distinct *hypostasis* – in the movement between Father and Spirit – is running in another direction, so to speak, so that his way of life is the coincidence of eternity and time in the sense that the eternal begetting coincides with the temporal mission, so that his fellow creatures are included within the identifiable life of God.[11] Or to put that in Jenson's terms: 'The space between the Father and Christ at his right hand accommodates the embodiment of the *totus Christus*'; in other words, we are to be found in God, between Father and Son, so that God can only know himself – as the relation between these two – with us lot plotted within him.[12]

If Jenson is right about this, we must imagine the Father eternally speaking a Word, who is directed towards the creature in such a way that the specific path of the existence of this Word is itself a two-way mutual communion, in that he is at one and the same time both God and man. This means God the Son simply is his subsisting relation to his Father *and* his subsisting relation to his brothers and sisters, with all the weight of Jenson's argument landing precisely on the twofold *is*.[13] He thinks Jesus lives unconditionally for us so that his *hypostasis* is defined by the utterly selfless relation that reaches death's definitive terminus, with the result being that the Father cannot have this Son without including those who define him at the terminus of his subsisting relation, i.e. his crucifiers.[14] In short, the Son is the man unconditionally for others, and thereby hypostatically one-with-us.

By pressing the two realities together in this way, Jenson accepts that both God and his creation only exist in the way they do because of God's unstoppable act of self-determining election, thereby constituting two mutualities in reciprocal relation through this one *hypostasis*. Or to put that more precisely, God and the world are one single act with two terms, with the hinge between the terms being the election of Mary's boy and Pilate's victim as the Father's eternal Son who is our brother. As a result, Jenson concludes:

> This human personality is then an identity of God: Toward the Father in the Spirit he lives the mutual self-giving that God is. And vice versa, this 'second' identity of the Trinity is simultaneously a human identity: With his mother and his executioner and you and me he has his place in the converse of human community. Thus, he is born in created time of the Virgin and in God's time of the Father, is condemned by Pilate, and is delivered over by the Father.[15]

With this point in mind, Jenson concludes that *both* the Father and ourselves turn towards the 'hanged man on Golgotha' to know – and therefore *be* – who we are.[16] Or, as Jenson states it, 'To understand what is behind the vast spaces, whether of the cosmos or of the human heart, the only thing we can do is what God the Father does as he rules them: Consider his Son Jesus.'[17] And that is because, 'From and to all eternity, God says to himself: "I am that man's Father," and rules all his decisions and acts by that self-identification'.[18] In other words, 'God knows Godself and us in the cross, just as we know ourselves and God in the self-same cross'.[19]

By setting things up in this way, Jenson thinks – to pick up this chapter's opening point about the staggering *Logos asarkos* – that it is a mistake to imagine some kind of spasmodic interruption between two steady states of being, by which some pre-existent eternity is distinguished from the temporal realm by time, as if God is eternally doing himself and then – in an eternity when there were no *thens* – decides to create a world and then do what he eventually does to save it. He instead wants us to believe there is only the one act of God in these two simultaneous modes, by which eternity and history coincide in the Son. Or, as Rowan Williams puts it, 'God's eternity is not a parallel track to what happens in the finite order'.[20] Which is to say, 'the procession of the Son from the Father is what we witness in the virgin birth', and thereon going forward.[21]

To press the point, Jenson claims the 'reality of Christ – his death, resurrection, and present Lordship – is not merely a set of events within what is created by some other act of God. It is a Trinitarian identity of the one act of God by which the world is'.[22] Or to put that in even starker terms: one act, two outcomes, with the difference between God and creation mapped across Holy Saturday. Or better, Saturday is the space within the event of their unification. It is infinity's spacious envelopment of the finite order.

To push the same point in yet a different direction, Jenson is arguing that 'God's relations to us are internal to him'.[23] He thinks there is no gap for God to cross, because, as Gatewood puts it, 'there never was nor could have been a Son that individually possessed the divine nature, nor could there have been a Jesus that was merely human. This one and the same person was and is always in relation to the Father through the Spirit as the Word of God.'[24] Just so, the begetting and conception coincide as the eternal beginning of what reaches its term on the cross and then springs into Life. Or, to put that in Jenson's words, he thinks, 'there is a spiral by which the birth of the Son eternally and his birth from Mary are not events separated on a merely linear timeline'.[25] But how on earth do we make sense of that?

As I read it, Jenson's proposal is best pictured spatially, in that what we are dealing with here is an 'implosion' and 'explosion' by which God does the difference between God and everything else as both are established in their distinct ways of being in the singular Nazarene.[26] Of course, we must admit that one single bidirectional act – that is at once eternal and historical – is incredibly hard to imagine, and so we have again reached the point where explanations will run aground, and there is nothing embarrassing about that. All theologians reach a point where their explanations cease, whatever theological method, model, schooling or metaphysics they draw upon in their run up to their silent wonder at an incarnate God. With Jenson, however, this common occurrence takes on a peculiar form, in that Jenson thinks our words fail us at the point where God is taken to be the bidirectional act of his own self-election. In short, God is eternally wondrous as the incarnate God. But, again, what does that mean?

If we momentarily lay aside the question of creaturely reality being somehow plotted within the life of God, we can see we are basically exploring the character of the eternal cause of God's self-determining act, including, in Jenson's case, the eternal cause's determination to be two vectors of relationality at once imploding and exploding in subsistence to himself. With this being so, we can see that we have run aground on the brute mystery of the sheer contingency of the Father's *fathering*, and – as any theologian knows – 'One cannot question one's way back behind the fact of the Father's Fatherhood'.[27] The *arche* can only be accepted as the brute given, in that 'The final contingency is simply the utterly underivable fact of the *Father* as *person*, of the *monarchos* before which there was not even nothingness'.[28] And we must leave it at that. But what is remarkable here is the way Jenson is claiming that what the Father eternally – and inexplicably – speaks is the enfleshed Son. As a result, the central issue becomes clear.

Jenson wants us to accept that we cannot enquire as to how the Father is the eternal speaking of this two-directional Word – who is Jesus – any more than we could explain what it means, for example, for the unbegotten Father to be at one and the same time the one who both *begets* and *spirates*. That is to say, none of us can spell out what it means for the Father to be 'rightly described as *fons trinitatis*',[29] by which the Father is thought to be two distinct modes of origination in his utter singularity as he begets the Son and spirates the Spirit, with this 'double relativity' thereby 'character[izing] the Father in his eternal personal perfection'.[30] As a result, if we are willing to accept the complexity of the Father's sheer givenness – especially the way the *filioque* can modify what one church has to say in distinction from another[31] – the apologetic point is obvious: Jenson cannot be expected to perform explanatory somersaults that no other theologian is trying to attempt. Instead, we should accept that every explanation fails to explain how the Father is the fathering of this Son in distinction from this Spirit, even if Jenson's own explanation terminates on the unusual claim that the single *hypostasis* of the eternal Son – mysteriously begotten of the Father – is at one and the same time both an implosion and explosion, i.e. bidirectional in being.[32]

To Jenson's credit, this caveat shows how his proposal is not as unreasonable as it first appears. We are happy for the three trinitarian *hypostases* to be distinguished by their modes of origination, and so accept the unbegotten Father is utterly mysterious in his capability – if that's the right word! – to do two distinct originations at one and the same time (without himself being two *hypostases*, which would seem to be the *prima facie* consequence of being the two subsisting relations of *begetting* and *spirating*). Just so, if the Father can singularly do himself two ways, so to speak, there is no obvious reason why one of the eternally generated *hypostases* – the only begotten Son – cannot himself be two ways of being in his sheer singularity, i.e. the theandric Godman who is at once imploding and exploding as a singularity. If anything, the acceptability of the Father's twofold generating strengthens Jenson's argument for a singular twofold Son.[33]

And if this is the case, the family resemblance between Jenson's understanding of the Son's two-way identity and the standard conception of the complexities of the triune relations of origination in the Father should at least buy Jenson some time – or perhaps even convince us he is on the right track. That is because the systematic link between the twofold generative act of the singular Father – *begetting* and *spirating* – and the twofold act of his thereby begotten Son enables us to see that Jenson is only relocating two long-standing conundrums, rather than inventing something entirely out of the blue. He knows his opponents are dealing with the double-originating power of the singular Father, as well as grappling with the staggering two-step ontology of the unfleshed Son's movement into an incarnate state, thereby attempting to make sense of the non-consequential difference between *begetting* and *spirating* and the way the Son is first involved in some eternal decision about taking on flesh and then – when there were no 'thens' – moving immutably from being *asarkos* to *ensarkos*. And with this being so, Jenson manages to simplify the double conundrum by proposing that the Son, like the Father, is a *hypostasis* who forever lives two ways at once, always. Unlike others, Jenson has no need to explain a timeless 'extension' of the unfleshed Word. And just so, Jenson in fact makes our task much simpler.

To put the point otherwise, whichever way you run at the question of the Son's identity, every theologian will have to bow their heads at some stage and confess in wonder that the Son 'became man'. Most of us have been happy to leave that 'became' simply hanging there, without ever attempting to explain its mysterious mechanics.[34] However, Jenson has spotted that this explanatory hole leaves the concept of 'became' open to definition, and, with that being the case, we can see that his account of God's act of election – by which the eternally enfleshed Word is simultaneously God's being and ours – constitutes Jenson's attempt to locate the 'became' in the Father's sheer contingency. As a result, his proposal cannot be written off as an illegitimate mutation of previously tried and tested certainties. Instead, he is in the same boat as the rest of us, albeit rowing very differently.

8.2 The questionability of Jenson's God

Of course, Jenson's proposal looks odd in comparison to the standard conception of 'became'. We will still assume the verb captures a two-state movement, so to speak, rather than indicate the sheer bidirectionality of the eternal *hypostasis* of the only begotten Son. But this doesn't mean the standard conception is right. As Jenson argues, we must 'note the extreme oddity of asking what things were like "before" the birth of one who is eternal God, which may at least suggest that we need to be careful in plotting divine events on a univocal time line'.[35] The bottom line is whether a God – resplendent in his timeless perfection – could decide to become man. And what exactly does a timeless decision even mean? Surely it implies there was a before and after for a timeless Being we assume simply *is*?

Of course, this is not to deny that Jenson's handling of the conundrum raises its own questions, and it is clear Jenson himself tried various approaches to getting to grips with what 'and became man' means. This included a period when he explored the idea as to whether the Son was always 'going to be born'[36] – or in more technical terms, was *incarnandus* – before Mary gave birth, thereby situating the Son's previous unfleshed identity in the trajectory of the Old Testament's plot line as the *Logos asarkos* always and forever hurtled through time towards Mary's womb as 'a pattern of movement'.[37] But eventually Jenson decided that this way of seeing things is unnecessary, sensing that it is only another attempt to dodge the sheer contingency of the Nazarene's identity as the eternal Son – spoken by the Father – by explaining it away with a prior unexplainable mystery. Ockham's razor therefore did what it always does, with Jenson accepting that we must simply affirm that Jesus is the Son he claimed himself to be, whose eternal origination and temporal birthing thereby coincide in his single *hypostasis*, and proceed to bend our metaphysics around that startling premise.[38]

In other words, Jenson begins and ends with the 'one and the same' Jesus, and determines his conception of time and eternity, causation and other pivotal concepts around that unshakeable belief, rather than try to shoe-horn Jesus into a fixed metaphysical framework that cannot handle his *theandric* reality.[39] His entire project therefore trades on the unshakeable premise that we cannot limit what it is possible for the Father to *father,* thereby calling on us to accept that he is 'the *monarchos*, the determining beginning anterior to which there is not even nothingness, the Father answers, and indeed can answer, to no instance but himself'.[40] As a result, we are in no position to decide whether the Father can forever be the speaking of this particular Son. Only the Father himself could prevent Jesus of Nazareth being 'the self-same God *as* God the Father precisely in and by his relation *to* God the Father'.[41] Put otherwise, why can't the Father eternally speak this enfleshed Word?[42]

Jenson's reason for refusing to conceive of an unfleshed Word has by now become clear. The Son is Jesus and Jesus is the Son, and that is an identity statement. But this means Jenson has drawn the eternal self-determination of God into the gospel narrative, and that in turn means our identity is similarly derived from the eternal deliberation surrounding God's identity, which is nothing other than the breathless question that the Son existentially poses on that hill on Good Friday: '*Will you still be my Father, even though I'm now tied up with these despicable brothers?*' The 'still' in the previous sentence is a deliberate insertion on my part, marking my attempt to indicate – in an inadequate way! – how Jenson understands God's being to be his positive faithfulness to all that he always decided to be in the Father's never-ceasing utterance of this peculiar Word, who is the Son in his sheer obedience as he twists and turns towards the Spirit's embrace into the Future that is God's life through the passage of his temporal infinity.[43] From one perspective, God's simplicity can therefore be understood as the Son's constancy to his identifying origination, by which he is at one and the same time faithful to his final identity, so that the character traits of his life – which are the plot waves of the story we tell – never deviate from a perfect expression of existential trust in his Father as the Son is eternally flung towards the End that is the Spirit of God's life. That is to say:

> Since the Lord's self-identity is constituted in dramatic coherence, it is established not from the beginning but from the end, not at birth but at death, not in persistence but in anticipation . . . he is eternally himself in that he unrestrictedly anticipates an end in which he will be all he could ever be.[44]

What Jenson is claiming here is that the triune persons need to be conceived as the distinct poles of the relations between them, and one of those poles – the Son – has a clear terminus: the hanged man extrinsically focused towards the creature *and* his Originator in his dying breath of

'Father forgive them, for they know not what they do.' In other words, Jenson is arguing that the crucifixion is the defining end of this vector which thereby constitutes the character of the one who says 'Yes' to the Spirit's envelopment of him into the Last Future that is unsurpassable. That is to say, Easter is the event of God's faithfulness to his decision to be the God he in fact is.[45]

Of course, we will find it hard to accept that the pole of that eternal relation is a crucified man. However, we need to say something like this in light of Jenson's proposal, even if we must at the same time accept some drastic consequences. That is because faithfulness is not the same as necessity, and thereby the concept brings with it the actual possibility that God could have undone himself in the freedom of doing himself. However, Jenson thinks the gospel narrative demands we say something like that, even if we now know the possibility to be counterfactual.[46] That is because God's doing of himself in the faithfulness of the journey from Beginning to End is repeatedly left open within the scriptural narrative, hanging there in the repeated refrain of 'will these bones live?' or 'take this cup from me?' or 'into your hands I commend my Spirit'. In other words, Jenson wants us to accept that Jesus lives faithfully from the transcendent horizon of his eternal origination and towards the transcendent horizon of his own end, and thereby defines himself as the presence of the eternity that brackets us, but in a way in which his utter commitment to that which is not God amounts to the posing of a question to God within God's own deliberative act by which God freely makes himself vulnerable within his own faithfulness to the outcome of the eternal Word that he speaks.[47] In short, the Son's faithfulness implies that God is free to be otherwise within that relation.

To put the point differently – and run with an insight from the previous chapter – Jenson thinks God asks God whether he is really willing to be this one, namely, God who lives for the ungodly even unto death so that his identity is bound to us. And a positive answer was by no means guaranteed. In short, Jenson's God is 'the one absolute contingency' of genuine self-actualization.[48]

There can be little doubt that Jenson's proposal includes within it the possibility that God could have undone himself in the act of election, thereby leaving us with a 'mutually betraying pantheon' by which God and everything ceases; the story of God could have taken an unexpected twist in ending in untranscended brutality.[49] To ignore this possibility is 'to misread the gospel', according to Jenson, because the canonical narrative of Scripture presents us with a God who is the pure contingency of could-have-been-otherwise, whose being is therefore the event of his own decision to be God-with-us, and so his own doing of that decision is in some sense questionable because of the sheer contingency of the plot's twists and turns in our presence. 'Will you still be my Father, if this lot are intrinsic to who I am?' Jenson's point is simply that the Father could have said 'No'.

As I understand it, the idea of God being 'questionable' is abhorrent to most theologians, not least if God is the simplicity of his actuality by which he has no potential because he is the pure act that he is, always and forever fully realized in his perfection. But in another respect, the word 'questionable' seems to run hand in hand with the idea of sovereign freedom, in that it gestures towards the way in which God is not imprisoned by anything, even himself, but instead Lords it over his own being. In other words, the idea of God being 'questionable' needn't be considered an unwelcome weakness, but instead seen as 'an ontological perfection', if God himself answers it, in that it signifies the power of God to entrust himself freely to himself for the other, without defence, which is his being-in-love.[50] That is to say, the ground of the act that God *is* is nothing other than the act that he is, which is to say that there is no extrinsic measure to underwrite its certainty other than its sheer actuality, because we cannot legislate what is necessary for God to be God. That is why Jenson argues that what happens at Easter must be considered contingent in its happening – i.e. a living out for the other unto death poses the question – which is thereby questionable only on its own terms. In short, God alone underwrites God, and he does so in the way of his free self-election. Or put otherwise, he doesn't choose this life in abstraction; the choosing is the *living*.

Of course, all of this is by-the-by in many respects. The 'questionability' of the sheer contingency of God's act of decision is secondary to the answer given to that question, i.e. it is the outcome of God's eternal deliberation that is key. Whatever mechanics make up the act, it is the God we are left with that should interest us (and not one who isn't now to be).[51] And for Jenson, the outcome of God's act is clear: the resurrection means God is the decision to be God for the ungodly. In effect, 'The Father has defined his deity itself by the appeal of that man, "Father, forgive them . . .": to be God *is* to be the one who says "yes" in that exchange'.[52] In other words, 'What the Spirit brings is the triumph of one whose personal character is that he does not cling to what he is or has, whose individuality is his freedom from his merely private self.'[53] That is to say, this God is resolutely public, and he is so with us. There simply is no God without the creature.

8.3 Creation comes after Easter

As we can now see, Jenson thinks the climactic act of God's faithfulness to himself happens palpably on that Easter morning when the Father says 'yes' to this Son – who is the Man for Others – thereby raising him into the future of the Spirit, so that God is the act of wedding himself to the ungodly in the act of resurrection.[54] Put otherwise, the triune structure of God's faithfulness to himself is the way in which this God is without potential, but he is what he is in the 'roomy' manner of threefold deliberation by which he may not have been fully himself from Beginning to End. That is to say, the narrative flow of trust and dependency and generosity and reception between the Father and Jesus in time combine as the mutual aspects of this singularly coherent life, which is somehow essential to making God to be the merciful God he freely chooses. And that means Jenson is claiming – and here comes the substantive point of the double homoousion of the Son's single hypostasis – that the mysterious transcendence implied by *became man* is acted out from the already-assumed position of utter commitment to the created order, for whom God is always-already set to die. Or to put that otherwise, faithfulness to a transcendent End is what makes the plot cohere as a whole, but love for the other is the story which is thereby told. In being for himself, he is for us.

Now this point is highly significant. Jenson thinks God eternally speaks precisely that love, the speaking of which God eternally is. Therefore, God is to be pictured as the converse of love in freedom, meaning he is stuck with us – and not in the abstract, but in the sense of what happened over Easter. As a result, Jenson is proposing something along the following lines: the only way the creature could separate itself from God is to take him in our hands and kill him, but God has always-already chosen the event of separation as his life in Jesus Christ, whose *hypostasis* – as an eternally subsisting relation that is its own term – is always and forever determined by its directionality to the cross. And this means that nothing can separate us from the love that God is, because the event of the creatures' attempt to separate is the definition of his life. Or, as Jenson puts it:

> He chose to happen for us as the Crucifixion, as the very event of our hatred and suffering – and is therefore the God who cannot be separated from us, for the very occurrence of what could have separated him from us he chose as his life.[55]

In effect, Jenson thinks we are stuck with God, just as much as God is stuck with us, because God has defined himself as the merciful one in relation to us. And by 'us', I mean his sin-sick enemies.

Now, there is again plenty more that needs to be said here, and we will need to run at this point from several directions, each of which will allow us to sharpen the question as to our own existence in relation to God's act of self-election over the Easter weekend. Of course, because the gospel deals with God's act towards us, creaturely consequences will always follow. If, for instance, the God of the gospel is somehow – and that 'somehow' is again what is up for grabs in this entire discussion – the cause of all being, then our existence is determined by his continuous act towards us, i.e. God being logically and ontologically prior to everything that is. A raft of divine attributes can be derived from this insight, in that it means God's omnipresence and omnipotence is thereby assumed, because of the fact that *everything* comes from him, and – looking at the same point from another direction – the existential form that the creature takes is likewise shaped by God's act of creation. We are what we are because of what he does. None of that is rocket science, at least not in theological circles.

But on Jenson's reading, things have become more complex. God's nature has been moved, so to speak, into the midst of created being. That is to say, God is himself being worked out – and in! – through the paschal mystery. And so we must conclude that 'God *is* what will come of Jesus and us, *together*'.[56] This implies that all reality is somehow determined right from the start – and right now – by this strange act which is 'not a something, however rarefied or immaterial, but a *going-on*, a sequentially palpable event, like a kiss or a train wreck'.[57] Or to put the point in the starkest of terms: the incomparable being of God, from which all other beings derive, is situated slap, bang, middle of the history we are caught up in. As a result, we must say that all creation springs from that cross and tomb, being derived from whatever we are denoting with the verb '*resurrect*'.

In other words, Jenson thinks that 'God is the event of the world's transformation by Jesus' love, the same love to which the world owes its existence', and, in putting the matter like that, we again spot how he has thrown everything up the air.[58] Jenson's attention to the gospel narrative means he is circling around the strange idea that the ground of all being is the event of raising this Nazarene. In effect, the pure act of what happened in the tomb is to be considered the *causa sui*, which is therefore not to be understood as one being among other beings, but the source of all being. This means Jenson can claim – to cite just one instance, taken from his reading of Barth – that 'Human being is being which *originates* in the event of its rescue from perversion and its exaltation into fulfilment in the existence of Jesus Christ.'[59] As a result, when asked 'What is it to *be*?' Jenson can simply answer, 'It is to have a part to play in Jesus' life story.'[60] Or put otherwise, 'saying that "Christ is risen!" is [always] the truest thing you could say about the world.'[61] But how on earth does that work?

In many respects, this question has been hovering on the horizon throughout this book, most notably when we explored the way in which any conception of eternity is the way in which we give meaning to time, thereby constituting it as a specific history by which we navigate the contingencies of our lives. Because Jenson has pulled the eternal bracketing into time – so that the infinite End breaks out at the terminus of a specific temporal trajectory – he must conclude that things exist only in direct relation to the narratable event of God's self-determination.[62] Or to put the point another way, because Jenson argues that 'were the gospel fully spoken, it would be a word about every item of reality',[63] he is on the verge of implying that everything that exists – and everything that happens to the existent – is somehow determined by its place within the singular story that God tells God about God, i.e. what happens with Jesus and his Father in the Spirit. And just so: if God is what happens with Jesus, everything must come logically after that event.

To put the point otherwise, the way Jenson has set things up means it is not only the End that breaks out in the middle, but also the Beginning. The incarnation of the Son 'is not a single punctual event on some time line exterior to it; but is foundational to all on that created time line that would be said to precede or follow it'.[64] Or to put that in even bolder terms, creation comes after Easter.[65]

Again, this is difficult to think, and on first hearing it sounds absurd.[66] As David Bentley Hart once noted, 'it is a fairly inflexible law of logic that no reality can be the emergent result of its own contingent effects'.[67] As a result, it is hard to see how *what we did to the Nazarene* can somehow be the primary cause of our existence. Nonetheless, Jenson thinks, 'it is Christ's resurrection and ascension that create the church; [and] thus Christ is agent precisely of the first creation and of the purpose of all creation'.[68]

Now, we must be careful not to overdo the sequentiality of the act of creation in relation to Easter. God is the triune movement towards himself from the poles of eternity, which takes us along in his wake through this event. Otherwise put, his relation to us is internal to him. Therefore, the precedence of resurrection over creation is more logical, than temporal, but only within the one single act that it is.[69] Thereby, 'the succession of . . . life [is not] plotted on a sort of neutral timeline, which would run as it runs whether or not the risen Lord were before the Father in the Spirit'.[70] It is instead best imagined as the event of the creature spiralling 'around the resurrected Jesus like a helix', with the beginning and end – and every moment in between – thereby being proximate to the infinite risen Lord. '[T]hat is, to be is to rise from the dead.'[71]

Of course, Jenson's mind-bending ordering of events demands that we rethink the nature of time. And to do that, it might be helpful first to map out the usual ordering of creation and Jesus, which will allow us to see how odd Jenson's proposal is.

8.4 The purified acts of the one pure act

Before I began to read Jenson, I had assumed that Jesus is the way he is – embodied as a specific version of humanity – because God had made human beings like that before we needed saving. In effect, the Son took on our previously established form. Jenson, however, thinks it is the other way around. That is to say, we are the way we are – 'the featherless biped', with two arms, a single head and so on[72] – because *that* is always and forever God's second hypostatic identity, who we are called to image as his companions.[73] In short, Jesus comes first, the rest of us after.[74]

Now, the metaphysical outworking of this will occupy us shortly, not least when we see the way the triune identities occupy time's poles, so that God envelops us as Beginning, End and specious Presence in such a way that our time spirals around the resurrected Son 'like a helix', with each successive moment – from creation through to eschaton – being equidistant from the epicentre of his resurrection from which all creation derives.[75] But I want to approach this aspect of Jenson's thought by way of a different question. Because Jenson is saying the eternal Word the Father speaks – thereby making himself Father – is the life of this one who journeys from virginal womb to lonely cross, he ends up asking whether the sin-sick death on a Roman gallows is essential to the relation between these two *hypostases*, eternally.

Of course, we usually think Jesus died because we sinned, thereby positing the counterfactual possibility that a Redeemer might not have been needed if Adam didn't fall. In fact, before encountering Jenson's work, I had studied the way God's decision to save us can be seen either through a supralapsarian or postlapsarian lens, and had even weighed up the options myself, finding that I struggled to conceive of the incarnation as a Plan B, so to speak. I therefore sided with those who believe God was always intending to become incarnate. In effect, the fall doesn't cause the taking on of flesh, but instead only impacts the form his already-decided embodiment would take.[76] That is to say, rather than the Son of God coming in the fullness of time to be met in celebration by his creatures – Love himself joyfully enthroned! – the fall means the Son ends up coming as the despised and rejected one, unfairly judged and finally executed outside Jerusalem's gates. In short, the Son's rightful throne was transformed into a gallows.[77] But I then discovered Jenson rules out both these options.[78] He refuses to accept that Jesus is any kind of deviation from God's primary intent, which means Jenson must take on 'the resultant burdens' of tackling the thorny issue as to whether sin and fall are somehow written into God's creative act, so that God is finally their author.[79]

In many respects, no other conclusion is possible for Jenson. He thinks, 'the Word that is Jesus was the Word spoken at the beginning', and so what actually happens with Jesus is what makes God to be the God that he is.[80] Creation and atonement are thereby drawn into the doctrine of God, which is exactly where you will find these topics in Jenson's *Systematics*.[81] He thereby rejects standard ordering – God, creation, fall, redemption and so on – and instead pulls everything into the one act of God, with the termination of God and creation being the crucifixion of the Son at the hands of the ungodly. As a result, all of reality is enfolded into the doctrine of God – even the bad bits – so that Jenson ends up singing his own version of the 'famous line from the Exultet of the Easter Vigil . . . "Oh fortunate sin *(felix culpa)* that occasioned such great redemption!"'[82]

Jenson's signature move makes this stark conclusion inevitable. Because the gospel narrative has all sorts of twists and turns within it – with the denouement of death being driven by a prior betrayal, with us turning away to eat and drink and be merry – he must draw these 'plot waves' into the creative act, at the risk of drawing them into God.[83] Of course, Jenson – just like other theologians – must in some sense conclude that all things are caught up in the pure act that is God, because where else could we live and move and have our being? If in the beginning there is only God – which is what creation *ex nihilo* implies – then there are only two possible 'places' towards which everything is heading: God or nothingness.[84] That is to say, God is not held in a larger container within which we could find some alternative, semi-autonomous space for ourselves, somehow at a distance from the 'space' that God is. We must somehow – and again that 'somehow' is what is up for debate – either be participating in him and with him and through him, or instead be falling away into non-being. As a result, it seems obvious that all the good and bad things that happen must be aligned to one or other of these trajectories.

Of course, this is usually done by keeping the bad stuff at an infinite distance from God, in effect, identifying them as a privation in being, a falling into nothingness. However, we can now see that Jenson is saying something more radical than that. Jenson thinks we only exist in the more concrete sense of the freedom of God's decisive choice in its sheer palpable occurrence, which is the event of God determining himself to always and forever be – to the very depths of his being – the merciful God who dies for the ungodly. God is therefore nothing other than the eternal mutual conversation of self-identification in which the Father's eternally spoken Word has genuine content, and that content is the sounding of the temporal resonance of giving oneself fully to the other that terminates on a gallows – generously fathering *this* Sonning, who therein is generously opening outwards towards the other who is met by the generously intruding Spirit who comes through the event of dereliction by which God makes God to be forever God-*with-us*. As a result, the being

JESUS IN THE TRINITY

of God is best pictured as an envelopment that includes us and thereby constitutes us as those spoken about by this God in this excruciating way.[85] Therefore – and this is the point to which this discussion has been heading – what God says, in the pure act that he *is*, is: '*Let me be purely for purified acts*'.[86]

We can now see what is most astonishing about Jenson's proposal. He thinks the internal trajectory of God's self-causing is not hidden from us in any normal sense, but is instead publicly worked out in what happens between Jesus, the eternal Son – who is our brother – and his Father in the life of the Spirit they share with sinners. Or to put that another way, Jenson runs with Luther's celebrated phrase that 'God made us to redeem us', but gives it his own twist. *God makes us by redeeming us to constitute himself.*[87]

Whatever consequences arise from this odd conclusion – which Jenson calls 'an awesome question'[88] – we can clearly see that it shatters our conception of time by placing Easter at the beginning of everything. It allows for no timeline in the standard sense of the word – or 'pseudo timeline', as Jenson sometimes calls it[89] – but is instead suggestive of something more akin to time spiralling around the resurrected Son, who is both Alpha and Omega breaking out in the middle,[90] so that all points on the spiralling line are equidistant from the span of Good Friday to Easter Sunday, which is the paschal epicentre, so to speak, by which time becomes historical in line with a bracketing eternity that envelops us from each of time's poles.[91] In other words, he is arguing that '"Let there be . . ." and "Christ is risen" are but two utterances of God within one dramatically coherent discourse'.[92] But – once again! – how on earth does that work?

8.5 Baptizing time

Jenson's proposal is clearly odd, although that doesn't necessarily make it false. It is not as if any of us are certain as to how the reality of created time works. We earlier noted how the greatest minds – such as Augustine's[93] – have struggled to make sense of the way in which the past and future relate to the present, with neither pole possessing any status outside the fleeting present moment. This means we should not rule out any new proposal, because no current construal of time can yet claim to be definitive. The point is therefore simple: we can agree with Jenson that created time is not necessarily Aristotle's timeline or Plato's revolving circuit around a point, and instead be open to the possibility that it is more gospel-shaped than that. Maybe the Spirit does bend everything around the aseity of the Father's act in raising the Son, because – as St Paul says – 'Everything there is comes from him and is caused by him and exists for him' (Rom. 11.36), with that pronoun picking out the resurrected Jesus.[94]

With this being so, we should explore Jenson's proposal further. He thinks Jesus is Lord, and seeks to discover what this means in relation to time. As he sees it, the envelopment of an unprecedented Beginning and from an unsurpassable End towards the presence of the resurrected Christ – who is the fullness of time by which it coheres from the start as a purposeful history by spiralling around him – is the best way to make sense of the claim that Jesus of Nazareth is Lord, in that 'time is the *accommodation* this life makes in itself for the particular History that the Son in fact and freely is, Jesus' history with what is not God'.[95] As I understand it, this again is not bizarre. In fact, Jenson is in some respects in good company. Many theologians have considered the Old Testament epiphanies, for example, to be epiphanies of the Son: Jesus is the rock in the desert, the one who wrestles with Jacob, etc., and have then proceeded to spell out the *'how can this be so?'*[96] As I read the Gospels, the resurrection appearances certainly suggest Jesus occupies a strange relation to time and space, with him appearing and disappearing by coming through closed doors to meet his disciples.[97] If we are happy for these episodes to inform our confession that Jesus is Lord, they could underwrite the idea that he is sovereign over time as well, so that past and future don't fall away from the fleeting present for him like they do for us. And if that is so, why can't the resurrected Jesus walk with Adam in the cool breeze of the evening, offering a gentle word to the crestfallen creature that 'It's okay, your redeeming Creator lives'?[98] And if that is so, why can't this retroactive causality be pushed even further, with this very same person rising from the grave to summon Adam first from the dust? Or to put that otherwise, perhaps 'the contingency of the world is *founded* in the contingency of Jesus's life, death, and resurrection'.[99]

Of course, this sounds strange, but Jenson counters that 'The Church has always dutifully taught that all things were created "in" Christ. But in most theology the meaning of that "in" remains utterly obscure.'[100] He thinks this is because our thinking remains hindered, which is to say:

> The claim that the incarnate Christ speaks in all Scripture sounds preposterous, I suggest, only because we unthinkingly make an (in itself rather naive) assumption about time: that it glumly marches on, that someone born in 4 B.C. could not have spoken to and through Jeremiah or that someone who died in A.D. 30 could not have spoken through, say, the seer John. But time, in any construal adequate to the gospel, does not in fact march in this wooden fashion. Time, as we see it framing biblical narrative, is neither linear nor cyclical but perhaps more like a helix, and what it spirals around is the risen Christ.[101]

In other words, if we avoid the trap of un-gospelized thinking, we can marvel at how it is the Father and the Spirit talking about the risen Jesus that launches creation *from* the epicentre of the Son's hypostatic identity, in that 'Time is our accommodation within the event of the Father's and the Spirit's meeting in the life of the Son'.[102] It is not as if we can rule this possibility out if we are dealing with a God who can raise the dead.[103]

To put the point otherwise, our existing conception of time cannot be unshakeable. We should question our very certainties about the concepts of time and causation, and ask whether they are fully baptized by the gospel message. And because we don't know how time or causation really work, Jenson is free to propose we begin afresh, taking the gospel as our non-negotiable starting point and doing things very differently from there. In short, we can begin with the assumption that 'the Son whose relation to the Father enables creation is the *incarnate* Christ'.[104]

Of course, this is an appropriate moment to remember that Jenson's entire project is an experiment, in which he is daring us to imagine that the specific hypostatic arrow from the annunciation through to the crucifixion is the Father's eternal Word. He invites us to think that this eternal Word really has a mother, and spiralling from there, a Babylonian king, an Egyptian pharaoh, a Judas Iscariot and a high priest called Ananias, and disciples and followers, a people Israel, Jacob, Isaac, Abraham, and Adam and Eve, and all the other things we find ourselves situated within. Everything is caused by the one event who God is, which is the resurrection of the Nazarene. In short, all things happen in God, and God happens at Easter.

As a result, Jenson concludes that 'You and I are here to play roles in Jesus' story'.[105] That is to say, we are embarked on an 'ontological adventure' of life with this risen One.[106] He then works out what this means about our status as creatures.

8.6 Wake before wedding

Jenson's way of putting things brings us back to the thorny issue – and that adjective is deliberately suggestive of the crucifixion – of the way in which betrayal, oppression and an entire litany of evil acts are somehow written intrinsically into the act that God is. It would seem that Jenson must move in that direction, because 'God the Son suffers all the contingencies and evils recorded in the Gospel and concludes them by suffering execution.'[107] However, when push comes to shove, Jenson refuses to give existence to evil, other than in the roundabout way of it coming closest to *being* at the precise point that God says 'no' to it as he raises the suffering Son into infinite life.[108] Or to put that point otherwise, evil is only ever what God has already ruled out in the self-determining act of creation, which is itself a judgement by which God determines that the creature will live forever because God has elected to die for his enemies so that death is no more.[109] Put differently, 'the goal of God's path is just what does in fact happen with Jesus the Christ', so 'sin and evil belong to God's intent precisely – but only – as they do appear in Christ's victory over them'.[110]

With that in mind, Jenson thinks evil only exists to the extent that it is eternally rejected by an intolerant God,[111] which is to say, 'It is the destiny of evil to cease. But this is not just its future destiny, it is also its origin. The last word about evil is also the first . . . [Its basis] *is its own overcoming*'[112] That is why Jenson thinks – again echoing Barth – that 'our confession of a good Creator is and will remain a great "nevertheless", a defiance of what we would otherwise conclude',[113] because there is no way to untangle God's act from the presence of evil in our midst. Although there can be no equivalence between God's 'yes' and his 'no', as if sin and evil are willed 'in order that' the good may be seen to triumph, Jenson thinks that theodicy – the justification of God – is yet another place where our explanations run aground. As he puts it, 'the Gospel does not *explain* the rule of history's hidden Lord'.[114] This is why the church has never really sought to explain evil, because an explanation would bring it into positive relation with the rationality of truth, thereby linking it to the transcendental of beauty and goodness. The church instead confesses that evil is ugly, absurd and an outright lie, finally amounting to no more than the 'incarnation of vacuity', as Jenson puts it, which is to say it is the impossible actuality of a privation in being that God will not countenance *from the start*.[115] Put otherwise, the 'bluster and disguises of this world's powers are become mere illusion', because evil begins with the attempt to un-create ourselves, which God has countered eternally by choosing to be the crucified God.[116]

With this being so, we must remember that Jenson thinks the vanquishing of evil is an 'actual historical conflict [that] occurred between an unholy alliance of Rome and Jerusalem and this lone Jew'.[117] That is to say, he has not slipped into the abstract here, or – to put that more positively – he thinks we are irresistibly caught up in the act by which God eternally does God, so that we might live forever as those for whom he dies. And just so, we cannot explain the evil we are caught up in exhaustively, because it is possessed – and thereby overcome – by the merciful God right from the start. Thus, we can only accept that our being is *simul iustus et peccator* – simultaneously justified and sinful – in that we are purified acts of the one pure act who is the eternal decision to die for the ungodly. As a result, just like the theory of atonement, Jenson's account of evil and sin can only 'be liturgically inhabited',[118] rather than explained by something more basic. Wonder is the final word.

If we run with Jenson on this, the question we are left with is whether the suffering we are experiencing is somehow real. In some respects – just like any good story – we can only wait until the end of time to make that call. In the intervening period, we can only trust – despite all the evil we perpetrate and suffer – that God is good. However, if Jenson is on the right track, we can also see that the End is best conceived as liturgical music. That is to say, we will forever be singing the praises – rhyming, dancing in utter reciprocal excitement – with the one who is nothing other than the eternal decision to die for us so we might live within the 'fugue' that is God in the eternal rhyming of the Easter event.[119] In other words, because God is the resurrected life that he infinitely possesses, Jenson offers us a vision of a God who we can't keep up with because he is the pure act that is the pure excitement of springing from the grave in the delightfully good beauty of his triune movement to embrace sin-sick creatures within his thereby defined life *from the start*.[120] That is to say, creation is definitively the registered musicality of *iustus et peccator* by which God is the temporal infinity of the threefold repetition of the particular note by which the temporal arrows of whence and whither resound in the envelopment of time by this crucified Son who triumphs over our enmity. Everything that has ever existed is therefore a riff on his life, as it spirals like a helix around the victory of his self-giving love. And that sounds like good news to me. It means everything we do – for good or for ill – happens only to the extent that it rides the 'plot waves' of the story of God, crucified and risen, with that story being 'capacious enough' to accommodate our very worst, just as much as it can handle our occasional best. In short, 'the Father and the Spirit take the suffering of the creature – who the Son is – into the triune life and bring from it the final good of that creature, all other creatures, and of God'.[121]

Just so, if we push Jenson's musical metaphor further, we can say that the creature is sung into existence, being called as the counterpoint to the triune fugue which sounds out *as* Easter.[122] Our creation, salvation and perfection thereby find their place in the being of God, because that is what his threefold chord eternally sounds.[123] And that is to say, the 'very being of creation is this harmony, to be a creature is, in this respect, to be harmonized, to fit in an endlessly complicated web of mutually appropriate relations'.[124] And on that reckoning a sinner confesses that 'God is our end in that we will be taken into the triune life. *Deification* is our end.' In effect, our thankful gospelizing sounds the penitential note in the triune harmony, which the hopeful creature is finally delighted to sing as the essence of the purified act that the creature is from the start.

To put this complex matter more simply, Jenson is arguing that 'the world is a wedding', with all the singing and dancing and feasting that such events bring, but this wedding comes after the funeral of the forever living Groom to whom we are wed.[125] God's pure act of self-determination is thereby understood as the excitement of celebrating the purified act – which *is* the forgiven sinner – and ours is the delight of the liberated penitents who are thereby caught up in the infinite tune of Mary's boy in the wedding banquet of the Lamb. In other words, 'to be a creature is, in this respect, to be freed'.[126] And so:

> The difference between the average god and the triune God is that the latter has *room* in himself, and so has room in himself for others than himself if he so wills . . . there is a sort of familial society in God, and it is God's purpose to bring redeemed humankind into that family as the daughter-in-law.[127]

As a result, created being is a never-ending delight. The one and only God – who the gospel identifies – is so utterly for us unto death, 'and then yet again faithful',[128] that his very own singing is what purifies our reverberating being, so that our existence is the call to get more into tune, more into step, thereby keeping up with the excitement of God's eternal song and dance.[129] Of course, we will want to sound our own note this side of the End, thereby wanting to prise open a gap between ourselves and the God who *is* his dying for us, sometimes – as Jenson sees it – by kidding ourselves that this separation is for God's benefit, in that we allow him the privacy of his own being-at-a-distance.[130] Jenson, however, knows this won't work. The only way to separate the God of the gospel from ourselves is to kill him, but that event of separation – the opening up of a metaphysical gap – is what God has eternally chosen as his life in Jesus, and therefore nothing can separate us from him. As a result, we can only repeat the refrain: this crucified man is one of the Trinity; one of the Trinity died so that the creature might live; Jesus is Lord and we are his purified acts, and so the 'goal of all things is a holy community', populated by God with forgiven sinners.[131] In short, there is room in God even for us. And that is good news.

Notes

1 Robert W. Jenson, *Systematic Theology*, Vol. 1, *The Triune God* (New York: OUP, 1997), 138–44.

2 In some respects, Jenson simply learns from Barth that 'the doctrine of the person of Christ may not be separated from the doctrine of His work. Rather, since he is what he does, the doctrine of His person must be at the same time the doctrine of His work.' Robert W. Jenson, *Alpha and Omega: A Study in the*

Theology of Karl Barth (Thomas Nelson and Sons, 1963; reprint, Eugene, OR: Wipf and Stock, 2002), 124. As Steve Wright has also commented in personal correspondence, 'Jenson is prepared for this move by his Lutheranism [and it] arises in large part from the denial of the *extra calvinisticum*.'

3 On the way 'person' is something diachronic and not abstractable in snapshot, see Robert W. Jenson, 'Christ as Culture 3: Christ as Drama', *International Journal of Systematic Theology* 6.2 (2004), 194–201.

4 Hence, 'a trinitarian identity is a "relation . . . in the mode of substance"'. Jenson, *Systematic Theology*, Vol. 1, 109.

5 From Barth, Jenson learns, 'the Incarnation is always an event, always to be described with present-tense action verbs. There is no other being of Christ than the movement of God to man and of man to God.' Jenson, *Alpha and Omega*, 125.

6 For concept of drama as a coherent and narratable life, in which what happens with Jesus is constitutive of our life and God's, see Jenson, 'Christ as Culture 3', 194–201.

7 Tee Gatewood, 'A Nicene Christology? Robert Jenson and the Two Natures of Jesus Christ', *Pro Ecclesia* 18 (2009), 32.

8 Robert W. Jenson, 'Gratia Non Tollit Naturam Sed Perficit', *Pro Ecclesia* 24.1 (2015), 122.

9 Jenson, *Alpha and Omega*, 126.

10 Thanks to Steve Wright for help with the phrasing here.

11 On the Son's hypostatic identity being wholly for us, see Robert W. Jenson, *The Triune Identity: God According to the Gospel* (Philadelphia: Fortress, 1982; reprint, Eugene, OR: Wipf and Stock, 2002), 171.

12 Robert W. Jenson, *Systematic Theology, Volume 2, The Works of God* (New York: OUP, 1999), 348.

13 For example, Jenson's emphasis can be seen clearly in the italicization of '*the one whose*' in Jenson, *Systematic Theology*, Vol. 2, 99.

14 For a statement of the idea that 'Jesus so attached himself' that the Father is 'stuck' with us, see Robert W. Jenson and Solveig Lucia Gold, *Conversations with Poppi about God* (Grand Rapids: Brazos Press, 2006), 20.

15 Robert W. Jenson, 'How Does Jesus Make a Difference?' in *Essentials of Christian Theology*, ed. William C. Placher (Louisville: Westminster John Knox Press, 2003), 202.

16 Jenson, *Systematic Theology*, Vol. 1, 229.

17 Jenson, 'How Does Jesus', 202.

18 And Jenson adds: 'No other God has *this* Son. Nor would any other want him.' Robert W. Jenson, 'The God of the Gospel', *Baltimore Paper*, 14–15. See also Jenson, *Systematic Theology*, Vol. 1, 229.

19 Steve Wright, personal correspondence.

20 Rowan Williams, *Christ The Heart of Creation* (London: Bloomsbury Continuum, 2018), 158.

21 Steve Wright, personal correspondence.

22 Robert W. Jenson, 'Creation as a Triune Act', *Word and World* 2.1 (1982), 41.

23 Jenson, *Triune Identity*, 120.

24 Gatewood, 'Nicene Christology', 31.

25 Robert W. Jenson, 'For us . . . He Was Made Man', in *Nicene Christianity: The Future for a New Ecumenism*, ed. Christopher R. Seitz (Grand Rapids: Brazos, 2001), 84.

26 For an example of Jenson working out how the 'external' relations in time *are* the internal relations, and not simply a mirror of them, see Robert W. Jenson, 'Jesus in the Trinity: Wolfhart Pannenberg's Christology and Doctrine of the Trinity', in *The Theology of Wolfhart Pannenberg: Twelve American Critiques, with an autobiographical essay and response*, ed. Carl E. Braaten and Philip Clayton (Minneapolis: Augsburg, 1988), 188–206.

27 Robert W. Jenson, 'The Hidden and Triune God', *International Journal of Systematic Theology* 2.1 (2000), 9.

28 Robert W. Jenson, 'Election and Culture: From Babylon to Jerusalem', in *Public Theology in Cultural Engagement*, ed. Stephen R. Holmes (Milton Keynes: Paternoster, 2008), 53.

29 Jenson, 'Wolfhart Pannenberg's Christology', 200.

30 Emmanuel Durand O.P., 'Perichoresis: A Key Concept for Balancing Trinitarian Theology', in *Rethinking Trinitarian Theology*, ed. Robert J. Wozniak and Giulio Maspero (London and New York: T&T Clark, 2012), 186.

31 For Jenson's thoughts on the *filioque*, see Robert W. Jenson, 'Lutheranism and the *Filioque*', in *Ecumenical Perspectives on the Filioque for the 21st Century*, ed. Myk Habets (London: T&T Clark, 2014), 159–66.

32 Robert W. Jenson, 'Karl Barth on the Being of God', in *Thomas Aquinas and Karl Barth: An Unofficial Catholic-Protestant Dialogue*, ed. Bruce L. McCormack and Thomas Joseph White (Grand Rapids: Eerdmans, 2013), 51.

33 To my knowledge, Jenson never defended his work in this way. However, that may be because he was concerned to move the conversation on from relations of *origin* to think about relations of fulfilment and eschatology, i.e. to find an Archimedean point for the Spirit. However, Jenson does spend time working out how the Father can be both Father and the person of the Trinity, thereby proposing that there is more than one way to be a person. See Jenson, *Systematic Theology*, Vol. 1, 108, 119–24.

34 As Jenson states, 'no one has ever suggested a plausible answer; the arbitrary metaphysical posit of a "*Logos asarkos*" persists mostly because people cannot think of a better idea'. Robert W. Jenson, 'Conceptus . . . De Spiritu Sancto', *Pro Ecclesia* 15.1 (2006), 106.

35 Robert W. Jenson, *Ezekiel* (London: SCM Press, 2009), 44.

36 Jenson, *Systematic Theology*, Vol. 1, 141.

37 Jenson, *Systematic Theology*, Vol. 1, 141.

38 Jenson, 'For us . . .' 84.

39 Hence his argument that '"From" [two natures] did not in Cyril's use have chronological meaning, as if there were first two actual natures who then came together. It is "from" the realm of possibility that two natures emerge into one hypostasis'. Jenson, *Systematic Theology*, Vol. 1, 131.

40 Robert W. Jenson, 'Triune Grace', *Dialog* 41.4 (2002), 288.

41 Jenson, 'How Does Jesus', 194.

42 Jenson, *Systematic Theology*, Vol. 1, 165.

43 In stark terms, 'The Lord's deity is his faithfulness'. Robert W. Jenson, 'Jesus, Father, Spirit: The Logic of the Doctrine of the Trinity', *Dialog* 26.4 (1987), 249. Jenson therefore thinks the theological concept of 'word' is best understood 'in the exact same sense in which we until recently spoke of "a gentleman's word"', i.e. it is personal faithfulness to a promise. Robert W. Jenson, 'The Triune God', in *Christian Dogmatics*, ed. Carl E. Braaten and Robert W. Jenson (Philadelphia: Fortress, 1984), 104.

44 Jenson, *Systematic Theology*, Vol. 1, 66.
45 Jenson, *Systematic Theology*, Vol. 1, 220.
46 Because it amounts to the 'crisis of the total biblical narrative', in Jenson, *Systematic Theology*, Vol. 1, 65–6.
47 Jenson thinks this is 'the only real question', amounting to the way in 'which the Hebrew Scriptures in a real sense conclude . . . "Son of Man, can these bones live?" (Ezek. 37:3).' Jenson, *Triune Identity*, 39.
48 Jenson, 'For us . . .' 77.
49 Jenson, *Systematic Theology*, Vol. 1, 65.
50 Jenson, *Systematic Theology*, Vol. 1, 64.
51 Jenson, *Systematic Theology*, Vol. 1, 221.
52 Robert W. Jenson, 'Jesus in the Trinity', *Pro Ecclesia* 8 (1999), 317.
53 Jenson, *Systematic Theology*, Vol. 1, 219.
54 Jenson, *Systematic Theology*, Vol. 1, 191.
55 Robert W. Jenson, *A Religion Against Itself* (John Knox Press, 1967; reprint, Eugene, OR: Wipf and Stock), 41.
56 Jenson, 'The Triune God', 101. Second emphasis added.
57 Jenson, *Systematic Theology*, Vol. 1, 214.
58 Jenson, *Systematic Theology*, Vol. 1, 221.
59 Jenson, *Alpha and Omega*, 98.
60 Jenson, *Alpha and Omega*, 170.
61 Steve Wright, in personal correspondence.
62 Jenson – like others – is clear that the *End* breaks out in middle. See, for example, Jenson, 'Lutheranism and the *Filioque*', 164.
63 Robert W. Jenson, *Story and Promise: A Brief Theology of the Gospel About Jesus* (Philadelphia: Fortress Press, 1973; reprint, Eugene, OR: Wipf & Stock 2014), 76.
64 Jenson, 'Election and Culture', 58. Again, Jenson blocks off our retreat to John's prologue. See, for example, Colin Gunton and Robert W. Jenson, 'The *Logos Ensarkos* and Reason', in *Reason and the Reasons of Faith*, ed. Paul J. Griffiths and Reinhard Hütter (London: T&T Clark, 2005), 81.
65 As Jenson puts it by quoting St Paul, 'it is a single concept that God "gives life to the dead and calls into existence the things that do not exist"'. The point here is that the order can be considered important, even if ever proved accidental. Jenson, *Systematic Theology*, Vol. 2, 14.
66 I suspect something like this idea thought first struck Jenson during his doctoral research into Barth's doctrine of election. You can see Jenson grappling with the strange relation between creation and reconciliation in Barth's work in Jenson, *Alpha and Omega*, 117–19.
67 David Bentley Hart, 'The Illusionist', *The New Atlantis* (Summer/Fall 2017), 118.
68 Jenson, 'Creation as a Triune Act', 41.
69 For Jenson's reasoning behind the claim that creation and redemption of singular yet distinct within the triune act of God-with-us, see Jenson, *Systematic Theology*, Vol. 2, 3–16.
70 Robert W. Jenson, *Unbaptized God: The Basic Flaw in Ecumenical Theology* (Minneapolis: Fortress, 1992), 146.
71 Jenson, *Triune Identity*, 182.
72 Jenson takes this phrase from Bertrand Russell, but cannot find the original source. Jenson, *Systematic Theology*, Vol. 2, 56.

73 Again, Barth's influence is clear. See, for example, Jenson, *Alpha and Omega*, 97.

74 For one example of Jenson looking to shape our understanding of reality around the eternal Son, see Robert W. Jenson, 'Christ as Culture 1: Christ as Art', *International Journal of Systematic Theology* 6.1 (2004), 69–76.

75 This is Jenson's way of avoiding Augustine's 'oxymoronic root metaphor' of 'a point perpendicular to a straight line yet equidistant from all points on it'. Jenson, *Systematic Theology*, Vol. 2, 32.

76 For the 'Plan B' view, see Jenson, *Alpha and Omega*, 21, and critique 48–51.

77 For how the incarnation can be conceived without a Fall, see Jenson, *Alpha and Omega*, 55–64.

78 See Jenson, *Systematic Theology*, Vol. 1, 71–4.

79 Jenson, *Systematic Theology*, Vol. 1, 73.

80 Jenson, 'Election and Culture', 58.

81 As his reading of Barth taught him, 'the entire reality of what has been called "the way of salvation" stands in force from all eternity'. Jenson, *Alpha and Omega*, 83.

82 Jenson, *Systematic Theology*, Vol. 1, 73. To be clear, Jenson thinks the ancient prayer 'is false'. That is because, 'If virtue merits nothing from God then surely sin does not. And where God sets himself against something there is nothing *felix* about it.' Jenson, *Alpha and Omega*, 52–3.

83 See Jenson, *Systematic Theology*, Vol. 2, 20–4.

84 Robert W. Jenson, 'Creator and Creature', *International Journal of Systematic Theology* 4 (2002), 216–21.

85 Jenson, 'Creation as a Triune Act', 40.

86 Put otherwise, 'Thus the Father's preoccupation with the Son, Jesus' intrusion into the outward flight of the Father's consciousness, does not restrict the Father's consciousness but is rather his consciousness's opening to its universal scope.' Jenson, *Systematic Theology*, Vol. 1, 220.

87 As he puts it, 'it is in that we *will* be what we will be with him, that we *are* at all. God creates by transforming'. Jenson, 'Creation as a Triune Act', 42.

88 Jenson uses this phrase when analysing Barth's reordering of reconciliation prior to the fall. Jenson, *Alpha and Omega*, 40.

89 Robert W. Jenson, 'Once More the Logos Asarkos', *International Journal of Systematic Theology* 13 (2011), 131.

90 Perhaps circumstantial, but Jenson deals first with Omega, before he gets to Alpha in Jenson, *Alpha and Omega*.

91 See Robert W. Jenson, 'Liturgy of the Spirit', *Lutheran Quarterly* 26.2 (1974), 189–203. Paul Cumin makes a strong case for seeing Jenson's account as an inversion of Plato's concept of time circling around the still point of eternity. For Jenson, God envelops the creation – which is given room within the *taxis* of his being – by perichoresing around the baptized. Paul Cumin, 'Robert Jenson and the Spirit of it All: Or, You (Sometimes) Wonder Where Everything Else Went', *Scottish Journal of Theology* 60.2 (2007), 161–79.

92 Jenson, *Systematic Theology*, Vol. 2, 68.

93 Jenson, *Systematic Theology*, Vol. 2, 29–31.

94 As Jenson says, 'If the claims about Jesus are true, time is odd over against our expectations of it. It is this oddity about time that is God'. Jenson, *Triune Identity*, 168. Scripture quotation taken from the New Jerusalem Bible (London: Darton, Longman & Todd, 1985).

95 Jenson, 'Creation as a Triune Act', 40.

96 See for example, Irenaeus, *Against Heresies*, 4.10.1. For an example of Jenson's approach, see Jenson, *Ezekiel*, 42.

97 Jenson, *Systematic Theology*, Vol. 1, 197.

98 This would exemplify Jenson's belief that 'That Jesus lives means that his love, perfected at the cross, is now active to surprise us. That Jesus lives means that there is a subject who has us as his objects, and wills our good in a freedom beyond our predicting.' Jenson, *Systematic Theology*, Vol. 1, 199.

99 Robert W. Jenson, *Canon and Creed* (Louisville: Westminster John Knox Press, 2010), 94. Emphasis added.

100 Jenson, *Alpha and Omega*, 93.

101 Robert W. Jenson, 'Scripture's Authority in the Church', in *The Art of Reading Scripture*, ed. Ellen F. Davis and Richard B. Hays (Grand Rapids: Eerdmans, 2003), 35.

102 Jenson, *Unbaptized God*, 145.

103 In effect, God creatively touches particular points from the Resurrection, and his act is more like a hyperbar than a flat omni-presence. On this matter, see Jenson's uses of 'meter bars' and 'hyperbars' to show how God is not limited by our conception of passibility and impassibility. Robert W. Jenson, 'Ipse Pater non est impassibilis', in *Divine Impassibility and the Mystery of Human Suffering*, ed. James F. Keating and Thomas Joseph White, O.P. (Grand Rapids: Eerdmans, 2009), 117–26. Jenson was averse to static states from childhood, when he realized – around the age of eight – that there is little difference between a perpetual state of bliss or torment if both are changeless: 'if heaven just goes on and on and on, and hell goes on and on and on, there's not a whole lot of difference between them'. Jenson and Gold, *Conversations*, 15.

104 Jenson, 'Election and Culture', 59. Emphasis added.

105 Robert W. Jenson, *A Large Catechism* (Delhi, NY: American Lutheran Publicity Bureau, 1991), 23.

106 Jenson, *Systematic Theology*, Vol. 1, 55.

107 Jenson, *Systematic Theology*, Vol. 1, 144.

108 See, for example, the discussion in Jenson, *Alpha and Omega*, 38–9 and 101–7.

109 Jenson, *Alpha and Omega*, 34–7.

110 Jenson, *Systematic Theology*, Vol. 1, 73, and see Vol. 2, 17–20.

111 If not, Jenson thinks we can only agree with 'Luther's rationalist' that God is 'a sheer Malevolence'. Jenson, *Systematic Theology*, Vol. 2, 21.

112 Jenson, *Alpha and Omega*, 102–3. Of course, Jenson knows the gospel is central to make this judgement. Otherwise again, 'As Martin Luther once said, if we judge by how God visibly created affairs, we must conclude "either that God is not or that he is wicked"'. Robert W. Jenson, *Lutheran Slogans: Use and Abuse* (Delhi, NY: American Lutheran Publicity Bureau, 2011), 7.

113 Jenson, *Systematic Theology*, Vol. 2, 23.

114 Jenson, *Alpha and Omega*, 158. As he adds, 'The Gospel of forgiveness does not establish the unity of God's will through a series of "in order thats".'

115 See Robert W. Jenson, 'Much Ado About Nothingness'. See also, Jenson, *Systematic Theology*, Vol. 2, 130–2. Jenson thinks the devil's days are numbered, but 'What his mode of nonbeing thereafter will be need not concern us; the universe will be rid of him' (Vol. 2, 334).

116 Jenson, *Systematic Theology*, Vol. 1, 193.

117 Jenson, *Systematic Theology*, Vol. 1, 193.
118 Jenson, *Systematic Theology*, Vol. 2, 24. But see the extensive discussion of sin, nonetheless, across Vol. 2, 133–52.
119 Jenson, *Systematic Theology*, Vol. 1, 235.
120 In fact, '*to be* God is always to be open to and always to open a future, transgressing all past-imposed conditions'. Jenson, *Systematic Theology*, Vol. 1, 216. Emphasis added.
121 Jenson, *Systematic Theology*, Vol. 1, 144. Parenthetical dashes added.
122 Jenson, *Systematic Theology*, Vol. 2, 39. This is perhaps why Jenson prefers 'counterpart' to 'image' when discussing the distinct calling of the human in creation (Vol. 2, 15–16).
123 Jenson, *Systematic Theology*, Vol. 1, 236.
124 Jenson, *Systematic Theology*, Vol. 2, 41.
125 Robert W. Jenson, 'Aspects of a Doctrine of Creation', in *The Doctrine of Creation: Essays in Dogmatics, History and Philosophy*, ed. Colin E. Gunton (London: T&T Clark, 2004), 23.
126 Jenson, *Systematic Theology*, Vol. 2, 41.
127 Robert W. Jenson, 'The Trinity and Church Structure', in *Shaping Our Future: Challenges for the Church in the Twenty-First Century*, ed. J. Stephen Freeman (Boston: Cowley Publications, 1994), 20.
128 Jenson, *Systematic Theology*, Vol. 1, 217.
129 See Jenson, *Systematic Theology*, Vol. 1, 235. In step with Jonathan Edwards, Jenson thinks music is vital, because 'what God thinks is precisely tunes, coherent sequences of events'. Robert W. Jenson, *America's Theologian: A Recommendation of Jonathan Edwards* (Oxford: OUP, 1988), 47.
130 Jenson, *Canon and Creed*, 90–1.
131 Robert W. Jenson, 'What Kind of God Can Make a Covenant?' in *Covenant and Hope: Christian and Jewish Reflections*, ed. Robert W. Jenson and Eugene B. Korn (Grand Rapids: Eerdmans, 2012), 7.

PART FOUR

And So

9

What on Earth Do We Do?

9.1 A theology of the humdrum

We have now tackled some seriously weighty issues, and no doubt Jenson's analysis of God's act of self-determination will have raised many questions. This is only to be expected if we are dealing with a description of the reality of God's triune nature, because none of us can expect to speak the conclusive word on that subject. The theological task knows no end, if only because God is utterly alive as the act of his own existence. Any proposal will therefore raise questions, and the joy is in the conversation.

With this being recognized, I want to use this chapter to explore how Jenson's constructive proposal impacts his readers directly, in the sense that Jenson cultivates a particular posture towards the reality we inhabit. Thankfully this task will be quite easy, at least in comparison to the previous chapters. That is because Jenson's feet are planted firmly on the ground despite his high-flying explorations. That is to say, his doctrine of God is in fact *a theology of the humdrum.*

Jenson believes the God of the gospel is precisely what happens in the life Jesus lives with his Father and the Spirit they share. Because Jenson thinks the Son is always and forever the enfleshed life of this specific man, there is no need for us to evacuate our own historical existence in order to engage with this particular God. God the Son is eternally plotted within the exact same reality as we ourselves are, albeit in a radically different manner as its creative Lord. God the Son thereby defines the meaning of our lives by drawing us into spacious continuity with himself in the enveloping relations of the triune aseity, and with the second Person of the Trinity making his eternal dwelling with us, there is nowhere else for us to travel. Put otherwise, God's relation to us is interior to him. 'We already live, move, and have our being in God even as rebellious creatures'.[1]

Because of the way Jenson sets things up, he must reject any attempt to detach ourselves from the history God creates. He therefore criticizes any tendency to curve in on ourselves in an attempt to venture towards some spiritual realm that is somehow divorced from the embodiment of our everyday lives.[2] Of course, Jenson knows our standard belief in a *timeless* God at some stage impels us to leave our religious symbols behind to get to the real thing, in effect thereby navigating the imagined distance between eternity and the lives we live.[3] But Jenson thinks the gospel puts a stop to this approach, because the eternal enfleshment of the Son means we are free to celebrate the way in which the Spirit creatively draws each of us into union with Jesus in our concrete specificity before our Father, by which our own personhood is constituted – as an analogue to the eternal Son – in the two-way communion of enfleshed God and enfleshed neighbour within the particular nexus of historical relations we inhabit. In short, there is nowhere to flee.

In other words, Jenson thinks we are called to love this particular God and our particular neighbours as the act of our particular purified being, and all of this is to happen within the contours of our own particular history within the plot line of God's gift of himself to us. Because 'to receive myself from God and be directed towards him is . . . to receive myself from and be directed toward a fellow human', our lives are to be – *simultaneously* – a 'self-transcendence from and to God and from and to one another'.[4] Therefore there must be no flight to a spiritual realm, and any attempt to encourage one 'must be repudiated no matter how embedded in piety'.[5] That is because, 'The Gospel relocates God; it says: The Life you seek – it is Jesus! The Bread you seek – it is Jesus! It is the words you now hear and the food you now eat!'[6]

Of course, we'll need to dig into the details of this shortly, especially the way Jenson critiques *and* applauds the religious lives we live. However, what I hope we can already sense, is the way his theology – from at least this perspective – makes for an easy read. By celebrating the sheer contingency of God's decision to be this particular God, Jenson can celebrate the particular contingencies of our own plotted existence.[7] Jenson's readers therefore get the impression they are right to be precisely where they are, so long as they are really there and not trying to escape the concrete embodiment that marks our existence.[8] And that qualification is important. Jenson has plenty of negative things to say about the way we tend to deny the timely nature of our embodied lives, tempted as we are to slide out of the ongoing flux of our dynamic temporality to seek a more stable bedrock beyond the accidental changes that make up our personal existence in relation to our neighbours.[9]

As this suggests, Jenson encourages his readers to make their current temporal location their primary abode in relation to the risen Jesus, because there is no other God than the one within which our brother eternally *is*. If this point is accepted, there is – as always! – a difficult counterpoint with which Jenson's reader must reckon. Jenson is intent on showing how we can remain where we stand, but only by arguing that where we stand is somehow within the timely being of a God who is himself always on the move within the act of his own existence. In effect, Jenson wants to keep things grounded, but only at the risk of throwing everything up in the air by redefining history as a timely existence in which we are enveloped by the triune God, who continually opens up our future to new possibilities by which we are freed from the fixity of the past and able to venture ever on and ever new into the depths of his life within the unending possibilities the gospel event opens through its identification of God and creature within the one act God is.[10] Jenson's readers are therefore at once comforted by the fact that there is nowhere to escape, but at the same time utterly disorientated by the call to live more fully within a temporal process that is essentially a dynamic suspension before, with and behind the infinite dynamic *taxis* of the triune God, who is himself moving at pace as the eternal melody of the 'fugue' that is Jesus and his Father within the Spirit, as the Three draw us into step with themselves.[11] Or, as Green argues, eternal life is a dance, and we are already caught up in it.[12]

To put this point in Jenson's terms:

Perhaps one may in almost unintelligible summary speak of an infinite implosion of love, of a created community pressed and agitated into perfect mutuality by the surrounding life of the triune God.[13]

That is to say, the temporal plot of our specific life is part of the creative movement within the strange life of God by which our existence is derived from God's own continuous excitement of making more and more room within his own life for us.[14] Much has already been said about the way Jenson makes the case for this, especially how he thinks the Father, Son and Spirit mutually constitute God's eternity as a temporal infinity in which they occupy the eternal poles of past, present and future in the imploding perichoresis of the act of raising Jesus, by way of which that which is not God is drawn into his presence. We have traced how he argues that God wills to be this one life from eternity, eternally spoken by the Father before whom there is 'not even nothing', only this Word. And from eternity, the Spirit seals this one as the one beyond whom there is 'not even nothing', only this Word. With these two 'personal poles of eternity' thereby marshalling the timely Son along his way with us, the act of resurrecting this one is the *aseity* of this threefold singular event of God making God-with-us. In effect, we are drawn into a world that *is* already God-with-us as we are summoned from nothingness.

With this complexity noted, a counterpoint follows. The reader's sense of '*being-at-home-in-God's-time*' is yet another way in which Jenson's proposal stands out from the crowd. Too often I close a theology book with the odd feeling that it has pulled me in a different direction. My attention has been directed – whether intentionally or not – towards a God who is himself unmoving in his sheer timelessness, and therefore devoid of time's essential character, and thus standing contrary – and stationary – to all that characterizes my current existence. And because this God is constant, immutable, impassible, simple and always-already everything he will forever be, what I need to do is somehow apply the existential handbrake and turn to face him in utter silence, awestruck at the sheer difference – or indifference – of the timeless realm that beckons. But reading Jenson feels different. He argues that time is not evaporating into the vanishing point of an impassible, simple and utterly remote Absolute, and therein shows that there is no need to identify something in me by which I am timelessly attached to that claustrophobic God. Therefore, our religious mode need not arm us with an arsenal of pietistic tactics, by which we can chip away at the temporal contingencies of our own situated relationships, somehow getting smaller and smaller, and finally collapsing into an interior silence in an attempt to get *everywhere* and *always*.[15] That is to say, the rough edges of our particularity need not be erased in the hope that we can be immersed in a faceless and hidden mystery. Put otherwise, 'the gospel is the last word from God, the object of *final* reliance', so 'there is no call to move on to higher things', unless the gospel 'is false'.[16]

As this suggests, Jenson thinks the gospel enables us to celebrate the humdrum particularity of our own religious life. His theology thereby encourages us to be the particular people we are, embodied in our specific temporal and spatial locality, so that where we are in our contingent specificity is intrinsic to who we are as persons structured in relation to God and each other, and by which we have no need to find an alternative landscape to which our disembodied souls can depart.[17] We are free to celebrate how our lives are inescapably accidental in their contingent movement, thereby helping us make sense of the radical contingency of the life we now live, rising from our beds, heading off to work, labouring and toiling, saying grace with our families, enjoying life in its rich variety, before heading off to St Cuthbert's, St John's or wherever it is that God calls us on a Sunday, because we know there is nothing more substantial than the particularity of such contingencies, *even with God*. In short, we must, 'resist conceptual abstraction and the spiritual move beyond materiality and particularity and commitment in time'. And that is highly unusual.[19]

In many respects, none of this is rocket science. However, Jenson's brilliance lies in managing to create a metaphysical structure by which we can celebrate how Christians find themselves doing odd rituals in odd communities, sprinkling infants in fonts, reading exotic texts, as we sing songs and consume bread and wine, all of which happens downstream from a strange event that is meant to have determined our lives for the good. We therefore need not fear how we face new questions within a post-Christian culture which has deconstructed everything to the extent that we now wait for 'the advent of nothingness',[20] plagued by bureaucratic forms and an all-pervading technology that seeks to impose order on the projected chaos, all the while hearing the command to feed the hungry, house the homeless, make peace with our enemies and seek justice, as suspicious and sceptical people enquire as to how on earth we can believe one man from a wandering tribe is the infinity of God. Jenson celebrates such challenges, with no need to bypass the sheer contingency of these facts. In contrast, their intrinsic oddity is all to the good, because that is precisely how things stand with God – or better *move* with Jesus and his Father in the life of the Spirit they share. In short, it is contingency all the way down, and all the way across.

To put the point otherwise, Jenson argues that 'There is no *other* body of Christ to have to be transported to or supernaturally identified with the loaf and cup – or with the sound of the preacher or the hand that washes the initiate or with the mutual sight of the gathered believers. The author of Colossians meant it: "in him all things hold together. He is the head of the body, the church . . ." (1:17–18)'.[21] Jenson thus refuses to posit some substantially ideal church, invisible beneath the specific manifestations we inhabit, via which we can escape the sheer contingency of the historical lives we live by accessing something irresistibly necessary.[22] Contingency is the heart of the gospel, and so our own lives need no excuse for being a thread of genuinely contingent decisions by which the future opens up within the freedom of possibilities that are never necessities, but that together – in their episodic actuality – make us the particular *hypostases* that we will be when we rise from the grave.

What we therefore end up with is a manifesto for the humdrum practicalities of everyday life, by which Jenson advocates the inhabiting of our temporal specificity more fully, by living in step with the risen Jesus here and now, playing our parts in the ongoing life of God-with-his-creatures by which justice and peace are established as the Spirit draws all of the hopeful penitents into the life of his always enfleshed Son. In other words, our particular lives have very distinct features, which is exactly what to expect if together we are the body of a fully featured Lord. In short, 'One of the Trinity is a Palestinian Jew, who came eating and drinking . . .' and so similar humdrumities are good enough for us. Or to put that negatively, 'No other God has a *church*. None other would want one.'[23]

9.2 A religion against itself

As the previous section indicated, Jenson's work at once celebrates the religious life while critiquing its escapist tendencies. In this respect, it again dovetails neatly with Barth's, although with a Jensonian twist.

Barth burst onto the theological scene after the horrors of the First World War, the devastation of which made him reject the theology he had been taught. The young pastor was thereby drawn into the 'strange new world within the Bible',[24] with his resulting *Römerbrief* soon dropping like a 'bombshell on the playground of the theologians'.[25] In it, Barth railed against the religious project of modernity, and attacked its attempt to domesticate God, with his central thesis still possessing the power to shock: *religion is unbelief*.[26]

In making this claim, Barth was of course working with a particular definition of religion, in that – in every form – it amounts to certain practices and rituals by which a person can prepare to encounter God.[27] Religion is essentially the means by which we navigate our way towards the light at the end of the tunnel, with none of us thinking we could arrive in the presence of the gods empty-handed. We therefore bring our best works, be that seasonal harvests, first-born livestock, pious acts or epistemological achievements. However, Barth spotted that these religious acts – in every case – constitute the means by which we offer *something* that can function as a '*Therefore*'; that is, a mechanism by which we force God's hand to make him welcome us.[28] Or, as Jenson puts it, 'all religion, Jewish and Christian included, is used by its devotees to evade and drown out the word from God by which it is called'.[29]

Barth's brilliance was in seeing that the gospel is instead the great '*Nevertheless*' to this sinful posturing,[30] in which God breaks out like 'a flash of lightning',[31] thereby shining in the deep darkness of our lives, and just so allowing nothing to get in between him and us, which – as Barth sees – is precisely the apocalyptic '*Krisis*' that stops us from domesticating God, because it means there is no time or space in which we can prepare to meet one who is so free to be present.[32] Or, in Jenson's terms: Barth sees there is no metaphysical gap to traverse, because God is always-already free for us before we can do anything about it.[33]

Barth's original diagnosis is therefore stark: in the face of our religious quest, God rises up 'like a boxer's closed fist',[34] smashing our idolatrous projects, but with a judgement that pardons.[35] That is to say, Barth knows God's relation to creation is defined 'at the Cross, where God's "No" is miraculously his "Yes"',[36] so that from beginning to end our lives are graced, with God being too quick to give us any time to respond to him religiously.[37] However, Barth also needed to say something positive about our religious projects, if only to underwrite the grounds of his sustained attack on them. Barth therefore argued that the Christian religion is best considered 'the highest form of religion', but only because it is intrinsically 'set against itself', as Jenson puts it.[38] That is to say, the Christian – like all others – still brings their gifts to God, but only in a way in which we cannot kid ourselves in the process, as if our offerings constitute a 'therefore' by which we strong-arm God. Instead, we approach God by faith, trusting that his merciful judgement will transform our gifts into his predetermined gift to us, who is the crucified saviour. Or, as Jenson puts it, 'Religion is man's attempt to provide that completion of his life which he cannot find within it. Faith is his knowledge that this attempt is doomed – and needless, since Jesus Christ completes our life without our works.'[39]

In effect, Jenson sees that Barth's positive view of the Christian religion is in some respects *eucharistic*.[40] The gathered church brings the bread and wine into the presence of God as an inadequate offering of 'the work of human hands', but, in so doing, depends entirely on the Spirit's transformation of our poor offering into the rich plenitude of the living presence of the crucified Son.[41] In other words, our religious work becomes God's gracious act for us, which is his life.

Regardless of the metaphysical details of this 'wondrous exchange'[42] – i.e. issues surrounding the various theologies of sacramental presence – Jenson contends that the church's religious practices work in much the same way. We effectively deny religion by doing religious things that say 'grace' – which is to say that the religious acts of the Christian say 'God dies for the ungodly', and just therein they remind us that there is no landscape from which we can barter with this God, no place on which we can claim a foothold of independence because God is already always free for us.[43] In short, our act is relativized by mercy, and therein justified.

To put this otherwise, the work God does for us is already to have done himself as God-with-us, and so from beginning to end, everything we do is a celebration of grace, even as we attempt to parade our piety as our own righteous work.[44] Or to put that in a slightly different register, Jenson thinks the true religion is 'the end of religion', because what we do in church celebrates the fact that there is no gap that our religious practices can traverse. As a result, Jenson concludes that 'The great religious need of late antiquity is not filled by the gospel; it is abolished.'[45]

Throughout his work, Jenson can therefore be found railing against our religious abstractions, constantly rejecting the way we attempt to erase our own particularity by using the metaphysical gap between Jesus and the Son as a means by which we can legitimize our own self-idealized projections to do with sex, gender, political theory and even 'a beach-boy guru', who is little more than an eternal psychotherapist, by projecting from our desires onto the unfleshed light at the end of the tunnel (or the 'human' Jesus discarded at the other end).[46] Jenson will attack this approach from numerous angles, but the common refrain is that there is no need to fly from the historical contingencies of the gospel towards an idealized realm, because this is no 'gap' if Jesus is the Son. As a result, 'the true God blesses and the gospel agitates no religious dynamism not identical with God's own active presence, no religious seeking or journeying that only leads to him.'[47] Which is why Jenson refuses to prioritize eyes-shut contemplation or retreat from the politics of the world, instead calling on us to pray with our eyes open and march with banners unfurled, and do all the things that we are called to do in the here and now of our concrete specificity.[48]

Jenson's occasional writings are therefore a constant celebration of prayers before meals or conversations with grandchildren, or married life and the local church, or political action and ethical decisions, all of which are seen to be somehow most basic because they constitute our embodied participation in the history of God with us.[49] In short, our relation with God terminates in these acts, and not in another realm. Thus, 'We can honor and obey the divine majesty of God "in himself" only by refraining from the religious quest for "God in himself" beyond his temporal revelation.'[50]

To put the point otherwise, because Jesus of Nazareth is not 'an image or an illustration or paradigm of God; rather, as the Creed puts it, he *is* "very God"',[51] then a lot of what we hear in church is misleading:

> If I hear the gospel promise of grace and am by that promise directed *elsewhere* as to the actual place of that grace, there is a move I now have to make upon which my sanctification depends. There is no way to avoid this conditioning of the gospel's promise so long as the church's speaking of the gospel and actual participation in grace are thought to be two events.[52]

But because the risen Son is with us and for us, as the Spirit of the community we are, then there is no metaphysical tunnel to separate us from the Light.[53]

In this respect, Jenson's theology amounts to a sustained analysis of the third article of the Nicene-Constantinopolitan Creed, just as much as it is clearly a reading of the second. There in the Creed, as Jenson reads it, the Christian discovers the coincidence of ecclesiology with pneumatology – in that 'as the Spirit shows his face, the church appears'[54] – and, just so, Jenson will run with this equation in much the same way as he does with his 'hyper-Cyrillean' Christology.[55] He thinks the Spirit is the giver of life, which is to be identified with baptism and the forgiveness of sins and the resurrection of the dead, as well as the one holy catholic and apostolic church, with no gap for our performance to bridge between the church and this living one.[56] That is to say, 'The Spirit's role as the one who frees the Father and the Son is concretely his role as the one who frees the Christian community.'[57]

This insight comes into clearest expression in Jenson's sacramental theology, in which he argues that baptism and Eucharist are doing precisely what they signify. Sacraments are not mere signs – as if signs can gesture adequately across a metaphysical chasm – because the sacraments are the actuality of God the Spirit's active presence in our midst, the means by which God remains identifiable by being pick-out-able *by* and *with* these events, despite the utter contingency of them.[58] That is to say – to pick up an earlier point – Jenson knows things could have been different, in that we might practise a 'lifelong haircut as initiation' or 'beer and bread' as our table fellowship, but that doesn't undermine the authority of what is, because the Spirit is freely taking up the contingent elements of water, bread and wine to make of them what the Father wills; that is, the presence of Jesus with us. As Jenson puts it:

> *That* baptism is the concretion of the repentance which the Christian mission opens is of course historically contingent; had Israel lived and the church begun in the arctic, the rite would doubtless have been different. But in this sense, the entire origin of the gospel is contingent.[59]

In other words, Jenson argues that the sacraments are Jesus present objectively to his church, amounting to his 'mode of availability' by which we – just like Israel – can point and say '*There!*' and just so address the living Lord.[60] And in being so constituted, the church is the presence of this God to the world, by which the Spirit enables Christ to be present to us by delaying the End, so that there is genuine time for us to be.[61] As a result, if someone wants to know where God is, Jenson will point them towards a particular altar at a particular time – 10 a.m. at St Cuthbert's, or some concrete equivalent[62] – and that is because the church in its contingent specificity is rendered by the patient Spirit 'to be the gateway of creation's translation into God'.[63] Thus:

> [We] will say that the consecrated bread and cup on the altar, the mouth of the preacher and the open page of the Scripture, the basin or torrent of water . . . mark the earthly places to which we may look to be looking to heaven, to the whence of God's coming; they are the created markers setting the boundary within creation which God rends to come to us.[64]

As this sketch begins to suggest, Jenson thinks 'each celebration is already a wedding feast'.[65] He therefore wants his readers to be much more confident in the ecclesial life they inhabit.[66] Because our liturgical actions are aligned by God to God's decision to be God-with-the-creatures, our preaching, breaking bread, bathing in fonts, absolving, pronouncing peace, intercessory prayers, distribution of gifts and the like are all bound up with the providential deliberation that is the ongoing conversation by which God constitutes the way that God *is* God-with-us and we-are-with-God. In effect, they are 'the *recursive* shape' of the Spirit bending all things to 'the inexhaustibility of the relation between Jesus and all that proceeds his [final] advent to establish his Kingdom'.[67]

As a result, Jenson thinks that when an ordained priest says, 'Almighty God, who forgives all who truly repent' etc., the specific act is itself the act of God's forgiveness happening right there.[68] In effect, God is so utterly committed to the pick-out-able places of churchy intensity that they do what they simultaneously signify. In short, repentance is a turning towards the reality we already inhabit, and that reality is church.[69]

Most remarkably, therefore, Jenson is arguing that the church's 'communal spirit is identically the Spirit that the personal God is and has'.[70] This move is no doubt rooted in an early epiphany, by which Jenson realized the psalms are in fact real prayers of an actual people to the actual God who got them out of Egypt, which so startled the young Jenson that he thereafter celebrated the particular contingency of our own personal conversation with God. We can see this worked out in the unusual section of the first volume of his *Systematics*, in which Jenson deals briefly with theories of atonement.[71] This section shows the extent to which his work is one long advocation of liturgy.[72] Rather than try to explain the atonement by using a theory by which the historical act can be related to some deeper economy in abstraction from the actuality of what happened on the cross, Jenson encourages his readers to perform the most basic narrative liturgically if they want to know the reality of the story, beyond which we cannot venture.[73] He thereby replaces theories of the atonement with the *Triduum*, believing that the acting out of the drama is itself part of the drama of God's continued act with us. In short, we recount what it in fact costs God to be in fact this God for us.[74] In other words, no theory is needed to mitigate the brute actuality of God's presence, with no liturgy mediating some faraway reality that we then play out. The eucharistic act is therefore the epicentre of God's being – and our being as purified acts – by which the reality of God is always God-with-us. In effect, the Eucharist is the End, because it is inside, so to speak, the *taxis* of a God who is not at a distance but instead 'in our face', and thereby no more capturable than the living God ever could be, but not in the sense that we can't point him out by telling his story and saying '*The Crucified one is here with us!' 'There he is, the hanging man Risen.' 'Partake of his flesh and blood.' 'Commune with your Maker!'*

In other words, because Jenson removes the gap between Jesus and the Son, he makes everything very real. There is no metaphysical space for us to navigate, because this God is essentially locatable here on the altar, here in this bath, these people, this place, in continuity with the way he has been eternally identifiable as this particular man. And that of course impacts his reader. It can inspire the preacher, for example, because Jenson shows there is no need for us to get people from their current location, through the gospel narrative, and away to another reality that is somehow more basic than the story we have just proclaimed in their midst.[75] The preacher must simply exegete Scripture to work out 'what needs to be said to be saying the gospel right here', and can trust that God is present in the very words by and with which he is willing to be identified.

In my experience – both personal and anecdotal – Jenson's work does boost the confidence of the clergy, and for the good in my opinion. The church is freed to do what the church *is*, and to do so with joyful authority and confident reverence. People thereby encounter a church that believes what God is doing in our midst, rather than being met by our unbelief in the plain words we say, with an insecure clergy thereby offering a blushing disbelieving gesture towards some distant God who is stripped of the sheer contingency of Mary's boy and Pilate's victim. Of course, Jenson's ecclesiology can make people nervous, alert as we are to the ongoing terrors of clericalism from which modernity was meant to free us.[76] But, as Jenson sees it, anyone who therefore argues for the 'priesthood of all believers' will tend to mean 'the laicizing of all priests',[77] but the danger is that any 'gap' thereby created between the priest's liturgical action and God's act in our midst is fertile ground for the cynicism and despair that too often plagues the church in our day. Jenson wants us to believe in the church, because it is bound up with God. In short, God means what we say.

In some respects, Jenson's high view of the church is just another way to show that our humanity cannot bear the weight of pointing to a distant God. He knows God – as Barth had taught him – must instead be the 'object and hidden subject' of our endeavours, enabling us to do what it is that we do.[78] Jenson's high view of the priesthood must therefore be seen as the height of humility, in that it is the acceptance of a *given*, rather than an achievement of a task. The gospel 'instructs celebrants and preachers and teachers so to teach and preach and structure worship as to open hearers to the righteousness which is not our own works but in the work of God',[79] and the inescapably odd fact is that 'God promises his Kingdom with a toast, his life with an invigorating wash'.[80]

Of course, every theologian must posit some trajectory towards an identity between God's act and our act in the end, in other words, a concept of divinization, *theosis* or some participation in God's life. If not, we risk suggesting that we all end up on a journey into nothingness, because where else could we land other than there or within God?[81] Just so, with a correlation between God's act and our existence needing to be posited somewhere at some time, many of us want to bump the identity into the future, where post-mortem we can mysteriously share in the life of the kingdom, thereby preserving the gap between God and ourselves today. Of course, Jenson accepts that 'our knowledge of God is now "through a glass darkly," [but that is] because it is knowledge across the eschatological boundary, across the discontinuity of our own death and resurrection'.[82] However, as happened with Jesus, the Spirit will bring that very future into our presence today, bending our existence around the risen Son as he opens up the infinity that is the life he shares with his Father so that the church's life is already 'the beginning of the end of the world'.[83] Thus, as Gatewood notes:

> The implication [of Jenson's work] is that we do not as the church need a hermeneutic of transcendence to perceive the secret of God's action in Christ. We do not need to move beyond or get behind Scripture to access the true nature of Christ or God. This is the case because there is not an ontological divide between the life of God and the kind of events that the Gospels report . . . What the Father speaks to be God and to woo his people to his side can be heard, touched, seen and narrated without ontological distortion.[84]

In other words, deification is not dissolving into some abstract essence, but to share in the life of the Three, with the Three, as the Three envelop us here.[85] As a result, 'When the church speaks, she begins, "It seems good to the Holy Spirit and to us . . ."'[86]

To put the point otherwise, Jenson thinks Christians are called to live ahead of time – quicker than time! – in that the existence of the Christian is entirely futuristic in being radically opened by the Spirit to the life of the Son in relation to his Father. The Spirit 'is the present force . . . of the divine *goal*',[87] which means the breaking of bread, the sermon preached and the like is akin to an eschatological flash mob in which the End which is God is with us now. Thus, from this dynamic state of perpetual 'anticipation', we are freed to break bread like it is really Jesus, preach like the gospel is happening here, pronounce absolution and peace like God means it, demand justice, embrace our enemies, baptize like it is life and death, and bury like it is death and life, and primarily amid it all pray like we are partners in God's providential conversation by which our voice is incorporated as a counterpoint into 'the triune deliberation we call providence'.[88] In short, believe that 'the whole revolutionary point of the gospel is that God is not lost, to be quested after; we are'.[89]

9.3 From here to eternity

To recall, Jenson thinks the gospel makes us claim some very strange things about God. That is because our speech about him is centred on what happened to one locatable Israelite, who we believe has been raised from the dead into infinity. This man is therefore the 'speakable eternity' we pick out as we address God. However, we are now beginning to see how Jenson's gospel logic cashes out into a scandalously particular ecclesiology. He thinks the church centres itself on a variety of specifiable acts, by which we think God is embodied in our midst. And, with this being so, we can see that Jenson needs to join up the ecclesial dots, so to speak, so that the particularity of our local church – in its episodic instantiation through time, constituted by the baptism of new converts and the death of others – coheres as one. In short, the church must somehow be identified in continuity with what it proclaims.[90]

As we might expect, Jenson thinks the unity of the episodic church is ultimately the work of the one true God, who alone is what makes the disparate gatherings one in communion. But again, Jenson makes the case for God's act without ever leaving the historical contingencies of the realm we inhabit. That is to say, he refuses to find the universal in abstraction from our particularity, as if there is a substantial form of the church standing beneath the accidents that define us. Instead, by reading the gospel in the way that he does, Jenson can set the single narratable event of Jesus in temporal relation to all other events and thereby incorporate our existence into the one act that God is.

Let me put the point another way. Because God does himself in the midst of time, Jenson knows that God should not be imagined as somehow relating to us from above, as it were, but instead be thought to extend himself across time – both past and future – as he keeps it in step with his risen Son. Or to put that better, God doesn't extend himself through time, but instead bends time around himself 'like a helix', so that all points in the sequence are equally present to the risen Lord. Of course, the way to conceive of that 'bending' is open to question, but the point here is that the risen Jesus is time's meaning, which he exercises as Lord.[91] Jesus is thereby conceived as the active agent, who functions as the substantial meaning of every accidental occurrence by drawing it into positive relation to his own life by actively situating it – by the Spirit – within the 'plot waves' of his own hypostatic individuation. In short, his own life, death and resurrection is capacious enough to accommodate our lives in his eternal velocity towards us via the double horizon in which God *is* the God who dies for the ungodly. Jenson's point is therefore simple: everything that exists is related to Jesus of Nazareth, by positing him as its liberating hope or merciful judge.

Because Jenson thinks everything is to be identified in relation to the risen Jesus, material consequences follow. Time is curved around Christ by the Spirit, and – in that sense – the temporal reality we inhabit isn't to be conceived as either a line or a circle. Instead, it is a dynamic relation to a specific person, realized by the Spirit opening the relation of past to present and making new possibilities in relation to Jesus. This works in the sense that God – just as he is his own space – is also his own time, but only as the time he is making for us. That is to say, by opening himself to the other, God essentially creates room, which is his own futurity, who is the Spirit, who is already ahead in the created heavens but comes to liberate us by relating us to the merciful Christ. Time is therefore an opening expanse of each existent thing to the heavenly possibility, who is nothing other than the resurrected Christ in relation to his Father. In other words, the Spirit – contrary to the inward posture of sin – effectively curves us outward, so to speak, as he liberates the ecstatic nature of our hypostatic relation both to God and neighbour.[92] Of course, this account can only make sense if the gospel is God's personal event within time that defines time by bracketing it and opening it up to its final historical meaning in his own infinity. But because Jenson thinks it is, he can celebrate the fact that Jesus' resurrection sparked a series of temporal events, which can be loosely grouped together as news-spreading about this event in relation to that event.[93]

To put the point otherwise, Jenson thinks the story of the narratable event of Jesus' resurrection needs to be told – that is, witnessed to by its believers – by which God creates a sort of rippling out of news-spreading through time.[94] People hear the news and are invited to join in spreading the news, in effect calling on others to join the strange community that is defined through baptism as the ongoing proclamation of the original event by which – we claim! – all existence will finally be determined. The Christian community is therefore the peculiar community that carries the strange claim about time's meaning – who is the eternal God – through the intervening time, within the temporal space that is opened up by that interruptive event in which we venture further into the life of this merciful God. Or, as Jenson adapts Barth's doctrine of creation, 'the church is the external form of the covenant'.[95] Or to put that yet a different way: 'were it not for the church there would be no world'.[96]

As this begins to suggest, Jenson understands the Christian – through their baptism – to be drawn into the event that is itself the *telos* of all events, thus living ahead of time, as it were, by being successively connected via a thread to what happened in a specific garden tomb in AD 33, which is time's beginning and end. What is most remarkable, however, is that the connection between the Christian and the resurrection is not a gesticulation towards some distant event behind us, with Christians now signalling across a new divide, albeit more like Lessing's ditch than a metaphysical chasm.[97] Instead, the church points to what it is itself enacting, namely, being part of God's self-identification *by* and *with* events in our history, so that what we point to is precisely in our midst.[98] Again, the Eucharist to us, and from there outward, us to the world.[99]

Of course, this amounts to a drastically high doctrine of the church, because Jenson is refusing to see the contingency of our current existence as a problem to be solved. However, this doesn't mean we are free of anxiety.[100] The church is something of a 'detour', in that Jenson thinks it is situated in the space that opens between the resurrection and the End as the nations are incorporated into Israel's life.[101] With this temporal space opened out, the Christian can only believe that *something* happened when Pontius Pilate was the governor of a small outpost of a particular empire, on a specific hill just outside Jerusalem's gates, where a man was put to death and laid in a tomb, which was followed by the claim that this one and the same man has been raised from the dead, now living with death behind him so that he is truly the infinite one. But because this strange event didn't happen to me under Elizabeth II just outside London – nor to you under So-and-So in the suburbs of Wherever – there remains the question of how we are connected with it. How on earth – and that is the right word – does the gospel get to me in both its own contingent particularity and mine?[102]

With this question, we finally get to Jenson's *prolegomena*. Traditionally, a prolegomenon sets out a theologian's epistemic justification for the theology that follows, so that what we say about God is underwritten by an account of the way we know it to be true. Jenson, as we might expect, is suspicious of modern approaches to this issue, by which the solvent of scepticism drives us to seek some watertight assurance about the veracity of our knowledge before we commit ourselves to our findings. He is more at home in the pre-modern tradition, in which 'we believe in order to understand', and so he waits until the final pages of the first volume of his *Systematics* to present a vision of our participation in the God he has already described. In short, he offers an *epi*legomenon; who God *is*, in his triune harmony, is what has enabled us to delight in the truth of his beautiful goodness in Christ, thereby justifying the theological task as nothing other than the sounding of a counterpoint within the triune 'fugue' we are already hearing.[103]

As Jenson sees it, this approach – offering a retroactive theological rationale for the preceding theology – is the only way to stop the prolegomena smuggling in an unbaptized metaphysics, which will invariably end up 'turn[ing] against the legomena' as we search for a non-Christian justification for our theological speech.[104] Again, textbook Barth in many respects. Nonetheless, Jenson still offers a prolegomenon of sorts before he launches into his doctrine of God, in which he explains how we can trust the message we have come to believe. It is worth us taking a look at what he says, because the remarkable thing is that he can celebrate the span of time between the event of the resurrection and us, rather than apologize for it and work his way around it. That is because – to sound the familiar refrain – Jenson believes that time is not alien to this God, and so it needn't be an epistemological problem for us either.

9.4 Telephonic existence

To explain how this works, Jenson sets out his theory of gospel knowledge, in which the church – considered as a verb, with God as the subject – exists through time in the ongoing pivoting of confessional witness to the resurrection of Jesus of Nazareth.[105] In effect, the gospel message migrates through time by travelling *from* and *to* and *with* particular people, who thereby enable it to journey through the generations, from there to here, with no evacuation of the contingencies of this travelling because God himself is with us in time. The Christian is thereby freed to accept the existential riddle of their temporal existence – and the underdetermined nature of our experience of time – while resisting any absolute answer to that quandary, as if there was some algorithm that is simply mathematically self-evident about the nature of God. Instead, Jenson celebrates that Christians are really hearing news, which posits the eternity that is bracketing the time we are caught up in.

To put the point otherwise, Jenson thinks the gospel message – as an item of news – is intrinsically odd, in that it will always rupture into the tramlines of our self-determination as a merciful exclamation: '*Surprise! One man has been raised! And your future is good because it is the friend of tax collectors and sinners who defines your time in history!*' This news can never be justified, because it is always surprisingly new. In short, the gospel is forever unexpected.[106]

However, by making this move, Jenson is claiming that the gospel can only ever be trusted, so that *faith* – as the mode of our knowing – will never get us to the point of certainty on the basis of any watertight evidence, but is instead the 'appropriate mode of knowledge' for what remains sheerly contingent.[107] Therefore, the Christian can only ever be a news-hearer and news-spreader, who is thereby drawn into a community whose identity is that very purpose, namely, broadcasting the sheerly contingent.[108] As a result, Jenson thinks our speech about God is at one and the same time directed towards the church, in the freedom of the church to remind the church to be the church and not some other community, while also being directed to the world in an outward proclamation which is an ongoing invitation: *'Have you heard? The God of Israel raised Jesus from the dead. He lives with death behind him, and in his infinity, he is the Last Judge. So come and discover the true meaning of life.'*

The Christian is thus determined by the hermeneutical pivoting from hearing the gospel to proclaiming it afresh, a hearing and a speaking in which theology is 'working out what needs to be said to be saying the gospel' to these potential converts and to our forgetful selves.[109] Or, as Jenson puts it in one place:

> To speak the gospel to my fellows and myself, I cannot, therefore, merely repeat formulas from my days in Sunday school. I must speak of Jesus as the hope of the new possibilities and new threats that open today and tomorrow in their life and mine. Therefore I must think, and not merely recite. 'Theology' is this thinking. We must ask: given that such-and-such *was* said to us (e.g., by missionaries, parents, friends) . . . what are we *now* to say that will function as gospel? We must propose sentences of the form: 'To say the gospel now, let us say "---" rather than "---"'. What goes in the first blank is either a proposed sample of the gospel itself or some stipulation about it; the whole sentence is a piece of 'theology'.[110]

As this suggests, Jenson thinks theology is intrinsically a work of the missional church, amounting to 'criticism of yesterday's preaching in preparation for tomorrow's, [and so] it is precisely in systematics that theology is *repentant*'.[111] In other words, particular people are called to engage the gospel at particular times and places in response to questions posed by the event and the situation in which that event is now proclaimed, with the meaning of our baptized lives centring on the common call to live within the bracketing of time and from that point announce the identity of the Last Judge, thus exposing the meaning of time as the history God has for us. That is to say, we are purified acts whose existence is *telephonic*.

By understanding it in this way, Jenson can celebrate our temporal existence. Time with us is the essence of this God, and so we need only 'ride the plot waves' of the story he is telling himself. Just so, it isn't a problem that we are born at a different time and in a different place to Jesus, and Irenaeus, Athanasius, Augustine, Aquinas and so on, because there is no ugly ditch separating us from them.[112] Instead, history is rightly a temporal *tradition*, which needs neither backstroke nor evacuation to decipher its meaning because it is connected by an authoritative series within the event that *is* God. In other words, Jenson accepts that we have all heard a form of the message via someone's humdrum speech, which has drawn us into a community that is nothing other than the repetition of that same message in continuous new forms. We are therefore part of a 'leap-frogging mutuality'[113] – which Jenson learns from Von Rad aligns with Israel's witness[114] – in which the ups and downs of promise and faithlessness twist and turn as the message makes its way from the garden tomb to us and beyond.[115]

With that being recognized, Jenson knows the contingency of this structural movement still begs the question, in that we have to ask *how can we know that what we are hearing is trustworthy?* In response, he offers a simple analogy, making passing reference to a game called '*telephone*'.[116] This game involves a group of children sitting in a circle with one of them whispering a message to their neighbour. The message then migrates from one player to another, and the fun of the game is in witnessing how the message gets corrupted in the process. The question we face is whether the gospel has been corrupted as it passes along the historical line towards us.

Close to the epicentre of God's self-determining act, Jenson thinks things were simple. News of the resurrection was shared by the apostles, who had heard of it from the women who ran from the tomb. The apostles could easily draw out the good news of the message, remembering the character of the one who had been raised. They could thereby discuss what Jesus was like, telling stories about how their friend ate with so-and-so and said this-and-that, and thus celebrate why it is unconditionally good news that this identifiable one lives with death behind him. And note: if the apostles got it wrong, Jenson thinks the trail runs out. There can be no necessary reason that could bridge the gap between the apostles' mistaken knowledge and God's infinity.[117] Our faith is inescapably dependent on their witness.

So to make the point: if we could teleport ourselves back to the first century, we could hear the gospel and then unpack it in conversation with an apostle, and if things got contested we could head off to Jerusalem or Rome to check with Peter and James, or John on Patmos etc.[118] In short, the eyewitnesses could tell us why the news of this resurrection is good, even if they couldn't prove that it is necessarily true. But the question that exercises Jenson is what happens when the apostles die out?[119]

Jenson thinks the need to remain faithful to the apostles' teaching created the threefold authority of canon, creeds and bishops, which combine to enable the church's faithful tradition by functioning as 'an interim surrogate for living apostles'.[120] In effect, the church began to canonize authoritative witnesses to their teaching, which it then placed alongside Israel's Scripture as a faithful hermeneutic of the decisive event.[121] The assembled texts thereby tell of Jesus, 'who is the one who . . . xyz', with these texts becoming 'the norm without a norm' by which our witness is governed, while other texts – such as those by 'Thomas' or 'Philip' – were deemed unfaithful.[122] Of course, Jenson celebrates the way these authorized texts are themselves contingent, albeit inspired by the Spirit, in that they didn't drop timelessly out of sky, but are themselves historical in the sense of being written by a particular hand on a dusty road and addressed to the contemporary issues of certain congregations, such as Corinth's.[123] This is no problem for Jenson. Scripture is sufficient for the use the church sets it, rather than needing to be watertight in conveying necessary truths.[124] So, to return to the analogy: Jenson argues that the first whisper is accompanied by a scribbled note as it is passed round the circle, which captures the message accurately. As a result, the chance of the message being preserved through time becomes much higher.

However, Jenson accepts that Scripture – both Israel's and the church's – can be read in different ways. He therefore argues that around the same time as the canonization of texts, a series of ecumenical creeds began to be formalized.[125] Derived from early rites of initiation, these creeds functioned as a rule for reading, effectively saying, *'if you read the scriptural witness to the apostles' teaching faithfully, you will say "I believe in God the Father, maker of heaven and earth, etc"'*.[126] In other words, the scribbled note in the children's game is accompanied by an executive summary, which is clearly printed and easy to read. And there's more. At the same time, the church introduces a mechanism to regulate its tradition live, as it were, thereby creating the teaching office of the bishops, which emerges in succession to the apostles with the charge of ensuring that any churches in their jurisdiction teach the gospel in accordance with Scripture, as per the creedal rules of reading, and thereby in line with the apostles' teaching.[127] In short, the scribbled note and printed summary are accompanied by people with good hearing, who eavesdrop into the current whispering of the message with the authority to correct it whenever the message gets distorted.[128]

Now, this all makes good sense to me. But Jenson knows it remains somewhat precarious, in that one mistake could lead to another, with three mistakes little better than one, if they all collude in false witness. As a result, Jenson finally places the buck in God's hands, arguing that the risen Jesus alone can ensure – if he is risen into infinity[129] – that the temporal church bears faithful witness to himself through time, with Scripture,

Creed and bishops thereby being 'agitated and guided' by his living Spirit, by which God self-testifies in the mutuality of the Three to the time he has for us.[130] So back to the game: Jenson wants us to imagine that the original Person – who is the message – walks around double-checking that the bishops' oversight of the verbal communication is attuned to the scribbled note of Scripture and the executive summary of the creeds, which continues in its infinity so that the living Word is able to ensure that the gospel we hear is faithful to his end.[131] In short, 'We are not the agents of the risen Lord's identification; he is.'[132] Or to put Jenson's point a slightly different way, the medium is the message, because we are the body of the risen incarnate Lord identified *by* us and *with* us. In short, the message is alive.[133]

As we can no doubt see, Jenson has set things up so that it is no longer a problem for us to be located here and now, seemingly removed from the epicentre of God's act, because God's act is the envelopment of time by the threefold one who is the eternal history that envelops ours from the mutual arrows of time. It is Jesus of Nazareth, who we crucified, but who was raised by the one he named Father into the life of the Spirit they share, who addresses us by way of these peculiar and odd things that we do when we gather in our churches. Of course, this is a circular argument in many respects, but that circle is benign if true. And, for Jenson, that 'if' is finally inescapable. He never intends to reach some self-evidentially demonstrable reason, which rests on the self-diagnosed necessity of our own assumptions. *Faith* is the correlate of contingency, and contingency isn't a problem, so we can dare to trust God because we are unconditionally free within the sheer contingency that is God's own life. In short, Jesus lives with death behind him, and we are caught up within the telephonic reality of that person's freedom. That is the freedom of our existence. We know by Spirit-enabled faith in the resurrected Jesus.

9.5 Not for those who desire certainty

An important point has now become clear. Jenson is not writing for timeless abstractions, any more than he is writing about a timelessly abstract God. He is instead writing about a very particular God for very particular persons at a very particular time and in a very particular place. To read Jenson's theology is therefore to be encouraged to stay 'nested',[134] so to speak, in the contingent nexus of our own lives, and there to be converted by living meaningfully within that nexus as we make our way through time in light of the specific infinity that is enveloping us, that of the Nazarene. Concrete, specific, particular and rough round the edges,

Jenson's theology is for the church today, because he calls on us to stay where we are in a new way, entering reality as it finally is, by emerging from this bath, eating this bread, drinking this cup and listening to the dramatized telling of the narratable event around which we spiral in an envelopment that is the meaning of life and determines what we should do together as a people who bear witness to the resurrected Son of Mary in the unbelieving world for which he died. In short, worship the living God in these contingent ways, and see what he will do with you.

And so this is the point where we would be wise to stop, because it shows how the bottom line for Jenson is this: if Jesus hasn't been raised, our theology – like Paul's and any good theologian – is most to be pitied.[135] Everything hangs on the resurrection, which alone drives Jenson's account of the sheer contingency of the God who decided always and forever to be the risen Nazarene. As a result, if we don't like being suspended in animated air – if we desire necessity, as it were – then Jenson is not the theologian for us.[136] However, if we dare to identify God as whoever raised Jesus from the dead, then Jenson can offer us a way to conceive of this God as precisely what happens here – a rippling outwards and inwards from the epicentre that is Easter, which is the 'pure excitement' of the single act that God is with us. Therein lies the risk.

Notes

1 Robert W. Jenson, *Systematic Theology, Volume 2, The Works of God* (New York: OUP, 1999), 322.

2 For example, see Jenson's analysis of the concept of the 'soul' within Christian piety, in Jenson, *Systematic Theology*, Vol. 2, 109–11.

3 See Robert W. Jenson, 'The Body of God's Presence: A Trinitarian Theory', in *Creation Christ and Culture: Studies in Honour of T. F. Torrance*, ed. Richard W. A. McKinney (Edinburgh: T&T Clark, 1976), 85.

4 Jenson, *Systematic Theology*, Vol. 2, 73.

5 Jenson, *Systematic Theology*, Vol. 2, 111.

6 Robert W. Jenson, *Alpha and Omega: A Study in the Theology of Karl Barth* (New York: Thomas Nelson and Sons, 1963; reprint, Eugene, OR: Wipf and Stock, 2002), 161.

7 On this, see the positive appraisal of centrality of the human in a vast universe, which pivots on God's interest in the specific 'specks' of historical particularity. Jenson, *Systematic Theology*, Vol. 2, 116–17.

8 This is not to deny the ethical implications of the gospel, or the call to live a different way of life. See Jenson's comments on church culture and the Law in Robert W. Jenson, 'Election and Culture: From Babylon to Jerusalem', in *Public Theology in Cultural Engagement*, ed. Stephen R. Holmes (Milton Keynes: Paternoster, 2008).

9 See, for example, his thoughts about the religious implications of the Greek metaphysics, and the fact that their God 'has to be searched for' in Robert W. Jenson, *The Triune Identity: God According to the Gospel* (Philadelphia: Fortress, 1982; reprint, Eugene, OR: Wipf and Stock, 2002), 59–60.

10 Jenson, *Systematic Theology*, Vol. 2, 25–6.

11 Robert W. Jenson, *Systematic Theology, Volume 1, The Triune God* (New York: OUP, 1997), 236. But Jenson will occasionally 'change from propositions to poesy' to provide incredible visions of what – this side of it – could never be described as humdrum, but which will nonetheless be the norm in what is to come. See, for example, Jenson, *Systematic Theology*, Vol. 2, 340.

12 Chris E. W. Green, *The End Is Music: A Companion to Robert W. Jenson's Theology* (Eugene, OR: Cascade, 2018), 9.

13 Robert W. Jenson, 'Eschatology', in *The Blackwell Companion to Political Theology*, ed. Peter Scott and William T. Cavanaugh (London: Blackwell, 2004), 407. In one place, Jenson offers an analogy for the final fulfilment: 'all humanity bound together by bonds as inward as those between parent and child and as ecstatic as those of sexual union'. Jenson, *Systematic Theology*, Vol. 2, 317.

14 The sense of space is captured by Jenson's use of infinite approachability in the culminating comments to his *systematics*: 'The point of identity, infinitely approachable and infinitely to be approached . . .' Jenson, *Systematic Theology*, Vol. 2, 369.

15 Jenson thinks the desire to flee to God will only 'create a God who is indeed all too plainly only *our* God or dash us against the true God where he is not ours'. Jenson, *Triune Identity*, 28.

16 Jenson, *Triune Identity*, 26.

17 See comments in Jenson, *Systematic Theology*, Vol. 1, 46.

18 Tee Gatewood, 'A Nicene Christology? Robert Jenson and the Two Natures of Jesus Christ', *Pro Ecclesia* 18 (2009), 49.

19 Jenson can indicate multiple times, in just one paragraph, how odd this all is. Jenson, *Systematic Theology*, Vol. 2, 123.

20 Robert W. Jenson, 'Second Thoughts About Theologies of Hope', *Evangelical Quarterly* 72.4 (2000), 345.

21 Robert W. Jenson, *A Large Catechism* (Delhi, NY: American Lutheran Publicity Bureau, 1991), 69. See also, Jenson, *Systematic Theology*, Vol. 2, 123.

22 As Jenson understands it, 'The concept of the invisible church has occasioned little but trouble through theological history, and no use will be made of it in this work. The church is not an invisible entity; she is the, if anything, all too visible gathering of sinners around the loaf and cup. What is invisible is that this visible entity is in fact what she claims to be, the people of God.' Jenson, *Systematic Theology*, Vol. 2, 174.

23 Robert W. Jenson, 'The God of the Gospel', *Baltimore Paper*, 17.

24 Karl Barth, *The Word of God and the Word of Man* (New York: Harper & Brothers, 1957), 28.

25 This is Karl Adams's celebrated phrase.

26 Or, as Garrett Green notes in his introduction to Barth on religion: 'The meaning of religion is death'. Karl Barth, *On Religion: The Revelation of God as the Sublimation of Religion*, translated and introduced by Garrett Green (London: Bloomsbury, 2013), 11. See 'The Meaning of Religion', in Karl Barth, *The Epistle to the Romans*, 6th edn, translated by Edwyn C. Hoskins (Oxford: OUP, 1968), 240–56. See also Jenson's analysis in Jenson, *Systematic Theology*, Vol. 2, 136–8.

Of course, the thesis that 'religion is unbelief' is developed in the second part of the first volume of his *Dogmatics*.

27 Jenson warns us of the difficulty of summary here: 'Trying to state Romans' position is a treacherous undertaking, for the book is a Socratic assault on all positions.' Jenson, *Systematic Theology*, Vol. 2, 136.

28 See the analysis of being *reckoned* in Barth, *Romans*, 123.

29 Jenson, *Systematic Theology*, Vol. 2, 83.

30 For one example of Barth's use of this word, see Barth, *Romans*, 95.

31 Barth, *Romans*, 343.

32 Barth, *Romans*, 32, and at length 362–74.

33 In Jenson's terms, 'God puts himself as an unavoidable object in our way, and so makes moot the question of our meaning in seeking him.' Jenson, *Systematic Theology*, Vol. 2, 138.

34 Barth, *Romans*, 259.

35 This is clearly expressed in paragraph 61 of *Church Dogmatics* IV.1, where Barth moves almost seamlessly from 61.2 *The Judgment of God* to 61.3 *The Pardon of Man*.

36 Robert W. Jenson, 'A Dead Issue Revisited', *Lutheran Quarterly* 14.1 (1962), 55.

37 As Jenson puts it, 'Sin is helpless. It cannot achieve its goal, the establishment of a life separated from grace. For grace gets there ahead of it and grace is exactly God's victory over this attempt [to separate]'. Jenson, *Alpha and Omega*, 105.

38 See Robert W. Jenson, *A Religion Against Itself* (John Knox Press, 1967; reprint, Eugene, OR: Wipf and Stock, 1967).

39 Jenson, 'Dead Issue', 55.

40 Jenson knows Barth did not see it quite like this. Jenson, *Systematic Theology*, Vol. 2, 138.

41 The phrase can be found in the liturgy at the preparation of the gifts.

42 For an analysis of this patristic concept in Jenson's theology, see Joseph L. Mangina, 'Blood on the Doorpost: Atonement and Sacrifice in the Theology of Robert Jenson', in *The Promise of Robert W. Jenson's Theology: Constructive Engagements*, ed. Stephen John Wright and Chris E. W. Green (Minneapolis: Fortress, 2017), 182–6.

43 Robert W. Jenson, *Canon and Creed* (Louisville: Westminster John Knox Press, 2010), 90–1.

44 Jenson learns from Barth that sin amounts to the refusal to believe in God's gracious act for us before there is even an 'us'. Jenson, *Alpha and Omega*, 38.

45 Robert W. Jenson, 'The Triune God', in *Christian Dogmatics*, ed. Carl E. Braaten and Robert W. Jenson (Philadelphia: Fortress, 1984), 126–7.

46 For example, 'Jesus in the Trinity', 309, 318. See also Jenson, *Systematic Theology*, Vol. 1, 50–3.

47 Jenson, *Systematic Theology*, Vol. 1, 107.

48 This is shown by the way Jenson moves directly from an examination of the *imago dei* to an analysis of 'politics and sex'. Jenson, *Systematic Theology*, Vol. 2, chapters 18 and 19.

49 Again, most comprehensively, see Jenson, *Systematic Theology*, where Jenson works out his proposal in the interpersonal realms of politics and sex. For example, he analyses the Nazi horrors and abortion on demand in light of misconceptions of the *imago dei* and reductions of humanity to the animal realm (Vol. 2, 56–8); the

relation between sensuality, physical 'plumbing' and sex (Vol. 2, 88–90); family life as 'the essential institution of any community' (Vol. 2, 90–3); and lists 'minor or major mysteries of communion', which includes family meals and parental blessings (Vol. 2, 260).

50 Jenson, *Triune Identity*, 27.

51 Robert W. Jenson, *Essays in Theology of Culture* (Grand Rapids: Eerdmans, 1995), 91.

52 Robert W. Jenson, 'Basics and Christology', in *In Search of Christian Unity: Basic Consensus/Basic Differences*, ed. Joseph A. Burgess (Minneapolis: Fortress Press, 1991), 53.

53 As Jenson puts it, 'That grace is God's completely free act of choice means that it is not caused or motivated by anything other than itself. Therefore there is nothing that can undo it, nothing that can call it into question . . . Therefore it is Gospel'. Jenson, *Alpha and Omega*, 142.

54 Jenson, *Systematic Theology*, Vol. 1, 89.

55 Jenson, *Systematic Theology*, Vol. 1, 148.

56 See, for instance, Jenson, *Systematic Theology*, Vol. 1, 107. For an interesting analysis of the Spirit's relation to liturgy, see Robert W. Jenson, 'Liturgy of the Spirit', *The Lutheran Quarterly* 26 (1974), 189–203.

57 Jenson, *Systematic Theology*, Vol. 2, 173.

58 They 'are not results or illustrations of God's infinity, they *are* that infinity'. Jenson, *Systematic Theology*, Vol. 1, 219.

59 Robert W. Jenson, 'The Mandate and Promise of Baptism', *Interpretation* 30.3 (1976), 278.

60 For example, Jenson, *Systematic Theology*, Vol. 2, 123 and 213.

61 Jenson, *Systematic Theology*, Vol. 2, 178–9.

62 Jenson, *Systematic Theology*, Vol. 2, 124.

63 Jenson, *Systematic Theology*, Vol. 2, 179.

64 Robert W. Jenson, 'On the Ascension', in *Loving God With Our Minds: The Pastor as Theologian*, ed. Michael Welker and Cynthia A. Jarvis (Grand Rapids: Eerdmans, 2004), 337.

65 Jenson, *Systematic Theology*, Vol. 2, 216.

66 For an account of nature of church, see Jenson, *Systematic Theology*, Vol. 2, 213–14.

67 Jenson, *Systematic Theology*, Vol. 1, 219. For a critical analysis of Jenson's pneumatology in relation to his ecclesiology, see John W. Hoyum, 'Robert Jenson's Pneumatological Contribution: An Engagement', *Pro Ecclesia* 28.2 (2019), 178–92.

68 Jenson, *Large Catechism*, 56. See also Jenson, *Systematic Theology*, Vol. 2, 177.

69 In one essay, Jenson argues that Stanley Hauerwas's work grounds Barth's concept of creation as the external form of the covenant by making the church the external form of the covenant. Of course, we have already noted that external and internal don't quite work within Jenson's vision of God, because God's relation to us is internal to him. Robert W. Jenson, 'The Hauerwas Project', *Modern Theology* 8.3 (1992), 285–95.

70 Jenson, *Systematic Theology*, Vol. 2, 181.

71 Jenson recognizes that 'no theory of atonement has ever been universally accepted', which frees him to offer his own version. Jenson, *Systematic Theology*, Vol. 1, 186.

72 As Jenson understands it, he is not alone: 'The school of [trinitarian] logic was the church's liturgy.' Jenson, *Systematic Theology*, Vol. 1, 92. Jenson was himself a liturgist for the Evangelical Lutheran Church of America, crafting their authorized eucharistic prayers, for example. See Jenson, 'Liturgy of the Spirit'.

73 Jenson, *Systematic Theology*, Vol. 1, 190.

74 Jenson, *Systematic Theology*, Vol. 1, 190–3.

75 Put negatively, Jenson thinks the failure to recognize that 'we will never get past the Jewish prophet and sufferer, the friend of sinners and radicalizer of Moses' is 'why the church's preaching and catechesis are mostly so dull'. Robert W. Jenson, 'What if It Were True?' *Neue Zeitschrift für Systematische Theologie und Religionsphilosophie* 43.1 (2001), 11.

76 For a summary account of these concerns, see Zerra's analysis of the way ecclesial authority functions in relation to the work of the Spirit. Luke Zerra, 'Escaping the *Libido Dominandi*: Authority and Accountability in Jenson's Ecclesiology', *Pro Ecclesia* 28.2 (2019), 193–209.

77 Robert W. Jenson, *Lutheran Slogans: Use and Abuse* (Delhi, NY: American Lutheran Publicity Bureau, 2011), 23.

78 Colin E. Gunton, *The Barth Lectures*, ed. P. H. Brazier (London: T&T Clark, 2007), 46.

79 Jenson, *Lutheran Slogans*, 10.

80 Jenson, *Systematic Theology*, Vol. 2, 92.

81 Robert W. Jenson, 'Creator and Creature', *International Journal of Systematic Theology* 4 (2002), 219.

82 Jenson, *Systematic Theology*, Vol. 1, 230. See also his account of the saints' knowledge of God. Jenson, *Systematic Theology*, Vol. 2, 341–6.

83 The phrase is Rowan Williams's. But see, for example, a series of rifts on the ontology of church in relation to time in Jenson, *Large Catechism*, 50–1.

84 Gatewood, 'Nicene Christology', 38.

85 Jenson, *Systematic Theology*, Vol. 2, 318–19.

86 Robert W. Jenson, 'A Lesson to Us All', *Pro Ecclesia* 3.2 (1994), 133.

87 Robert W. Jenson, 'Lutheranism and the *Filioque*', in *Ecumenical Perspectives on the Filioque for the 21st Century*, ed. Myk Habets (London: T&T Clark, 2014), 164.

88 Robert W. Jenson, 'Choose Ye This Day Whom Ye Will Serve . . .', in *Essays on the Trinity*, ed. Lincoln Harvey (Eugene, OR: Cascade, 2018), 18.

89 Robert W. Jenson, 'Review: Risk and Rhetoric in Religion: Whitehead's Theory of Language and the Discourse of Faith, by Lyman T. Lundeen', *Lutheran Quarterly* 24.4 (1972), 411.

90 In talking about the unity of the church, it is worth recalling John Flett's and David Congdon's critique of Jenson, in which he is charged with bankrolling the priority of Western culture over genuine difference. John G. Flett, *Apostolicity: The Ecumenical Question in World Christian Perspective* (Downers Grove: Intervarsity Press, 2016), 103–38; David W. Congdon, *The God Who Saves: A Dogmatic Sketch* (Eugene, OR: Cascade, 2016), 175–6.

91 Jenson, *Systematic Theology*, Vol. 2, 127.

92 Hence the human person is 'an "eccentric" entity' that exists in the act of transcending itself towards God and neighbour. Jenson, *Systematic Theology*, Vol. 2, 64–5, 73.

93 See discussion of the church's purpose in Jenson, *Systematic Theology*, Vol. 1, 3–5.

94 As Jenson puts it, 'Christ's reality includes ours without swallowing it up, without abolishing us as persons, in that God *reveals* to us what has already happened to us'. Jenson, *Alpha and Omega*, 134–6.

95 Jenson, 'Hauerwas Project', 285–95.

96 Robert W. Jenson, 'The Church's Responsibility for the World', in *The Church's Responsibility for the Earthly City*, ed. Carl E. Braaten and Robert W. Jenson (Grand Rapids: Eerdmans, 1997), 1. Put otherwise, humanity outside the church is an 'abstraction' from 'anima ecclesiastica'. Jenson, *Systematic Theology*, Vol. 2, 289.

97 As Jenson learns through his analysis of Barth, 'Barth laughs at Lessing's "great gulf" as a pseudo-problem', because there is no gap to traverse. Jenson, *Alpha and Omega*, 148 n2.

98 Jenson, *Systematic Theology*, Vol. 1, 13.

99 Jenson, *Systematic Theology*, Vol. 2, 168.

100 From one angle, anxiety could be generated by the fact that God is not our wish-fulfilment. Jenson thinks the church says to the convert: 'We are here to introduce you to the true God, for whatever he can do with you – which may well be suffering and oppression.' Jenson, *Systematic Theology*, Vol. 1, 51.

101 Jenson, *Systematic Theology*, Vol. 2, 170–3.

102 Or, as Jenson puts it, how do we keep up with 'what he is up to next'? Jenson, *Systematic Theology*, Vol. 1, 233.

103 Jenson, *Systematic Theology*, Vol. 1, 224–36.

104 Jenson, *Systematic Theology*, Vol. 1, 9.

105 Jenson, *Systematic Theology*, Vol. 1, 4–5.

106 Jenson, *Systematic Theology*, Vol. 1, 168.

107 Jenson, *Systematic Theology*, Vol. 1, 68.

108 Jenson, *Systematic Theology*, Vol. 2, 199.

109 Jenson, *Systematic Theology*, Vol. 1, 14.

110 Eric W. Gritsch and Robert W. Jenson, *Lutheranism: The Theological Movement and Its Confessional Writings* (Philadelphia: Fortress, 1976), 3–4.

111 Robert W. Jenson, 'Wilhelm Dilthey and a Background Problem of Theology', *Lutheran Quarterly* 15.3 (1963), 222.

112 Jenson, *Systematic Theology*, Vol. 2, 278–82.

113 Robert W. Jenson, 'Aspects of a Doctrine of Creation', in *The Doctrine of Creation: Essays in Dogmatics, History and Philosophy*, ed. Colin E. Gunton (London: T&T Clark, 2004), 23.

114 Robert W. Jenson, 'A Theological Autobiography, to Date', *Dialog* 46 (2007), 49.

115 Jenson, *Systematic Theology*, Vol. 1, 14.

116 Examples of use: Jenson, *Lutheran Slogans*, 27; Jenson, *Systematic Theology*, Vol. 1, 25–6.

117 Jenson, *Systematic Theology*, Vol. 1, 27.

118 Jenson, *Systematic Theology*, Vol. 1, 23.

119 Jenson, *Systematic Theology*, Vol. 1, 23.

120 Jenson, *Systematic Theology*, Vol. 1, 23. On this, see Zerra, 'Escaping the *Libido Dominandi*', 193–209.

121 Jenson, *Systematic Theology*, Vol. 1, 27; Vol. 2, 272–6.

122 Jenson, *Systematic Theology*, Vol. 1, 32.

123 For example, Jenson celebrates how the book of Proverbs can be authoritative today. Jenson, *Systematic Theology*, Vol. 2, 276.

124 Jenson, *Systematic Theology*, Vol. 1, 23–35.

125 Jenson, *Systematic Theology*, Vol. 1, 35–9.

126 Jenson, *Systematic Theology*, Vol. 2, 281.

127 Jenson, *Systematic Theology*, Vol. 1, 39–41. See also the chapter on ordained ministry and the magisterium, Vol. 2, 228–49.

128 Jenson knows that if Israel and the New Testament writers got it wrong, we are all wrong. Jenson, *Systematic Theology*, Vol. 1, 26–8.

129 See discussion of the mysteries of communion in Jenson, *Systematic Theology*, Vol. 2, 251–60, and also on the Word and the icons, Vol. 2, 270–88.

130 Jenson, *Systematic Theology*, Vol. 1, 25, and see the way Jenson also applies this to Israel and the church, Vol. 2, 194.

131 Jenson, *Systematic Theology*, Vol. 1, 172–3.

132 Jenson, *Systematic Theology*, Vol. 1, 173.

133 I am grateful to Donna Lazenby for this phrasing. For an example of Jenson stressing the identity between God and the proclaimed message of God, see Jenson, *Systematic Theology*, Vol. 2, 61.

134 The use of this word finally provides an opportunity to rectify an error. My friend Christopher C. Roberts regularly uses the term 'nested within, and accountable to, the doctrine of creation' to explain natural law, and he suggested its use when helping with a previous publication of mine. Unfortunately, an administrative error with the final document led to the omission of the footnote that credited Chris with the idea. Generous as ever, Chris did not mind, but we were rightly worried that his own future use of the phrase would now need to reference me. This footnote thus clarifies the origin of the term, and thereby corrects my error in *A Brief Theology of Sport*.

135 As Jenson puts it, 'if some day the Hidden Imam in fact appears as judge of the living and the dead, Christians will be able to tell that our hope has been disappointed'. Jenson, *Triune Identity*, 172.

136 As Jenson points out, the apostle Thomas did not accept 'the verification of a disputed empirical proposition, but . . . "believed"'. Jenson, *Systematic Theology*, Vol. 1, 200. In another essay, Jenson argues a related point: the disciplines of 'worldly learning' are used by God to ensure – through their critical rigour – that the 'props by which we give our life security and meaning apart from him' are broken down. 'God is determined that *he* shall be our refuge and not we ourselves'. Robert W. Jenson, 'The "Triplex Usus" of Worldly Learning', *The Lutheran Quarterly* 14.2 (1962), 121. However, to balance this, Steve Wright has noted – in personal correspondence – how Jenson does 'advocate a certain irascible certainty, which may nevertheless be ambushed by God or disproven by the church over time'. That is to say, he resists 'lack of closure', which comes across clearly in a review of Rowan Williams's work. Robert W. Jenson, 'Review: *On Christian Theology*, by Rowan Williams', *Pro Ecclesia* 11.3 (2002), 367–9.

10

Concluding Postscript

10.1 Sins of omission

Let me be clear. There is much more that needs to be said about everything that has been covered, and – even worse than that – there is plenty of material that has been overlooked. I have only touched the surface of Jenson's extensive writings, in which no stone is left unturned. Of course, this book is intended only as a guide, and so it was never meant to be encyclopaedic. As a result, I mustn't worry too much about what has been omitted, because even Jenson accepted that 'the fate of every theological system [is] to be dismembered and have its fragments bandied about in an ongoing debate'.[1] Such is the case here.

However, I am all too aware I have underplayed the role of Israel in Jenson's theology, which could mean that I have got things wrong. As I see it, this deficiency is linked to my attempt to abstract the structure of Jenson's metaphysics from his theology, thereby creating something that is quite static and that would have been better narrated as the story of Israel and her Christ. Jenson, in contrast, prefers to show rather than tell, thereby tracing the long arc of God's act with and through his covenant people. For better or worse, I have not shown this feature of his thought. Instead, I have told and tried to explain.

With this recognized, I think the reader can still be assured the book is a helpful guide. Whatever Jenson says about anything – including Israel – is always determined by his central conviction that God is precisely what happens between Jesus and his Father in the life of the Spirit they share with us. Whether he is tackling a theology of Scripture, angels, church order, providence, heaven and hell, or a literary reading of Dante, it will always be the concrete actuality of God's triune identity that shapes what Jenson says.[2] In other words, the systematic cohesion of his work depends on his signature move, with that key unlocking every door. The risen Jesus is the second Person of the Trinity, and so we should work out whatever needs to be said about the issue in hand from that premise alone.

Of course, Jenson's stubborn approach to Christology means he has put all his eggs in one basket. If he was wrong about the coincidence of

PART FOUR | AND SO

eternity and time in Jesus, then everything he said comes tumbling down. But Jenson believed he had no choice. He was convinced that the fleshy Jesus is no clue or pointer towards a more basic reality, as if the Nazarene is only a living signpost who gestures across an unbridgeable chasm towards an unfleshed Word, but instead embraced the 'one Lord Jesus Christ', as Nicaea put it, and thereby decided it is this 'one and the same' – in Chalcedonian terms – who is the single subject about whom everything we have to say about God and the reality of his creation is to be predicated. In other words, there is simply the Godman, Jesus of Nazareth, who is the eternal God, born of Mary, whose singular life is the eternal event of God's self-determination within which the crucified Son puts it to the Father whether or not he will always and forever be the Father of this very one who lives so fully for his killers that his hypostatic being is wedded to us. With the resurrection being the Father's resounding 'yes', that exchange in the Spirit is what constitutes God's eternal being-for-the-creature, leaving us with one act, two terms and a God who is the sheer contingency of that 'pure excitement'. Everything follows from this.

This all sounds like good news to me, though of course I am not the best judge as to whether it is. We must admit that Jenson may have got his theology entirely wrong, and – as I said in the opening pages of the book – most theologians think his project ultimately fails. With only a few minor exceptions, the secondary literature invariably applauds Jenson's efforts as it ventures a seemingly devastating critique. Suspicion tends to centre on whether his theology is little more than the latest version of a paganized pantheism, within which his pseudo-Hegelian desire to draw God into our subjective orbit historicizes God's being to such an extent that Jenson's God needs creation to be the God that he is. In short, his God isn't the sovereign God that the church confesses. Instead, God is disfigured into our own image, with everything thereby collapsing into a solipsistic one. As a result, the critics think Jenson's theology is at best borderline heretical, and his work should be avoided – or at least handled with extreme caution.

However, I am not sure we can rush to condemn Jenson in this way, without at least identifying where the logic breaks down. We can't simply reject the conclusions he reaches without first spotting where the missteps take place. However, aside from coming in for criticism about the way he reads the Cappadocians and Augustine, it is hard to find any criticism of the signature moves Jenson makes, with most interlocutors simply gunning for his conclusions instead of his premise and the argumentative trail that follows. And that should give us pause for thought. To put it simply: where exactly does Jenson go wrong in his christological argument? Is Jesus really the Son he claimed to be? Or is Jesus somehow related to the Son? And if it is the former, do Jenson's conclusions follow?

To draw those questions together, what Jenson finally asks is whether the church's metaphysics has been evangelized. On one hand, Jenson thinks that it has. The church's novel interpretation of the interrelation of persons and nature within its account of the doctrine of God gives the Christian a new way to understand what is most basic to reality. However, he thinks the metaphysical baptism was more akin to a sprinkling than full immersion, and so he dares us to plunge even deeper into the conceptual waters; and what harm can there be in that? In other words, we must remember Jenson is inviting us to join him in an ongoing project which he believes has never been completed. He wants to encourage his peers to probe the presuppositions with which we work and ensure these primary building blocks are shaped by the gospel, rather than the substance metaphysics that dominates the tradition. Of course, if we remain in the standard metaphysics, it will be easy to raise objections. We can quickly dismiss the absurdity of Jenson's claims and thereby proceed happily on our way, confident that his odd proposal will soon be consigned to history as a late-modern aberration of the church's faithful teaching. But whether that turns out to be the case remains to be seen. It is early days in the reception of Jenson's work, at least from an ecclesial perspective. In short, the experiment has only just begun.

Of course, if Jenson's revisionary work does identify the true God, he needn't worry about the way his theology is currently received, even if he now finds himself in a minority of one. He knows the church's teaching has often hung like a thread, with theologians like Athanasius having to stand *contra mundus*.[3] Jenson therefore makes a virtue of his minority status, pointing out that the overcoming of dominant voices has been central to the establishing of orthodoxy, which he think shows any development 'is surely the work of the Spirit'.[4] As a result, we have no way of knowing whether the living God will want theologians to be reading his work in 40 years or 400 years or 4,000 years, any more than Athanasius' peers did.[5] However, if God does use Jenson's work in the future, people will be amazed at how little we engaged with his work in his lifetime. 'America's greatest theologian' remained pretty much unknown at the time of his death.

However, I do think it is important to devote time to the study of Jenson's theology. Even if we end up disagreeing with his proposals, our labours will not have been in vain. We will become better theologians for having allowed him to interrogate the metaphysical framework we inhabit, and – even more importantly – begin to question whether we have really taken Jesus seriously.[6] And that is the crux. Jenson once joked that Hegel only got one thing wrong, in that he had confused himself with the Last Judge, with Jenson wryly noting how 'that is quite a fault'.[7] Jenson, in contrast, may have got only one thing right, although surely it is the best to get. Our speech about God should be centred on the strange message about the odd event in that garden tomb, where Mary's boy and Pilate's victim was raised from the dead, and if that message is ever proven to be false the Christian has nothing to say.[8] But if it is true, Jenson has found his 'one thing', with the theological task becoming a prolonged investigation into whatever the verb 'resurrect' denotes.[9]

Jenson certainly attempts to do just that. As Steve Wright says, his 'project is revisionary metaphysics to the extent that he wanders through the halls of Christian thought and turns all the objects he finds to face the risen Christ'.[10] Or to put that point polemically: not enough theologians get me excited about the risen Jesus in the way that Jenson does, and excitement about Jesus is never a bad thing. That is why I encourage you to read Jenson's theology, and to give him a fair hearing in the process. I hope that this book will have helped in that task, having introduced you to Jenson's startling doctrine of God and the signature moves that shape it, although – as I said at the beginning – there is finally no substitute for reading the primary texts. At which point, a bibliography, which in many respects is the purpose of this book.[11]

Notes

1 Robert W. Jenson, *Systematic Theology*, Vol. 1, *The Triune God* (New York: OUP, 1997), 18.

2 Robert W. Jenson, 'Dante's Vision', *Studies in Christian Ethics* 30.2 (2017), 167–9.

3 See his discussion of the minority of Nicenes, for example. Jenson, *Systematic Theology*, Vol. 1, 104.

4 Robert W. Jenson, 'Christ in the Trinity: Communicatio Idiomatum', in *The Person of Christ*, ed. Murray Rae and Stephen R. Holmes (London: Continuum, 2005), 62. Jenson also notes how 'the weapons of the Spirit have been initially beleaguered minorities or even individuals'. Robert W. Jenson, 'Jesus in the Trinity', *Pro Ecclesia* 8 (1999), 308.

5 God will judge theological systems. Jenson therefore noted – when weighing up his disagreement with Barth – that there is always room for gratitude 'before the Lord of theology, if [a theology] teaches His grace, [because it therefore] teaches rightly'. Robert W. Jenson, *Alpha and Omega: A Study in the Theology of Karl Barth* (Thomas Nelson and Sons, 1963; reprint, Eugene, OR: Wipf and Stock, 2002), 146.

6 Jenson's positive appraisals of others will still often critique them for lacking christological focus; see Jenson, 'Dante's Vision', 167–9.

7 Robert W. Jenson, *The Knowledge of Things Hoped For: the Sense of Theological Discourse* (New York: OUP, 1969), 233.

8 'Christian faith must be in this fashion historically vulnerable.' Jenson, *Systematic Theology*, Vol. 1, 174.

9 Jenson's poem on the Epiphany makes the point: 'the easterners were wise' because they took 'one clue sufficient for the venture'. Robert W. Jenson, 'Epiphany', *Theology Today* 60.4 (2004), 559. For further examples of his poetry, see Blanche Jenson, 'You shall love the Lord with all your mind', *Pro Ecclesia* 27.3 (2018), 248–54.

10 Stephen John Wright, 'A Precise Mystery', in *The Promise of Robert W. Jenson's Theology: Constructive Engagements*, ed. Stephen John Wright and Chris E. W. Green (Minneapolis: Fortress, 2017), 9.

11 The bibliography has not been annotated, but Jenson's titles do a pretty good job in mapping the terrain. If the reader wants a first port of call, I would recommend Jenson, *The Triune Identity: God According to the Gospel* (Philadelphia: Fortress Press, 1982; reprint, Eugene, OR: Wipf & Stock, 2002). That being said, there is probably nowhere better to head than Jenson's two-volume *Systematic Theology*.

Bibliography

Selected Works by Robert W. Jenson

'About Dialog, and the Church, and some Bits of the Theological Biography of Robert W. Jenson', *Dialog* 11.1 (1969), 272–8.

'Afterword', in *Trinitarian Soundings in Systematic Theology*, edited by Paul Louis Metzger, 217–20, London: T&T Clark, 2005.

Alpha and Omega: A Study in the Theology of Karl Barth, New York: Thomas Nelson & Sons, 1963. Reprint, Eugene, OR: Wipf and Stock, 2002.

America's Theologian: A Recommendation of Jonathan Edwards, Oxford: OUP, 1988.

'Anima Ecclesiastica', in *God and Human Dignity*, edited by R. Kendall Soulen and Linda Woodhead, 59–71, Eerdmans, 2006.

'Aspects of a Doctrine of Creation', in *The Doctrine of Creation*, edited by Colin E. Gunton, 17–28, London: T&T Clark International, 2004.

'Basics and Christology', in *In Search of Christian Unity: Basic Consensus/Basic Differences*, edited by Joseph A. Burgess, 45–63, Minneapolis: Fortress Press, 1991.

'The Bible and the Trinity', *Pro Ecclesia* 11.3 (2002), 329–39.

'The Body of God's Presence: A Trinitarian Theory', in *Creation, Christ and Culture: Studies in Honour of T. F. Torrance*, edited by Richard W. A. McKinney, 82–91, Edinburgh: T&T Clark, 1976.

'Can We Have a Story?' *First Things*, March 2000. www.firstthings.com/article/2000/03/can-we-have-a-story.

Canon and Creed, Louisville: Westminster John Knox Press, 2010.

'Choose ye this day whom ye will serve . . .' in *Essays on the Trinity*, edited by Lincoln Harvey, 14–19, Eugene, OR: Cascade, 2018.

'Christ as Culture 1: Christ as Art', *International Journal of Systematic Theology* 6.1 (2004), 69–76.

'Christ as Culture 3: Christ as Drama', *International Journal of Systematic Theology* 6.2 (2004), 194–201.

'Christ in the Trinity: Communicatio Idiomatum', in *The Person of Christ*, edited by Stephen R. Holmes and Murray A. Rae, 61–9, New York: T&T Clark, 2005.

'The Church's Responsibility for the World', in *The Church's Responsibility for the Earthly City*, edited by Carl E. Braaten and Robert W. Jenson, 1–10, Grand Rapids: Eerdmans, 1997.

'Conceptus . . . De Spiritu Sancto', *Pro Ecclesia* 15.1 (2006), 100–7.

Conversations with Poppi about God, with Solveig Lucia Gold, Grand Rapids: Brazos Press, 2006.

'Creation as a Triune Act', *Word & World* 2.1 (1982), 34–42.

'Creator and Creature', *International Journal of Systematic Theology* 4 (2002), 216–21.

'D. Stephen Long's *Saving Karl Barth*: An Agent's Perspective', *Pro Ecclesia* 24.2 (2015), 131–40.

'Dante's Vision', *Studies in Christian Ethics* 30.2 (2017), 167–9.

'A Dead Issue Revisited', *Lutheran Quarterly* 14.1 (1962), 53–6.

'A Decision Tree of Colin Gunton's Thinking', in *The Theology of Colin Gunton*, edited by Lincoln Harvey, 8–16, New York: T&T Clark, 2010.

'Election and Culture: From Babylon to Jerusalem', in *Public Theology in Cultural Engagement*, edited by Stephen R. Holmes, 48–61, Milton Keynes: Paternoster, 2008.

'Epiphany', *Theology Today* 60 (2004), 559.

'Eschatology', in *The Blackwell Companion to Political Theology*, edited by Peter Scott and William T. Cavanaugh, 407–20, London: Blackwell, 2004.

Essays in Theology of Culture, Grand Rapids: Eerdmans, 1995.

Ezekiel, London: SCM Press, 2009.

'The Father, He . . .' in *Speaking the Christian God: the Holy Trinity and the Challenge of Feminism*, edited by Alvin F. Kimel, Jr, 95–109, Grand Rapids: Eerdmans, 1992.

'For Us . . . He Was Made Man', in *Nicene Christianity: The Future for a New Ecumenism*, edited by Christopher Seitz, 75–87, Grand Rapids: Brazos Press, 2001.

'The Futurist Option of Speaking of God', *The Lutheran Quarterly* 21.1 (1969), 17–25.

God After God: The God of the Past and the God of the Future as Seen in the Work of Karl Barth, New York: Bobs-Merrill, 1969. Reprint, Minneapolis: Fortress Press, 2012.

'The God of the Gospel', *Baltimore Paper*. Accessed 7 November 2018. https://afkimel.wordpress.com/2018/08/28/the-god-of-the-gospel-by-robert-w-jenson.

'God's Time, Our Time', *Christian Century* 123 (2006), 31–5.

'Gratia Non Tollit Naturam Sed Perficit', *Pro Ecclesia* 24.1 (2015), 115–23.

'Gregory of Nyssa: The Life of Moses', *Theology Today* 62 (2006), 533–7.

'The Hauerwas Project', *Modern Theology* 8.3 (1992), 285–95.

'The Hidden and Triune God', *International Journal of Systematic Theology* 2.1 (2000), 5–12.

'How Does Jesus Make a Difference?' in *Essentials of Christian Theology*, edited by William C. Placher, 191–205, Louisville: Westminster John Knox Press, 2003.

'How My Mind Has Changed: Reversals', in *How My Mind Has Changed: Essays from the Christian Century*, edited by David Heim, 46–52, Eugene, OR: Cascade, 2012.

'How the World Lost Its Story', *First Things*, March 2010. www.firstthings.com/article/2010/03/how-the-world-lost-its-story.

'An Interview with Robert W. Jenson', *The Christian Century* (May 2006), 31–5. Accessed 21 June 2019. www.religion-online.org/article/an-interview-with-robert-w-jenson.

'Ipse Pater non est impassibilis', in *Divine Impassibility and the Mystery of Human Suffering*, edited by James F. Keating and Thomas Joseph White, 117–126, Grand Rapids: Eerdmans, 2009.

'It's the Culture', *First Things*, May 2014. www.firstthings.com/article/2014/05/its-the-culture.

'Jesus, Father, Spirit: The Logic of the Doctrine of the Trinity', *Dialog* 26.4 (1987), 245–9.
'Jesus in the Trinity', *Pro Ecclesia* 8 (1999), 308–18.
'Jesus in the Trinity: Wolfhart Pannenberg's Christology and Doctrine of the Trinity', in *The Theology of Wolfhart Pannenberg: Twelve American Critiques, with an autobiographical essay and response*, edited by Carl E. Braaten and Philip Clayton, 188–206, Minneapolis: Augsburg, 1988.
'Joining the Eternal Conversation: John's Prologue and the Language of Worship', *Touchstone* 14.9 (2001), 32–7.
'Justification as a Triune Event', *Modern Theology* 11.4 (October 1995), 421–7.
'Karl Barth on the Being of God', in *Thomas Aquinas and Karl Barth: An Unofficial Catholic-Protestant Dialogue*, edited by Bruce L. McCormack and Thomas Joseph White, 43–51, Grand Rapids: Eerdmans, 2013.
The Knowledge of Things Hoped For: the Sense of Theological Discourse, New York: OUP, 1969.
A Large Catechism, Delhi, NY: American Lutheran Publicity Bureau, 1991.
'A Lesson to Us All', *Pro Ecclesia* 3.2 (1994), 133–5.
'Liturgy of the Spirit', *The Lutheran Quarterly* 26 (1974), 189–203.
'The Logos Ensarkos and Reason' with Colin E. Gunton in *Reason and the Reasons of Faith*, edited by P. J. Griffiths and R. Hütter, 78–85, New York: T&T Clark International, 2005.
'A Lutheran Among Friendly Pentecostals', *Journal of Pentecostal Theology* 20 (2011), 48–53.
Lutheran Slogans: Use and Abuse, Delhi, NY: American Lutheran Publicity Bureau, 2011.
'Lutheranism and the *Filioque*', in *Ecumenical Perspectives on the Filioque for the 21st Century*, edited by Myk Habets, 159–67, London: T&T Clark, 2014.
Lutheranism: The Theological Movement and Its Confessional Writings with Eric W. Gritsch, Philadelphia: Fortress, 1976.
'The Mandate and Promise of Baptism', *Interpretation* 30.3 (1976), 271–87.
'No other God has this Son. Nor would any other want him', Lecture transcribed by Alvin Kimel, *Eclectic Orthodoxy*, 12 September 2017. https://afkimel.wordpress.com/2017/09/12/no-other-god-has-this-son-nor-would-any-other-want-him/.
'On the Ascension', in *Loving God With Our Minds: The Pastor as Theologian*, edited by Michael Welker and Cynthia A. Jarvis, 331–40, Grand Rapids: Eerdmans, 2004.
'On the Doctrine of Atonement', *Center of Theological Inquiry, Reflections* 9 (2006).
On the Inspiration of Scripture, Delhi, NY: ALPB, 2012.
On Thinking the Human: Resolutions of Difficult Notions, Grand Rapids: Eerdmans, 2003.
'On Truth and God: 1. Ipsa Veritas and Late Modernity', *Pro Ecclesia* 20.4 (2011), 384–8.
'On Truth and God: 2. The Triunity of Truth', *Pro Ecclesia* 21.1 (2012), 51–5.
'Once More the Logos Asarkos', *International Journal of Systematic Theology* 13 (2011), 130–3.
'An Ontology of Freedom in the *De Servo Arbitrio* of Luther', *Modern Theology* 10.3 (1994), 247–52.
'Parting Ways?' *First Things* 53 (1995), 60–2. www.firstthings.com/article/1995/05/001-parting-ways

'The Plot Not to Kidnap Kissinger', *Dialog* 11.2 (1972), 88–9.
'The Praying Animal', *Zygon* 18.3 (1983), 311–26.
A Religion Against Itself, Louisville: John Knox Press, 1967. Reprint, Eugene, OR: Wipf and Stock, 2009.
'A Reply', *Scottish Journal of Theology* 52.1 (1999), 132.
'Response: The Philosophy that Attends to Scripture' in *Symposium on Kenneth Oakes, Karl Barth on Theology and Philosophy*. Accessed 1 March 2019. https://syndicate.network/symposia/theology/karl-barth-on-theology-and-philosophy.
'Response to Watson and Hunsinger', *Scottish Journal of Theology* 55.2 (2002), 225–32.
'Reversals: How My Mind Has Changed', *Christian Century* (20 April 2010), 30–3.
'Review Essay: David Bentley Hart, The Beauty of the Infinite: The Aesthetics of Christian Truth', *Pro Ecclesia* 14.2 (2005), 235–7.
'Review: *On Christian Theology*, by Rowan Williams', *Pro Ecclesia* 11.3 (2002), 367–9.
'Review: Risk and Rhetoric in Religion: Whitehead's Theory of Language and the Discourse of Faith, by Lyman T. Lundeen', *Lutheran Quarterly* 24.4 (1972), 410–12.
'The Risen Prophet', in *God and Jesus: Theological Reflections for Christian-Muslim Dialog*, American Lutheran Church Division for World Mission and Interchurch Cooperation, 57–67, Minneapolis: American Lutheran Church, 1986.
'Scripture's Authority in the Church', in *The Art of Reading Scripture*, edited by Ellen F. Davis and Richard B. Hays, 27–37, Grand Rapids: Eerdmans, 2003.
'Second Thoughts About Theologies of Hope', *Evangelical Quarterly* 72.4 (2000), 335–46.
'Some Platitudes about Prayer', *Dialog* 9 (Winter 1970), 60–6.
'Some Riffs on Thomas Aquinas's De Ente Et Essentia', in *Theological Theology: Essays in Honour of John Webster*, edited by R. David Nelson et al., 125–30, London: T&T Clark, 2015.
Song of Songs: A Biblical Commentary for Teaching and Preaching, Louisville: John Knox Press, 2005.
Story and Promise: A Brief Theology of the Gospel About Jesus, Philadelphia: Fortress Press, 1973. Reprint, Eugene, OR: Wipf & Stock 2014.
'Story and Promise in Pastoral Care', *Pastoral Psychology* 26.2 (1977), 113–23.
Systematic Theology, 2 vols, New York: OUP, 1997, 1999.
'A Theological Autobiography, to Date', *Dialog* 46 (2007), 46–54.
Theology as Revisionary Metaphysics: Essays on God and Creation, edited by Stephen John Wright, Eugene, OR: Cascade, 2014.
A Theology in Outline: Can These Bones Live? Transcribed, edited and introduced by Adam Eitel, Oxford: OUP, 2016.
'Three Identities of One Action', *Scottish Journal of Theology* 28 (1975), 1–15.
'The Trinity and Church Structure', in *Shaping Our Future: Challenges for the Church in the Twenty-First Century*, edited by J. Stephen Freeman, 15–26, Boston: Cowley Publications, 1994.
'The "Triplex Usus" of Worldly Learning', *The Lutheran Quarterly* 14.2 (1962), 121–25.
'The Triune God', in *Christian Dogmatics: Volume 1*, edited by Carl E. Braaten and Robert W. Jenson, 83–196, Philadelphia: Fortress Press, 1984.
'Triune Grace', *Dialog* 41.4 (2002), 285–93.

The Triune Identity: God According to the Gospel, Philadelphia: Fortress, 1982. Reprint, Eugene, OR: Wipf and Stock, 2002.
Unbaptized God: The Basic Flaw in Ecumenical Theology, Minneapolis: Fortress, 1992.
Visible Words: The Interpretation and Practice of Christian Sacraments, Minneapolis: Fortress, 2010.
'What if It Were True?' *Neue Zeitschrift für Systematische Theologie und Religionsphilosophie* 43.1 (2001), 3–16.
'What Kind of God Can Make a Covenant?' in *Covenant and Hope: Christian and Jewish Reflections*, edited by Robert W. Jenson and Eugene B. Korn, 3–18, Grand Rapids: Eerdmans, 2012.
'What's to Celebrate?' *Pro Ecclesia* 26.1 (2017), 7–10.
'Wilhelm Dilthey and a Background Problem of Theology', *Lutheran Quarterly* 15.3 (1963), 212–22.
'With No Qualifications: the Christological Maximalism of the Christian East', in *Ancient and Postmodern Christianity: Paleo-Orthodoxy in the 21st Century*, edited by Kenneth Tanner and Christopher A. Hall, 13–22, Downers Grove: Intervarsity Press, 2002.
'You Wonder Where the Spirit Went', *Pro Ecclesia* 2.3 (1993), 296–304.

Selected Secondary Literature

Busch, Eberhard, *Karl Barth: His Life from Letters and Autobiographical Texts*, translated by John Bowden, Grand Rapids: Eerdmans, 1994.
Cary, Philip, 'The Barth Wars; A Review of Reading Barth with Charity', *First Things*, April 2015. www.firstthings.com/article/2015/04/barth-wars.
Case, Jonathan P., 'Music of the Spheres – Part 1', *Crucible* 3.1 (November 2010).
——— 'Music of the Spheres – Part 2', *Crucible* 3.2 (September 2011).
Chalamet, Christophe, 'God's "Liveliness" in Robert W. Jenson's Trinitarian Thought', in *Recent Developments in Trinitarian Theology: An International Symposium*, edited by Christophe Chalamet and Marc Vial, 141–52, Minneapolis: Fortress Press, 2014.
Congdon, David W., *The God Who Saves: A Dogmatic Sketch*, Eugene, OR: Cascade, 2016.
Cornelius, Emmitt, 'Being Going to be Born to Mary: An Overview and Appraisal of Robert W. Jenson's View of the Incarnation as an OT Phenomenon', *Journal of the Evangelical Theological Society* 58.2 (2015), 353–66.
——— 'St. Irenaeus and Robert W. Jenson on Jesus in the Trinity', *Journal of the Evangelical Theological Society* 55 (2012), 111–24.
Crisp, Oliver D., 'Concerning the Logos Asarkos: Interacting with Robert W. Jenson', *The Southern Baptist Journal of Theology* 19.1 (2015), 39–51.
——— 'Robert Jenson on the Pre-existence of Christ', *Modern Theology* 23.1 (2007), 27–45.
——— *Word Enfleshed: Exploring the Person and Work of Christ*, Grand Rapids: Baker Academic, 2016.
Cumin, Paul, *Christ at the Crux: The Mediation of God and Creation in Christological Perspective*, Eugene, OR: Pickwick Publications, 2014.

――― 'Robert Jenson and the Spirit of it All: Or, You (Sometimes) Wonder Where Everything Else Went', *Scottish Journal of Theology* 60.2 (2007), 161–79.
Curtis, Jason M., 'Trinity, Time and Sacrament: Christ's Eucharistic Presence in the Theology of Robert W. Jenson', *Journal of Christian Theological Research* 10 (2005), 21–38.
Dempsey, Michael T., *Trinity and Election in Contemporary Theology*, Grand Rapids: Eerdmans, 2011.
Driel, Edwin Christian van, 'Karl Barth on the Eternal Existence of Jesus Christ', *Scottish Journal of Theology* 60 (2007), 45–61.
East, Brad 'Rest in Peace: Robert W. Jenson (1930–2017)', *Resident Theologian*, 6 September 2017. https://resident-theologian.blogspot.com/2017/09/rest-in-peace-robert-w-jenson-19302017.html.
――― 'What is the Doctrine of the Trinity For? Practicality and Projection in Robert Jenson's Theology', *Modern Theology* (Online Early View, 2017), 1–20.
Eitel, Adam 'The Resurrection of Jesus Christ: Karl Barth and the Historicization of God's Being', *International Journal of Systematic Theology* 10 (2008), 36–53.
Farrow, D., D. Demson, and J. A. Di Noia, 'Robert Jenson's Systematic Theology: Three responses', *International Journal of Systematic Theology* 1 (1999), 89–104.
Flett, John G., *Apostolicity: The Ecumenical Question in World Christian Perspective*, Downers Grove: Intervarsity Press, 2016.
Fryer, Gregory, 'A Parish Pastor Speaks of Robert W. Jenson', *Newsletter of the Center for Catholic and Evangelical Theology* (2017), 2–4.
Gaghan, Josh, 'Reason, Metaphysics, and their Relationship in the Theologies of Jenson and Aquinas', *New Blackfriars* 99.1082 (2018), 520–40.
Gatewood, Tee, 'A Nicene Christology? Robert Jenson and the Two Natures of Jesus Christ', *Pro Ecclesia* 18 (2009), 28–49.
Gathercole, Simon, 'Pre-existence, and the Freedom of the Son in Creation and Redemption: An Exposition in Dialogue with Robert Jenson', *International Journal of Systematic Theology* 7 (2005), 38–51.
Green, Chris E. W., *The End Is Music: A Companion to Robert W. Jenson's Theology*, Eugene, OR: Cascade Books, 2018.
――― 'Participation in Providence: Robert W. Jenson's Theology of Prayer', *Pro Ecclesia* 28.2 (2019), 167–77.
Gunton, Colin E., 'Immanence and Otherness: Divine Sovereignty and Human Freedom in the Theology of Robert W. Jenson', in *The Promise of Trinitarian Theology*, 2nd edn, Edinburgh: T. & T. Clark, 1997, 118–36.
――― (ed.) *Trinity, Time, Church: A Response to the Theology of Robert W. Jenson*, Grand Rapids: Eerdmans, 2000.
Guthrie, Shirley C., 'Book Review: Systematic Theology: Volume I: The Triune God, by Robert W. Jenson', *Theology Today* 55 (1998), 249–52.
Hart, David Bentley *The Beauty of the Infinite: The Aesthetics of Christian Truth*, Grand Rapids: Eerdmans, 2000.
――― 'The Lively God of Robert Jenson', *First Things*, October 2005. www.firstthings.com/article/2005/10/the-lively-god-of-robert-jenson.
Hauerwas, Stanley, 'How to Write a Theological Sentence', *ABC Religion and Ethics*, 26 September 2013. Accessed 6 November 2018. www.abc.net.au/religion/how-to-write-a-theological-sentence/10099600.
Hector, Kevin, 'God's Triunity and Self-Determination: A Conversation with Karl Barth, Bruce McCormack, and Paul Molnar', *International Journal of Systematic Theology* 7 (2005), 246–61.

BIBLIOGRAPHY

——— 'Immutability, Necessity, and Triunity: Towards a Resolution of the Trinity and Election Controversy', *Scottish Journal of Theology* 65 (2012), 64–81.

Henry, James Daryn, *The Freedom of God: A Study in the Pneumatology of Robert Jenson*, Lanham, MD: Lexington/Fortress, 2018.

——— 'Invitation to the Triune Conversation: Explorations of Prayer Through the Theology of Robert Jenson', *Dialog: A Journal of Theology* 52 (2013), 340–8.

Hinlicky, Paul R., 'Robert Jenson and the God of the Gospel', *The Christian Century*, 14 September 2017. www.christiancentury.org/article/critical-essay/robert-jenson-god-of-gospel.

——— 'Theology after the Death of God: On Robert W. Jenson', *Marginalia: Los Angeles Review of Books*, 26 April 2019. https://marginalia.lareviewofbooks.org/theology-after-the-death-of-god/.

Hoyum, John W., 'Robert Jenson's Pneumatological Contribution: An Engagement', *Pro Ecclesia* 28.2 (2019), 178–92.

Hunsinger, George, *Reading Barth with Charity: A Hermeneutical Proposal*, Grand Rapids: Baker Academic, 2015.

——— 'Robert Jenson's Systematic Theology: A Review Essay', *Scottish Journal of Theology* 55 (2002), 161–200.

Jenson, Blanche 'You shall love the Lord with all your mind', *Pro Ecclesia* 27.3 (2018), 248–54.

Kerr, Fergus, 'Comment: *God the Great Fugue*', *New Blackfriars* 83.972 (2002), 50–1.

Kimel, Alvin F., 'Robert W. Jenson: Reminiscences and Memories', *Eclectic Orthodoxy*, 7 September 2017. https://afkimel.wordpress.com/2017/09/07/robert-w-jenson-reminiscences-and-memories/.

Kline, Peter, 'Participation in God and the Nature of Christian Community: Robert Jenson and Eberhard Jungel', *International Journal of Systematic Theology* 13.1 (2011), 38–61.

Lee, Sang Hoon, 'Toward an Understanding of the Eschatological Presence of the Risen Jesus with Robert Jenson', *Scottish Journal of Theology* 71 (2018), 85–101.

——— *Trinitarian Ontology and Israel in Robert W. Jenson's Theology*, Eugene, OR: Pickwick Publications, 2016.

Leithart, Peter, 'The Adventure of Orthodoxy', *First Things*, October 2013. www.firstthings.com/web-exclusives/2013/10/the-adventure-of-orthodoxy.

Malysz, Piotr J., 'From Divine Sovereignty to Divine Conversation: Karl Barth and Robert Jenson on God's Being and Analogy', *Concordia Theological Quarterly* 71.1 (2007), 29–55.

Mattes, Mart, 'An Analysis and Assessment of Robert Jenson's Systematic Theology', *Lutheran Quarterly* 14.4 (2000), 463–94.

McCall, Thomas H., *Which Trinity? Whose Monotheism? Philosophical and Systematic Theologians on the Metaphysics of Trinitarian Theology*, Grand Rapids: Eerdmans, 2010.

McCormack, Bruce L., 'Election and the Trinity: Theses in Response to George Hunsinger', *Scottish Journal of Theology* 63 (2010), 203–24.

——— 'Grace and Being: The Role of God's Gracious Election in Karl Barth's Theological Ontology', in *The Cambridge Companion to Karl Barth*, edited by John Webster, 92–110, Cambridge: Cambridge University Press, 2000.

——— 'In Memoriam: Robert Jenson (1930–2017)', *International Journal of Systematic Theology* 20.1 (2018), 3–7.

——— 'Let's speak plainly: A Response to Paul Molnar', *Theology Today* 67 (2010), 57–65.
McFarland, Ian A., 'The Body of Christ: Rethinking a Classic Ecclesiological Model', *International Journal of Systematic Theology* 7 (2005), 226–45.
Molnar, Paul, *Divine Freedom and the Doctrine of the Immanent Trinity: In Dialogue with Karl Barth and Contemporary Theology*, London: T & T Clark, 2002.
——— *Faith, Freedom and the Spirit. The Economic Trinity in Barth, Torrance and Contemporary Theology*, Downers Grove: InterVarsity Press, 2015.
——— 'The Perils of Embracing a "Historicized Christology"', *Modern Theology* 30.4 (2014), 454–80.
Nicol, Andrew W., *Exodus and Resurrection: The God of Israel in the Theology of Robert W. Jenson*, Minneapolis: Fortress Press, 2016.
Ochs, Peter, *Another Reformation: Postliberal Christianity and the Jews*, Grand Rapids: Baker Academic, 2011.
Pannenberg, Wolfhart, 'Systematic Theology: Volumes I & II', *First Things*, May 2000. www.firstthings.com/article/2000/05/systematic-theology-volumes-i-amp-ii.
Riches, Aaron, *Ecce Homo: On the Divine Unity of Christ*, Grand Rapids: Eerdmans, 2016.
Scholl, Brian, K., 'On Robert Jenson's Trinitarian Thought', *Modern Theology* 18 (2002), 27–36.
Schlesinger, Eugene R., 'Trinity, Incarnation and Time: A Restatement of the Doctrine of God in Conversation with Robert Jenson', *Scottish Journal of Theology* 69 (2016), 189–203.
Swain, Scott R., *The God of the Gospel: Robert Jenson's Trinitarian Theology*, Downers Grove: IVP, 2013.
Tavast, Timo, 'The Identification of the Triune God: Robert W. Jenson's Approach to the Doctrine of the Trinity', *Dialog* 51.2 (2012), 155–63.
Verhoef, A. H., 'How is Robert Jenson Telling the Story?' *Scriptura* 98 (2008), 231–43.
——— 'The Relation Between Creation and Salvation in the Trinitarian Theology of Robert W. Jenson', *HTS Theological Studies* 69.1 (2013). https://hts.org.za/index.php/HTS/article/view/1191/3244.
——— 'Trinity, Time and Ecumenism in Robert Jenson's Theology', *Deel* 52 (2011), 247–56.
Watson, Francis, 'America's Theologian: An Appreciation of Robert Jenson's *Systematic Theology*, with some remarks about the Bible', *Scottish Journal of Theology*, 55.2 (2002), 201–23.
Webster, John, *God Without Measure: Working Papers in Christian Theology*, London: T&T Clark, 2016.
Wiles, Maurice, 'Book Review: Systematic Theology: Volume I: The Triune God, by Robert W. Jenson', *The Journal of Theological Studies* 50.1 (1999), 428–30.
Williams, Rowan, *Christ The Heart of Creation*, London: Bloomsbury, 2019.
Wright, Stephen John, 'The Creator Sings: A Wesleyan Rethinking of Transcendence with Robert Jenson', *Heythrop Journal* 53.6 (2012), 972–82.
——— *Dogmatic Aesthetics: A Theology of Beauty in Dialogue with Robert W. Jenson*, Minneapolis: Fortress Press, 2014.
——— 'Restlessly Thinking Relation', in *Essays on the Trinity*, edited by Lincoln Harvey, 140–61, Eugene, OR: Cascade, 2018.

——— 'Robert Jenson's Story of Creation', *Sapientia*, 24 January 2018. https://henrycenter.tiu.edu/2018/01/robert-jensons-story-of-creation/.
——— 'Sounding Out the Gospel: Robert Jenson's Theological Project', *Pro Ecclesia* 28.2 (2019), 149–66.
Wright, Stephen John and Chris E. W. Green (eds), *The Promise of Robert W. Jenson's Theology: Constructive Engagements*, Minneapolis: Fortress, 2017.
Zerra, Luke, 'Escaping the *Libido Dominandi*: Authority and Accountability in Jenson's Ecclesiology', *Pro Ecclesia* 28.2 (2019), 193–209.

Index of Names and Subjects

Aquinas
  and Aristotle 82 n15
  definition of divine persons 36 n59
  on existence and essence 15 n10
  Jenson compared with 7
Aristotle, theory of narrative 37–9
aseity 2, 118, 138, 141–3, 147
atonement 192
Augustine 118

Barth, Karl 110
  doctrine of creation 196, 206 n69
  doctrine of election 111–24
  theological development 8, 188–9
  wars of interpretation 120, 125 n9
  writing 3
begetting 54, 109–110, 122
Being 72–5
Bible, unity 26, 37
bishops 201–2
Bultmann, Rudolf 35 n40

Calvin 118–19
Chalcedonian Definition 97–8
'Chinese whispers' ('telephone' game) 200
Christ *see* Jesus
Christology 88–94
  in Barth's thinking 111–12
church
  as body of Christ 187
  particularity 195
  unity 207 n90
conceptual dissonance 23, 27
Congdon, David W. 82–3 n25, 207 n90
contingency 38–9, 82 n25, 184
  in everyday life 187
creation 51–2, 130–32, 164–7
  continuous 185
Cyril of Alexandria 96–7

ecumenism 17 n35
Edwards, Jonathan 146
either/or 149 n11
election 111–24
  as plot of gospel story 139
eternity 40–41, 45–9, 54, 138
  in Greek philosophy 74–5
Eucharist 189–93
evangelization 5–10
evil 170–71

faith 198
fall, the 166
Flett, John 82 n25, 207 n90
forgiveness 146–7, 173, 192
freedom 115–21, 147–8
future 30–32, 42–5, 116–20, 136–7, 145–6, 160–61, 185

Gaghan, Josh 7
Gatewood, Tee 99, 154, 156, 194

INDEX OF NAMES AND SUBJECTS

God
  action 52–3, 136–7
  aseity 2, 118, 138, 141–3, 147
  contingency 147, 157
  as creator 51, 130–32
  eternity 9, 45–9, 110, 120–23
  excitement of 1
  existence and nature 77, 116–18
  faithfulness 160–63
  as Father 54, 81, 157, 160
  freedom 120–21, 130, 162
  as fugue 1, 148, 197
  in Greek philosophy 64, 74
  identified 45–7
  name 80
  presence 52, 191–3
  self-determination 29, 31, 116, 118, 121, 123–4, 145–7
  storied nature 41, 54, 145
  suffering 98
gospel 28–9
  defines time 196
  mind-boggling nature 23
  as narrative 38–9
  particularity 14, 186, 197
  proclamation 198–9
  tradition 200–201
Gospels 30
Greek philosophy 64, 66, 68
  of *Being* 73–4
  of substance 69–74
  of time 73–4
  and trinitarian theology 90–93
Green, Chris 29, 50, 51
Gregory of Nazianzus 144

Hart, David Bentley 3–4, 165
Hauerwas, Stanley 5, 206 n69
Hegel 212
  on *Being* 72
helix 1, 8, 43, 165, 169, 195

history 40–48, 74, 99, 116, 120–24, 185
  God identified in 130, 135, 197, 199–200
Holy Saturday 156
Holy Spirit 145, 167, 184, 190–92, 194
Hunsinger, George 12–13, 20 nn77 & 80
hypostasis 71–2, 76–80, 94–6, 98–9, 102, 134–6, 153–8

identity 24
irrationality 20 n85
Israel 210

Jenson, Blanche 16 n16
Jenson, Robert W.
  academic career 5, 112
  critics of 211
  and the Lutheran Church 15 n7
  publications 3, 112
  theological originality 6–8, 113
  writing style 3–5
Jesus
  as bridegroom 172–3
  crucifixion 30, 32, 38–9, 41, 133–4, 146–7, 160–61, 163
  divine and human natures 89, 94, 96–100, 153–5
  divinity 27–8
  identity 24–6, 30, 37, 53, 160–61
  incarnation 7, 10–13, 153, 158–9, 183–4
  lordship 24, 26
  name 24–5
  resurrection 1, 28, 38, 47–8, 132–3, 139–42, 164, 198–9
  as Son/*Logos* 27, 91–3, 117–19, 155, 159–60

in the Trinity 3, 7, 9, 88, 153–8, 183
will 100–101
John Damascene 144

language about God 49
Leo I (Pope) 97–8
Logos 27, 91–2
Logos asarkos 10–11, 153, 156, 160
Luther, Martin 178 n112

Maximus 101
metaphysics 7
  of Barth 114
  evangelization of 212
  redefined by the church 110
  of substances 68–81
Molnar, Paul 12–13
music 173

names 24–5, 29
narrative 37–9, 40–41, 53
Nestorian controversy 96–7
Nicene Christology 114
Nicene-Constantinopolitan Creed 190

ousia 70–71

perichoresis 137, 144–5, 148
persons 32–3
  of the Trinity 67, 76–7, 97–8, 102
philosophy, not universal 66
physis 71
prayer 45, 50–51
preaching 193
predestination 118–19
prosopon 72, 76

religion 189
religious life 186–7

repentance 192
resurrection 28, 44
revelation, in Barth's theology 115
Roberts, Christopher C. 209 n134

sacraments 39–40, 191–2
Schwöbel, Christoph 4
self, in modern thought 77
sin 166
spiritual realm 184
Stobart, Andrew J. 112–13
story *see* narrative
substance metaphysics 68–81
Swain, Scott R. 126 n22

telephonic existence 198–202
Thomas (apostle) 209 n136
time 44, 48, 74, 166, 168–70, 198
  as the essence of God 199
  helix around God 195–6
tradition, gospel 200–201
trinitarian theology 14, 24, 63–7, 80–81
  in the early church 76–7
  and Greek philosophy 90–93
  see also Jesus, in the Trinity
Trinity
  immanence 136
  inner conversation 50
  as name summarising gospel story 24, 139

Williams, Rowan 156
witness 200–202
Wittgenstein, Ludwig 100
Word of God 51–2, 54, 117, 119, 166–7, 170
words about God 49–50, 143
Wright, Stephen John 15 n10, 19 n58, 209 n136, 213

www.ingramcontent.com/pod-product-compliance
Lightning Source LLC
Chambersburg PA
CBHW021943290426
44108CB00012B/946